THE IMAGES OF OCCUPATIONAL PRESTIGE

THE IMAGES OF OCCUPATIONAL PRESTIGE

Anthony P.M. Coxon
and
Charles L. Jones

ST. MARTIN'S PRESS NEW YORK

Contents

List of Figures

List of Tables

Preface

The world of work assumes an unparalleled importance in industrial societies, and it is mostly by virtue of his occupation that a man receives his livelihood and esteem from others. Not surprisingly, therefore, sociologists' attention has been focused upon the unequal access to, and distribution of, society's scarce resources, which they have usually categorised under the heading of social stratification.

Granted the fact that social institutions constrain man's activity to a considerable degree, there is none the less apparent unease about the role which people's conceptions play in the process of stratification. In large-scale national studies of mobility, the significance which the process has for the respondents is lost in the study of the aggregate, anonymous, individual. Yet even in these studies, recourse is had repeatedly to 'prestige scales' of occupations established from ordinary people's judgements and estimations of the world of occupations; no sociologist has gone so far as to banish the so-called 'subjective' aspects of stratification from his account, even if they turn up in surprising guises. One of the main aims of our study has, therefore, been to claim the 'subjective' for legitimate scientific concern, to insist that the sociological rhetoric of 'everyday knowledge', 'images of society' and 'occupational grading' be taken seriously and studied systematically as instances of cognitive sociology.

In fact our interest in occupational cognition arose initially in our independent studies of occupational allocation. Coxon had a long-standing interest in the recruitment, selection and socialisation of Anglican clergy, and Jones had studied the occupational choice processes of university under-graduates. In both areas, the conceptions which subjects have of their own future role and of related occupations loom large, and assume considerable importance when studying how and why people make the choices they do, whether they plan a systematic career, how they use social contacts (and are in turn used) — in short in the myriad processes which go to make up job-search, career plans and social mobility. Yet available accounts seemed to us to suffer in one of two ways: they either sacrificed generalisability by study-ing individual conceptions in full idiosyncratic detail, or they erected interest-ing explanations on the flimsiest of methodological foundations. What seemed necessary, we thought, was an examination of the social meaning of occupa-tions using the most sensitive and appropriate methods available.

Edinburgh formed the environment within which our research was conceived and carried out, and we owe a good deal to that fair city. It is entirely fitting that these volumes should appear in the Edinburgh series. A number of innovative and exciting developments which occurred whilst we were at the University of Edinburgh profoundly influenced our thinking. Within sociology itself, Edinburgh had become well known as a centre for studies in the sociology of work, of education and of sociolinguistics. Outside the Department of Sociology, the remarkable growth in cognitive studies in the School of Epistemics, the Department of Psychology and the MRC Speech and Communication Unit had considerable impact on our thinking, and directed our attention to the many 'qualitative formalisms' for representing such apparently intractable things as occupational belief-systems.

The result was a research project which many people — not least our funding agency — found difficult to fit within existing academic categories. The main questions we address are clearly and intentionally sociological. We are not primarily interested in personal idiosyncrasy nor directly in the psychological processes of perception which underlie many studies in cognition. But we do hold to the methodological principle that aggregation should follow inspection of individual differences, and not precede it. Secondly, we believe that it is a necessity, and not just a luxury, to pay attention to the cognitive basis of social action, if inferences are to be made about individual behaviour. Such a view has involved us in taking very seriously the language through which people express their conceptions of social reality, and many sociologists will find the juxtaposition of statistical and socio-linguistic analysis a curious one. It is our belief, however, that a methodology which is adequate to the complex, messy and apparently intractable complexity of social life will necessarily call upon procedures of different traditions. In our own case, we believe that the quantitive approach must be widened to incorporate cognitive aspects of human action, and conversely that ethno-graphical insights must be subject to a more rigorous representation.

THE THREE BOOKS AND THEIR ORGANISATION

In writing up the project research for publication, we decided from the outset to separate, as far as possible, the substantive from the technical. Most social scientists are not interested (and rightly so) in the full justification of method-ological niceties — written for the benefit of the technical expert — and many readers do not need to know the full details of the data analysis. Yet such information is necessary if our evidence is to be weighed and our conclusions checked. In addition to the substantive/technical distinction we recognise another divide between our work that is directly relevant to controversies in the field of social stratification, and those developments which take us into novel or unusual areas.

For these reasons, our research appears in three separate books. This first is concerned with subjective aspects of social stratification. The second is concerned more directly with the analysis of the social meaning of occupa-tions, and a third book will contain detailed information on the design techniques and methods used in the project, together with fuller information on a number of topics which, however intrinsically important, are peripheral to the main argument of the two substantive volumes.

Despite the considerable convergence in our interests and skills that occurred during the time of the research, there were — and remain — a number of important ways in which our perspectives diverge, and we have not attempted to disguise this fact. The authorship of the books is truly joint: in all our publications the order of the authors is simply alphabetical. Our practice has been for one of us to volunteer (or be persuaded) to produce the first draft of each substantive chapter, and this person keeps general oversight of the chapter through its many modifications. In this volume, Chapter 3 is primarily the work of Coxon, and Chapter 4 is primarily the work of Jones, but the other chapters are so much a joint activity that it is not now possible or desirable to separate out responsibility.

ACKNOWLEDGEMENTS

The research reported in these books was made possible by two grants from the (U.K.) Social Science Research Council over the period May 1972 — December 1975 (HR 1883/1: 'Occupational Cognition: Representational aspects of occupational titles', and HR 1883/2: 'Sociological aspects of subjective occupational structures'). We gratefully acknowledge this support. To our research staff we owe an especial debt of thanks for their hard careful and competent work. Mary McPherson, Ruth Lockhart, Remy Armstrong, Francoise Rutherford, Richard Feesey and Peter Firth bore the main brunt of the complex and exacting interview procedures; Steve Kendrick and Murray Dalziel preferred to work with data, and did so reliably and well; Sandra Rice, Kate Sadler, Brian Fletcher and Craig Stott provided valuable assistance on computing matters. An especial debt of gratitude is due to May Fraser, who served as secretary throughout the Project. In many unremarked ways she provided support, encouragement and continuity when they were most needed. She combined this with proficiency, reliability, devotion to work and a willingness to tackle material that was often unreadable. John Nimmo and his staff on the Centre for Research in the Social Sciences were an unfailing help in producing doumentation and providing reprographic services.

In a research environment as stimulating as Edinburgh it is difficult to single out specific people for the stimulus they provided. But we should like to mention Tom Burns, Frank Bechhofer, Brian Elliott, Mike Anderson, Jim Closs, David Muxworthy, George Kiss and his colleagues on the MRC Speech and Communication Unit, with whom we shared a concern about cognitive structures and their formal representation, and Andrew McPherson and his staff on the Centre for Educational Sociology.

Gratitude and thanks are due to many others who have helped us in different ways — Monnie Coxon, whose quiet support, good food and eminent common sense kept us down to earth; Hugh Trappes-Lomax, whose linguistic asides have always been valuable; Myrtle Robins and many others who have helped in typing at various stages; Stephen Davis our agent and John Winckler of Macmillan, who have helped us get our writing into publishable form; and finally to the 'Tuesday Club' at the Staff Club at Edinburgh, with whom we shared drink, ideas, food and friendship through several years.

A.P.M.C.
C.L.J.

Edinburgh, May 1977

1 Social Structure and Occupations

1.1 THE PERCEPTION OF OCCUPATIONS

Why is it that so many official forms and questionnaires contain questions about one's occupation, or one's father's occupation, or one's spouse's occupation? Why do introductions at cocktail parties or in bars so frequently involve the exchange of information about occupations? One plausible explanation is that occupational titles provide socially useful information about people. In the situation of informal social interaction, mere observation allows us to discover such things as the sex, age, accent, physical attractiveness, ethnicity, or whatever, of our co-participants. Being told the occupations pursued by the people one is chatting to seems to be thought of as adding to the information that could be gained solely by observation. When taken in context with age and sex, it gives some indication of a person's likely income bracket, educational level, housing area, and style of life. It also provides a starting point for further conversation.

In modern societies much information about people is communicated through third parties or through completed application forms, certificates, questionnaires or whatever. Feature stories in newspapers or on television commonly find it worth while to tell us the age, sex, race, residential area, *and occupation* of the characters in news stories.

Direct interaction need not take place between the person who applies for automobile insurance and the agent who writes the policy. The relationship between sociologists who send out interviewers or questionnaires to gather information from 'subjects' is similarly indirect. In such situations it seems that a person's occupation by itself is used as a major index of his (or her) position in (usually) industrial society. As it happens, empirically oriented sociologists have indeed found that even a crude coding of occupation is statistically related to a host of other characteristics. Some of these relationships are obvious; it does not take a social survey to tell us that architects (for example) have higher formal educational qualifications than builders' labourers, nor to tell us that stockbrokers generally earn more than teachers. We know these things from discussions with friends or from our exposure to newspapers and other media. Other statistical correlates of occupation, such as higher or lower suicide rates, and greater or lesser frequencies of sexual behaviour are less obvious and indeed are rather more difficult to explain.

The fact that there are enormous numbers of distinct occupational titles is a reflection of the highly specialised division of labour in large-scale societies. One important consequence of this is that the area of shared experience between people engaged in different specialisms is relatively small. Johnson (1972) has argued that the organic solidarity between people engaged in mutually dependent specialities is in a sense counterbalanced by a corresponding decrease in shared experience. The specialist engineer and the specialist nurse are neither competent to carry out the work of the other, and their occupational worlds have correspondingly little overlap. In Johnson's own words:

> . . . the emergence of specialised occupational skills, whether productive of goods or services creates relationships of *social and economic dependence* and, paradoxically, relationships of *social distance.* Dependence upon the skills of others has the effect of reducing the common area of shared experience and knowledge, and increases social distance. . .

In some ways, the phrase 'talking shop' sums up this point. 'Shop' is talk between specialists about their speciality, and it is considered impolite to make such talk in the presence of non-specialists who would be shut out of the conversation. Perhaps this is why so much talk revolves around the major areas of shared experience which seem to be television, sport and (in Britain) the weather. Almost everyone has had contact with some service occupations, such as schoolteaching and medicine, and of course, certain occupations have been made the subject of television 'soap-operas'. Studies have been carried out in North America in order to find out how television contributes to the knowledge that children acquire about occupations. The De Fleurs (1967) report that the occupations which are portrayed on television are learned about in rather standardised ways, and they ascribe this effect to the stereo-typed image of each occupation that television puts over.

HOW CAN AN OCCUPATION BE PERCEIVED?

The term 'perception' as applied to occupations does not refer solely to perceptual processes that occur when an individual is confronted with occupationally relevant stimuli. Rather it refers to the complex of beliefs and assumptions which exist in the individual's memory. The term incorporates the processes by which this complex came to be organised as it is, and how it is likely to incorporate new information. Thus studies of the 'perception' of occupations might be more accurately described as studies of how people form concepts about the occupational world, how they interrelate these concepts, and how they manipulate and evaluate them when making vocationally relevant decisions. Quillian (1968) frames one of the central questions as 'What constitutes a reasonable view of how semantic information is organized within a person's memory? (p. 216). In other respects, the processes involved in the perception of occupations may be similar to those studied under the label of 'the social psychology of rumour' (Allport and Postman 1947), or those of 'social memory' (Bartlett 1932), for what is involved here is the process by which an individual transforms a multiplicity of observations and hearsay into an organised set of attitudes and perceptions. This process of combining different kinds of evidence to form an attitude is studied as the process of 'impression formation' in social psychology (Asch 1946; Anderson 1962). If viewed over the formative years of life, it might be likened to the study of 'attitude development' as part of the life cycle. Proshansky (1966) has reviewed the literature on the development of children's attitudes toward ethnic groups, and the stages he identifies as 'ethnic awareness', 'ethnic orientation' and 'ethnic attitude' have a certain similarity to the stages of vocational development postulated by such writers as Ginzberg *et al.* (1951), and Super *et al.* (1957). Heise and Roberts (1970) have discussed the development of 'role knowledge' in more general terms. From a sociological point of view, one can raise questions about the 'social structuring' of such information, rumour and hearsay. One might ask for example, what social roles or social institutions are involved in the transmission of occupational information and how formal structures compare with informal systems (such as friendship networks) in getting such information (whether it be valid or invalid) to the individuals (see Granovetter 1974).

In asking how a particular set of occupations is 'averagely perceived' by a given group of people (and some thought should be given to what could be meant by an 'average perception'), one is raising questions about social stereotypes. In the language of advertising and market research (Harder 1969: 171) one is asking about the 'images' of occupations, rather in the same spirit as one might ask about the 'images' of competing brands of motor car (e.g.,Wells *et al.,* 1957, 1958). Erdos (1970) discusses the images of business corporations.

At the individual level, it has been a popular theme in the person-perception literature, that people use social stereotypes as identification rules (Cook 1971) to aid their daily perceptual decision-making. (Identification rules are rules of form — 'if it is an *A*, then it must posess the qualities *xyz*'.) Stereotyping (use of such identification rules) is often cited as being one of the cognitive processes that go to make up the 'implicit theories' that people hold about the external world. Tajfel (1969) in his review of the influence of social and cultural factors on perception defines a stereotype as

A set of characteristics attributed to a human group. Individuals who belong to the stereotyped group are assumed to be similar to one another with respect to those characteristics, and to differ with regard to the same attributes from other contrasting groups (1969: 327).

Triandis (1964) puts forward another definition:

Stereotypes are generalizations about the characteristics of groups of

people. They are part of the 'what goes with what' process which
organizes categories, places them in schemata, and orients the schemata
to make them consistent with the person's value orientations (p.23).

While the use of stereotypes can be an aid to accuracy in the perception of
persons and of social groups (Cronbach 1958) liberal social psychologists
have often felt called upon to warn their readers against uncritical acceptance
of (usually ethnic) stereotypes. Thus Cook (1971) says,

> Stereotypes have three characteristics. In the first place, they are very
> commonly wrong all or most of the time. [Cook is referring to ethnic
> stereotypes.] . . . secondly, they tend to be viewed over-inclusively, or to
> be rigidly held . . . thirdly, stereotypes often divide people up in ways
> that are felt to be inappropriate; it is thought that we should not make
> judgments — especially wrong ones — about people because they are
> Jewish, or manual workers, etc. (p. 61).

There are considerable possibilities for confusion when using the phrase
'social stereotype', because the term 'stereotype' brims over with surplus
meaning. Thus the noun 'stereotype' has subtly different applications from
the active verb 'to stereotype', and from the derived adjective, 'stereotyped'
(of perception, of cognition or behaviour patterns). Tajfel's definition of
social stereotypes has been given above, and it is clear from this that he
conceives it as a social and supraindividual concept. In visual metaphor a
social stereotype might be viewed as a large information hoarding, hanging
in the sky and visible to all, to be referred to or not as each individual
perceiver found convenient. The word 'sociotype' may be more appropriate
when this sort of model is envoked. The *Shorter Oxford English Dictionary*
defines the noun 'stereotype' (figurative) as, 'something continued or
constantly repeated without change', and the verb 'to stereotype' as meaning
'to fix or perpetuate in an unchanging form' (also figurative). For Tajfel,
stereotyping is a thing which individuals do:

> The general inclination to place a person in categories according to some
> easily and quickly identifiable characteristic such as age, sex, ethnic
> membership, nationality or occupation, and then to attribute to him
> qualities believed to be typical of the category (1969: 422).

The clinical use of the term 'stereotype' is again somewhat different, as it
incorporates the notion that the individual whose perception, cognition or
behaviour is said to be stereotyped is not simply making use of cultural
images or social stereotypes on the grounds (say) of the perceptual conven-
ience of doing so, but is in his personality-structure, rigid, unduly persever-
ative, reluctant to change set, or unable to learn from a changing environment.
For example, we may find that a single individual regularly treats what we
perceive as an internally differentiated class of stimulus objects, as if they
were all the same. The individual may indeed affirm that all these stimulus
objects *ought* to be treated in the same way, and he may deny the usefulness

of differentiating among them. In the classical example of ethnic stereotypes, the individual resists attempts to make him draw distinctions between
sub-sets of the category in question. In this sense, the word 'stereotype'
refers to the *structural* properties of one part of a particular individual's
cognitive organisation (what is referred to by some writers as 'cognitive
simplicity').

Clearly the word 'stereotype' is used markedly different senses by
different writers. This raises a major problem in research in the area of
occupational perception (and indeed in the area of social perception generally);
the relationship between the individual and aggregate levels of data (implying
problems about the relationship between processes at the individual and
social levels). Previous work has largely evaded the issue, the usual approach
being to characterise the cognitive structure of the individual by the 'average'
of some group (for example as a profile of arithmetic means on Semantic
Differential scales).[1]

Let us return to the metaphor for a social stereotype as a large information
hoarding, hanging in the sky, and visible to all, to be referred to or not as each
individual perceiver finds convenient. If a social stereotype is like this, then
how can it be measured? The techniques used in analysing social stereotypes vary in complexity from the content analysis of open-ended essays
reported by Mead and Metraux (1957), through Holland's (1963) use of a
sentence-completion task, to Sutton's (1971) use of 'quadratic discriminant'
analysis, and Coxon's (1971) of 'smallest space' analysis. Measurement
techniques have been reviewed by Ulrich *et al.* (1966) for the occupational
area, and by Cauthen *et al.* (1971) for stereotypes in general. Brigham (1971)
has discussed the various ways in which the 'stereotype' concept has been
used in psychology. Much use has been made of the Katz and Braly (1933)
technique, and also of Osgood's Semantic Differential. Thus methods
concentrate, perhaps mistakenly, on the aggregation of individual beliefs
into 'social beliefs' at the level of statistically defined groups. A few investigators have analysed properly collective representations, such as the content
of the mass media (e.g. Hirsch 1958; Jencks and Reisman 1962). Jencks and
Reisman analysed the files of *Crimson,* the Harvard student newspaper, and
also interviewed students and tutors, in order to assess the nature of the
popular stereotypes of the Harvard 'Houses'. Their report argues that these
stereotypes are used in a complex, metaphorical imagery by which students
describe themselves and each other. They remark,

> The impulse of the House resident to type the other Houses rests primarily
> *on a desire to say what he is not* . . . The stereotypes [held by] freshmen
> have a somewhat less placid quality, for them, these images are possible
> future roles (p. 754, emphasis added).

The Katz-Braly method which was applied to occupational stereotypes by
Walker (1958) consists of asking a respondent to look over a long list of
trait names, and for each 'object of perception' (e.g. the name of an ethnic

group or an occupational title), to pick the small number of traits that are seen as most characteristic of it (in Coombs' terminology, the experimental task used by Katz and Braly was 'pick 5 of 84'). The social stereotype of each object of perception is then defined as the set of traits which are ascribed to it (i.e. picked) by a large proportion of the respondents. Walker, for example, lists the five most frequent associated trait adjectives with each of the occupational titles she used. On this criterion the stereotype of the School Teacher was that he is well-educated, intelligent, tolerant, fair-minded, and friendly; that of the Coal Miner was that he is rough, tough, friendly, honest, and industrious; that of the Doctor was that he is intelligent, efficient, well-educated, humanitarian and practical.

In any experiment, each adjective will have been assigned to each object of perception (say to an occupation) with a certain frequency. For each occupation, the adjectives assigned to it can be arranged in a series of decreasing mention-frequency, say from left to right. Katz and Braly's index of strength of stereotype (or perhaps, of salience of the sociotype) measures the degree to which any particular occupation has a commonly agreed-upon meaning in some social group, and is measured as the smallest number of adjectives whose total sum of mentions is sufficient to account for half of the total votes cast. This makes the measure rather similar to a median. The theoretical maximum stereotypy score is one of half the number of traits 'picked', and the theoretical minimum is half the total number of traits in the list. Averaging the stereotype indices for ten ethnic groups, Katz and Braly (1933) found that about 8.5 adjectives were usually required (out of 84) to account for half the total number of 'mentions'. According to Walker other investigators have obtained average stereotype indices of 12.3. 12.6. and 15.3 (all in the field of ethnic stereotypes). Walker found stereotype indices varying from the highly stereotyped 'Doctor' with a value of 7.9, through 'Schoolteacher' with 7.7, to 'Trade Union Leader' with 15.5 (least strongly stereotyped), and she concluded,

> Comparing these results with those obtained in studies of ethnic stereotypes among students, it would appear that occupational stereotypes are approximately as strong as ethnic stereotypes (p. 123).

Measurement procedures imply theories about what is being measured and the model of a social stereotype which is embedded in the Katz-Braly procedure seems to be a chemist's 'concentration-model'. It has nothing to say about the content or structure of any individual's belief, as it defines a social stereotype in terms of how likely the individuals in the particular social group are to assign the same traits to some object of perception. The degree to which a social stereotype exists for a particular concept is often referred to as its 'strength', or its 'pervasiveness'. This 'strength' of a stereotype is measured in a statistical way as a function of the degree to which the distribution of trait-assignments depart from randomness. It is commonly implied (e.g. by such writers as Allport, 1954) that if aggregate-level cultural stereotypes are 'strong' or 'prevasive' in a statistical sense, then the beliefs of individuals must be strongly or intensely or rigidly held. But given group-level data (e.g., from the Katz-Braly technique, or the Osgood Semantic Differential technique), this need not be the case. To be sure, data from interviews show that some individuals hold such beliefs, but even with the availability of such 'intensity-measuring' techniques as Guttman's (Guttman and Suchman, 1947), such concepts as 'rigidity' of belief systems may very well elude the question-naire. The essential quality of rigid beliefs seems to be that they are resistant to *active probing* (e.g. Zimbardo and Ebbesen 1969: 102) and so the sophis-ticated interviewer will probably remain the appropriate tool for their inves-tigation. Even Holland (1963), in discussing the results from his semi-project-ive sentence completion technique (a technique which is concerned with the *distribution of associations,* and not with individual cognitive structures), allows himself to conclude that students perceive occupations in 'stereotyped' ways.

The study of social stereotypes is the study of cultural meanings and it was perhaps inevitable that the Osgood *et al* (1957) Semantic Differential method would be used to analyse the connotative meaning of occupational terms.[2] However, little attention has been paid to the fact that the use of this technique commits the researcher to being concerned with only one kind of meaning. The standard instructions for the semantic differential are,

Trust your first impressions and work quickly. Try not to spend more than a moment or two thinking about any one rating.

With such instructions, it takes an act of faith to believe that the responses will be true reflections of cognitive structure. Hudson (1968) warns that 'the test is exceptionally boring to do; and to some, infuriating' (p. 117). In terms of its known linguistic, theoretical and empirical deficiences, the aspects of occupational meaning that can be inferred by this procedure are severely restricted, being limited to connotative meaning, and not in fact providing the 'basic dimensionality' of a general semantic space, as is often claimed.

Despite these limitations, Beardslee and O'Dowd (1961, 1962) Hudson (1966, 1967a, 1967b) and a large number of other research workers have used the semantic differential to isolate and describe occupational stereo-types. Respondents are usually asked to rate a fairly large number of occupational titles or occupational roles on bipolar 7-point scales (see Heise 1969, for a discussion of methodological issues). The ratings are then averaged over individuals and the 'profiles' of the occupational titles on the bipolar scales are referred to as the 'occupational images'. Differences between the profiles of occupational titles are typically large and stable. For example, Beardslee and O'Dowd report that their respondents (male and female college students) viewed the Schoolteacher as

Low in wealth, social status and opportunity for advancement. He has little power in public affairs, and he cannot even command an attractive wife although he can count on a happy home life — just the opposite of the lawyer's situation. The teacher is considered intelligent, sensitive, and, like the professor, interested in art, but to a lesser extent. Furthermore, he is attentive to people and unselfish in his relations with them . . . Finally, the teacher is seen as lacking in confidence and in hard, assertive properties . . . the feminine component is high [and is] associated with a nurturant and at the same time dependent quality (1962: 616).

Another of the vignettes provided by Beardslee and O'Dowd is of the Scientist, who has a 'well-defined stereotype' as

A highly intelligent person with a strong tendency to be both individualistic and radical in personal and social outlooks. At the same time, the scientist is seen as socially withdrawn; he is indifferent to people, retiring, and somewhat depressed . . . he is believed to have a relatively unhappy home life and a wife who is not pretty. There is an air of strangeness about him: he is hard to like and comprehend . . . he focuses his powers in a rational and sensitive pursuit of answers to life's mysteries . . . the complexity of the scientist's nature must account for his being considered mildly interesting and colourful . . . In summary, there appears a picture of the scientist as a highly intelligent individual, devoted to his studies and research, at the expense of interest in art, friends and family. It should also be noted that the scientist is clearly a masculine figure in a desexualised way.

Beardslee and O'Dowd present portraits of the 'scientist's image' in the periodical *Science* (1961), and also in Sanford's *American College* (1962). It may amuse the cynic to note the former portrait seems a more favourable one than the latter, although the central core of a rational and cool intelligence is common to both. Beardslee and O'Dowd investigated the images of a large number of other occupational titles, including various types of specialised Scientists, and also College Professors, Engineers, Business Executives, Doctors and so forth. They claimed that a correlation of +0.91 between the average values attributed to the word 'Scientist' by students and by college professors (i.e., the Pearson correlation over the two profiles on 21 bipolar scales) was a telling argument of the 'social reality' of occupational images. They suggest that occupational images are apprehended in a similar way (within a linear transformation) by 'average perceivers' from fairly different culture-groups (i.e., that people agree about the meaning of the word Scientist). Biddle *et al* (1966) on the other hand, reports that the role requirements of the Schoolteacher are perceived differently by parents, pupils, school administrators and teachers, and Keil *et al.* (1967) refers to the literature on the 'cultural shock' which is supposed to be suffered by the neophyte Schoolteacher, as his or her preconceptions about teaching come up against reality. This raises interesting questions about how one might compare occupations with regard to their tendency to evoke Biddle's 'shared inaccuracies' or Beardslee's 'close agreement'.

Research on social stereotypes is in a peculiar position *vis-à-vis* its subject matter, because even more so than other areas of the social sciences it is itself subject to, and an inalienable part of, the processes that naïve researchers sometimes claim to report on in an objective manner. Thus Walker's (1958) report that there exists a social stereotype of the Lawyer as 'alert, calculating, well-educated, shrewd, clever'; the claim by Wells *et al.* (1958) that the Chevrolet owner is seen as 'poor, low class, ordinary, plain simple, practical, common, average, cheap, thin, little, friendly and small'; Coxon's (1971) word picture of the Town Planner who is 'of greatest social usefulness, needs most training, is most influential, most involved in formulating policy, most creative, hottest, most exciting, and is broadest in scope'; and the Hudson (1968) and Beardslee and O'Dowd (1962) reports on the images of various kinds of academic specialists all become part of the 'information environment', once they are published. By reporting the existence of a social stereotype, a social psychologist may be perpetuating it, disseminating it, or making it more salient. This does not mean that an embargo should be placed upon publications about social stereotypes. However, it is useful to bear in mind that one among many channels for the dissemination of popular stereotypes may be an 'academic channel'. The psychological and social processes involved in the presentation of scientific results have been indicated by Hirschi and Selvin's (1967) discussion of various fallacies in the presentation of research findings, e.g., the 'profile fallacy', which consists of summarising one's research by giving a brief profile of the 'typical' or 'average' person in some category of interest — e.g., describing the 'typical' delinquent, or the 'typical' authoritarian, or whatever, as having all of a set of characteristics which have each been separately averaged over a group. Hirchi and Selvin call this an illegitimate shift from the statistical properties of groups to the properties of individuals. Zigler and Child (1969) remark that 'word pictures' tend to be used by social scientists

> to emphasize the homogeneity of behaviour within a [social] class, and the heterogeneity across classes. . . . [and] Because it is irrelevant to the main process, little effort is ordinarily given to discussions of variability within a class, or of similarities across classes (p. 483).

But this is precisely the essential feature of stereotyping defined by Tajfel and Wilkes (1963) as '. . . [the feature of] exaggerating *some* difference between groups classified in a certain way, and of minimizing the same differences within such groups' (p. 113). Hudson (1971) has discussed a law of 'selective attention to data' and Berkowitz (1971) has demonstrated the existence of the classical processes of levelling, sharpening and assimilation to the typical instance or 'good' gestalt (Wulf 1938), in the summarizing of a classical experiment in textbooks of social psychology.[3]

If processes such as these occur in communications between academics, it does not seem over-elitist to suppose that they may also occur when individuals discuss the world of occupations among themselves. In the day-to-day world of discussion, individuals may exaggerate differences between and minimise those within; they may polarise issues, and discuss them in crude typologies; they may 'level', 'sharpen' and 'assimilate to the typical instance'; and yet they may only do such things to gain the effects of metaphor, imagery and contrast in communication. It may be that only the occupationally ignorant always think of occupations in the terms in which they are sometimes discussed; (in the same way, only the unsophisticated believe that conventional, scientific research reports reflect what was done in any accurate fashion.[4]

1.2   SOCIAL STRUCTURE: OBJECTIVE OR SUBJECTIVE?

The analysis of 'occupations' features centrally in a wide variety of sociological contexts. They are the main form of social identification and the most salient type of role-structure characterising industrial societies. 'Occupation' defines the work situation and is the articulation point between the systems for the distribution of economic, social and political resources. Within stratification theory *per se* it occupies a position of conceptual and empirical pre-eminence:

> Occupations are at once the most obvious and the most effective predictor of differential location within the structure of social inequalities
> (Runciman 1968: 55)

Within subdisciplines of sociology, occupations continue to occupy an important position. The professionalisation debate, role-conflict and social identity among schoolteachers, clergy, physicians; descriptions of the work situation of clerical workers are examples of this.

Over the past four decades, sociologists have increasingly relied upon occupation as an index of a person's social and economic status. Where any justification for this is given, it typically follows the line of argument put forward by North and Hatt, in a study carried out for the National Opinion Research Centre in 1947: that a man's job occupies a large slice of his daily life, that it influences his existence both inside and outside working hours and that it actually determines his social and his economic welfare (our use of the masculine pronoun here reflects the interests and assumptions of sociology). Some examples of this rhetoric are:

(1) 'A man's work is as good a clue as any to the course of his life and to his social being and identity' (Hughes 1958).

(2) 'A great share of men's waking hours is devoted to their occupational activities; the economic supports for group survival are provided through the pooled work of socially interrelated occupations; men's aspirations, interests and sentiments are largely organized and stamped with the mark of their occupations' (Merton 1958)

(3) 'Nothing stamps a man as much as his occupation. Daily work determines the mode of life . . . it constrains our ideas, feelings and tastes. Habits of the body and mind, and habits of language combine to give each

of us his occupational type People of the same occupation know one another, seek each other's company and frequent one another by necessity and choice' (Goblot 1961).

These arguments appeal to folk wisdom, but perhaps we should distrust them for that very reason. Folk wisdoms are notoriously flexible, having proverbs and aphorisms to fit almost any situation. Where absence does not make the heart grow finder, we are reminded that out of sight means out of mind. The reliance upon information about occupation has meant that books about social stratification are increasingly about occupational stratification, and that books about 'social ' mobility are increasingly restricted to 'occupational' mobility.

In this book, we are concerned with the ways in which people think about occupations and professions. We are concerned with subjective models of the occupational structure and with the way these relate to seemingly objective characteristics of occupations. In making such a study, we assume that occupational cognition may vary, that the conceptions which people have of the world of occupations are likely to differ according to their own experience of the social system.

'SUBJECTIVE' AND 'OBJECTIVE' SOCIAL STRUCTURE

The analysis of social stratification has usually rested upon a distinction being drawn between the 'objective' and 'subjective' structure. Interpretations of this distinction differ widely, but the core concept is that an individual's 'actual' location in the social structure may often differ from his own conception of it.

THE MARXIST ACCOUNT

The *locus classicus* of this question occurs in Marxist writings where the objective/subjective contrast usually refers to the extent to which individuals and groups correctly recognise their divergent group interests. In the popular account[5] the objective class structure is determined by the social relations of production, whose objectivity holds independently of a given individual's conception of them. In this account, cognition is simply the mirror-image of external reality, and 'subjective' consciousness or the awareness of the class structure is therefore thought of as derivative, brought into being in the course of class conflict. But the fact that different conceptions exist, even among the 'working class', poses serious theoretical problems (which have usually been discussed under the heading of 'false consciousness'). How do members of the working class come to hold a conception of the class structure which is not in accord with 'external reality', or with their 'objective class interest'? A common reply is that this is due to the fact that the ruling class promulgates a contrary image of common, national unity of interests, and are able to maintain it through manipulating power relations and the mass media.

Whilst this credits the ruling class with a good deal more foresight and knowledge than it has usually shown, it does locate the problem back where it belongs, in the relationship between ideas and social structure.

Later Marxists — and especially Lukács and Korsch — rejected this mechanistic account, and recognised that the problems associated with the relation between social structure and social consciousness could not be satisfactorily answered within a framework which viewed 'subjective' and 'objective' as antithetical, and which treated the subjective as simply derivative of the objective. Both Lukács (in *History and Class Consciousness*, 1922) and Karl Korsch (in *Marxism and Philosophy*, 1923) rejected the tendency (particularly evident in Leninist thought) to revert to crudely materialistic doctrines of the relationship between consciousness and the external world:

> We must discover . . . the practical significance of these different possible relations between the objective economic totality, the imputed class consciousness and the real, psychological thoughts of men about their lives (Lukács 1971: 51).

Lukács' refusal, at least before his recantation, to accept any simple object/subject antithesis produced a chain of thought which led to a radical form of sociological relativism. Its effect on other sociologists such as Mannheim was profound:

> All that concerned him [Mannheim] . . . was the reality of 'life-situations' as they confronted men and societies. Since that and that alone is the reality which people see from different 'vantage points' in the social structure, their ideologies can be 'relatively' true only with respect to that reality (Watnick 157).

THE 'REPUTATIONALIST' ACCOUNT OF STATUS STRUCTURES

A large number of empirical studies of status-communities have started from the study of such 'life-situations', as reported by members of the community, but in doing so they have encountered considerable conceptual and method-ological problems. By cutting links with the Marxian conception of the objective basis of stratification, they did not thereby avoid questions of the nature of an 'external' structure. In the 'reputational' tradition, the subject's own conceptions of the status structure are taken as *sui generis,* as the data from which the social scientist begins to piece together a coherent account. The best known example of research in this tradition is still Lloyd Warner's (1949) study of *Jonesville,* where he attempts to establish and systematise the relative location of families in terms of their symbolic status character-istics. Warner viewed the process by which status is defined as both relational and relativistic. The assignment of the location of a family, x, in the status structure is similar to the process of triangulation — persons located at different points in the structure provide different sorts of information and each

acts as a coordinate for fixing *x*'s position; this is relational information.
However, such information also tells us much about how the social position
of the speaker affects his judgement and in this sense it is relativistic. Given
two informants discussing a single person

> although the information gathered about him from the two will sometimes
> seem contradictory, each is telling the truth, from where he sees his status
> world, about the social position of the person under discussion (Warner
> 1960: 74).

Various problems of description remain, but it is clear that Warner views his
task as providing a coherent account of the subjects' own conceptions of
their status world. Certainly, he imposes upon his subjects constructs and
characteristics which may not be used universally, but the distinctions,
terminology and judgements are largely those of his subjects.

Unfortunately, the representation Warner makes of *'the'* status structure
of *Jonesville* is of more dubious validity. As in earlier community studies
(Davis *et al.*, 1941 : 65), Warner accepts virtually unquestioned the view that
'the stratification system' is a set of ranked classes, and yet the evidence for
this in the subjects' own accounts is equivocal, to say the least. Many of the
inferences that Warner himself makes about the conceptions of his subjects
illustrates well the contention by De Soto and Albrecht (1965) that social
scientists are as likely as anyone else to succumb to tendencies to oversimplify
social relations by expecting linear orderings, single orderings and end-
anchored orderings.[6]

THE COMPROMISE ACCOUNT

One of the most perceptive commentators on this style of research, as upon
the conceptual basis upon which it rests, has been Edward Shils (in Jackson
1968). He interprets status in the broader framework of 'deference', and in
so doing neatly dovetails the behavioural (action) and the attitudinal components of status.

Status judgements are thought of as based upon, and determined by, a
limited range of characteristics (called 'deference-entailing properties' by
Shils) which have typically been taken to include income, education, style
of life, ethnicity – and, especially, occupation. In common sociological usage
the term 'objective' is reserved for substantial characteristics (such as income
and length of education) which have an external quality, in the sense that no
cognisance need be taken of subjects' conceptions in arriving at acceptable
sociological assessments. By contrast, characteristics depending crucially upon
subjects' conceptions (such as 'self-definitions' of social standing) have
generally been taken to be 'subjective'. But this usage has by no means been
consistent. As Shils points out, the meaning of 'objective' has been extended
to cover *any* consensual, unambiguous status judgements which are not
thought to be matters of opinion, and are more or less quantifiable. As a

result, components of status which it is thought *ought* to be consensual and in fact are conformable to scaling procedures come to be invested with a distinct, substantial nature, whilst the more dissensual and attitudinal components are relegated to a subordinate and derivative category.

This confusion has had far-reaching consequences for the analysis of social status. The measurement of occupational prestige – the 'objective', substantial, evaluative component of status – has proceeded independently of the analysis of 'images of society'. As a result, subjects' conceptions and interpretations – which are an integral cognitive component of social status – have been virtually excised from the measurement of prestige, and the largely discursive qualitative and descriptive treatment which 'images of society' have received has confirmed the impression that they are inherently incapable of formal 'objective' treatment (Bulmer 1975).

The bifurcation of studies of status into prestige measurement and images of society dates largely from the 1940s, which saw the publication of Warner's 'Yankee City' studies, and Mapheus Smith's (1943) study of the 'prestige status of occupations', followed in 1947 by the now classic NORC national prestige scale.[7]

Warner's intention in what he called 'measuring social class' by the Index of Status Characteristics (he took social class and social status to be synony-mous) was to provide a systematic procedure for mapping assessments of an individual's occupation, source of income, house type, and dwelling area into a single index. The main purpose of the index is to allocate an individual to one of his six 'social classes'. The method which Warner used (1960 : 121-9) to produce his Index is interesting both because it is a *composite* index (formed by weighting and summing an individual's assessed rank on each of the four components of status), and because of the way in which he mixes 'objective' and 'subjective' elements in constructing the seven levels of each 'scale'. For example, the occupation scale was based not upon his subjects' judgements, but upon the Occupational Groups of the US Census devised by Edwards (1943), whilst the levels which Warner uses to define his income scale were based explicitly on distinctions which were made by the subjects themselves. The theoretical status of these procedures is interesting. If the 'measurement of social class' is intended simply to be a technical tool to make it easier to estimate the location of an individual on one of Warner's five classes then, like Duncan's use of regression techniques to provide a 'Socio-economic Index for All Occupations' (Reiss 1961: 196 *et seq.*), the techniques used to obtain such an Index have no substantive implications whatever. But if the Index is intended to say something about what characteristics of status are seen as most salient by the subject, and how he combines information in forming an overall impression or judgement of status – indeed, if the Index is intended to *represent* subjects' conceptions and beliefs in any way, then it is an entirely different matter. In this case, the unstated assumptions need to be made explicit and justified empirically. Since most of the assumptions he makes are clearly cognitive in form, they might be termed the 'cognitive cost' of Warner's procedure. Their general form is well specified by Shils (ibid. : 437):

(1) there is evaluative consensus throughout the society on the criteria (characteristics) in accordance with which status (deference) is allocated;

(2) there is cognitive consensus regarding the levels of each characteristic;

(3) there is consensus on the weights to be assigned to the properties (and between the judgement which a person makes of his own position and those which others make of it);

(4) equal attention is paid to, and equal differentiation is made between, the strata of the social structure.[8]

Each of these assumptions is highly debatable, and it will be our concern to investigate them in this book.

Whatever its shortcomings, Warner's study included avowedly 'subjective' aspects of status as an integral, and indeed fundamental part. Later studies, especially of 'occupational prestige', were much less sensitive to these issues, and as a result they can hardly be taken to represent status in any significant way. The only judgement required of the subject in a modern prestige study is typically that he should rate the 'general standing' of a large number of occupational titles on a five-point or nine-point scale. The task is straight-forwardly evaluative (although the ambiguity in the instructions given usually leaves room for doubt as to what sort of criterion is expected, and whether the subject is intended simply to report upon generally-held beliefs, or to give his own opinions). Once again, the technical details need not detain us,[9] but the 'cognitive cost' in such studies is yet more prohibitive, and the meaning of the task is problematic. The purpose of the measurement of occupational prestige none the less retains some reference to subjects' concep-tion of the status structure, as can be seen by the context of its development. In many cases, occupational prestige studies were preliminary investigations to the post-war studies of social mobility, especially in Britain (Moser and Hall 1954). As then construed, social mobility was concerned with the movement of men through an ordered set of occupational groups. Before the extent of movement could be assessed, the scale along which it took place had first to be established. It is perhaps worth asking why widespread 'lay' judgements (as opposed, say, to those of the Census Office) were thought relevant. The fact that they *were* testifies to the fact that 'subjective conceptions' were never considered irrelevant to 'objective' occupational prestige. In prestige studies, objectivity was equated much more directly with consensus, since the assessment of social mobility required a simple (uni-dimensional), unambiguous, ranking of occupations. The consensual occupa-tional scale in the NORC study was achieved simply, and virtually by fiat; arbitary weights were assigned to each of the rating categories and the average score for a given occupation then defined its prestige measure (Reiss 1961: 53). The rank order of these averages was then taken to represent 'the social-status continuum'. Later work (Reiss 1961) submitted the conceptual, methodological and technical basis of the NORC study to detailed and sophis-ticated criticism and evaluation, and in many instances emphasised many of the shortcomings alluded to here. Only limited ranges of the 88 occupational titles could be shown to scale unidimensionally, with more sensitive procedures. Even the central postulate of evaluative consensus (that subjects' evaluations are stable and reflect a single viewpoint) has been seriously undermined, not only on the grounds that the method of averaged ratings is too gross to enable differences to appear,[10] but also in terms of the original NORC data: Alexander (1972: 767) shows that

> systematic perceptual differences in status structures are a function of the perceiver's position.

If it is the case, as he goes on to argue (p. 772), that

> people respond to their perceptions of different status worlds rather than responding differentially . . . to similar perceptions of consensually defined status structures

then a main justification of the 'objectivity' of such structures is seriously undermined.

Nor, for that matter, do essentially *evaluative* judgements of prestige tell us much about the cognitions which underlie the evaluation. The need to separate cognitive and evaluative bases of judgement about occupations has increasingly been recognised by sociologists (Goldthorpe and Hope 1972: 38; Shils, 121 *et seq.;* Reiss, 106-7), but despite ingenious attempts to do so it will not in general be possible to 'retrieve' representations of occupational cognitions from purely evaluative data. The reasons for this are in part substantive, and in part methodological, and can well be illustrated by reference to theories of preference. Traditionally, preference has been construed as being the result of a subject evaluating a given set of 'objects' be they cars, occupations, commodity bundles or states of the world. The implicit — and important — assumption in comparing sets of individual preferences is that subjects perceive the alternatives in basically the same way. Preference is then viewed as some function of the prior cognitions, and the source of individual variability in preferences is located in differences in *evaluation*. Now prestige judgements are not necessarily to be identified with preferences, but the implications seem to be the same: in absence of *independent* information about perceptions (or conceptions) of the occupational structure, it is highly misleading to use prestige data to infer information about subjective occupational structure unless it can be assumed that the only source of variability lies in individuals' evaluations of that structure. But occupational prestige judgements *per se* give little direct information about the subjective occupational structure, or about concepts used to describe the occupational world, and if an integrated account is to be given of status, then it is necessary to have prior information on the way in which subjects organise information and on their cognitions of the occupational world before an account can be given of what prestige judgements mean.

Moreover, several other lines of research converge on the conclusion that in 'occupational grading studies' such as the NORC study, and the more recent British study (Hope 1972), cognition and evaluation are inextricably conflated, so that it is not at all clear what inferences may be drawn from grading data. Reiss (ibid.: 106) argues that by its very nature the NORC task requires subjects, at least in part, to report upon how they perceive the structure, rather then evaluate it, yet it is not possible to separate the two components: 'this suggests that any postulated "prestige" component ought to be measured independently of individual's perceptions of the structure'. An investigation of the semantic connotations of the NORC rating task was in fact made by Gusfield and Schwartz (1963), in order to understand what respondents did when they rank occupations. They conclude that the NORC scale

> did not reflect only a set of values applied to occupations but rather a set of perceptions about the social status which the occupations receive in the society (factual − normative) as well as a set of values (268).

The conclusion seems inescapable: to the extent that conventional occupational-prestige studies claim to represent in any significant way subjects' conceptions of the status structure, they fail. However useful scales of generalised 'goodness' of occupations (Goldthorpe and Hope: 31 *et seq.*) may be for some purposes they cannot represent in any direct way people's perceptions, interpretations, or the meanings which they ascribe to the occupational world.

1.3 IMAGES OF SOCIETY

If the development of occupational prestige studies represents an attempt to develop 'objective' consensual, quantitatively tractable aspects of status, the analysis of 'images of society' − its 'subjective' counterpart − has equally suffered from distortion and lack of rigour. The sociological literature on the images of stratification held by different social groups has certainly been rich. However, the evidence which underpins it turns out to be thin indeed, consisting to a very considerable extent of simple commentary by sociologists upon judiciously selected quotations from interviews. The basis for the quotations and the ground for inferring that subjects do in fact perceive a fixed number of classes, or a particular type of stratification are, to say the least, obscure (see Bulmer 1975).

In what way are subject's conceptions relevant to the analysis of social stratification? At one time, differing conceptions of society were viewed by sociologists as interesting primarily as an example of how people who were located at different points in the social structure categorized it in somewhat different ways. Karl Mannheim was prepared to argue

> Even the categories in which experiences are subsumed, collected, and ordered vary according to the social position of the observer (Mannheim 1936: 145).

In most empirical studies, a theoretical concern with 'images of society' has taken the operational form of enquiring about the number of classes or strata which individuals perceive, and about the names they give to social groups. The Marxian tradition, in this instance represented particularly well by Ossowski (1963), as well as by more conventional accounts (Willener 1957) has viewed differing conceptions and imagery of the class structure as arising from different class interests and experiences:

> *Different images of the same structure* do not merely express different propensities . . . they represent a stock of different experiences and observations resulting from differing practical interests (Ossowski 1963:7, emphasis added).

Two images which have received most attention have been the 'dichotomic' (where one group is set over against another) and the 'scheme of gradation' (where there are multiple divisions of a single continuum). These images tend to be associated, it is argued, with 'working-class' and 'middle-class' subjects respectively. In the American context, the first systematic and representative investigation of such images was Davis' (1941) *Deep South* study. He concluded that a basic six-class system existed in a Mississippi community, but that it was divided up and named in consistently different ways by members of the six classes. We shall return to these studies later; at present it is relevant only to note that an extremely rudimentary notion of differential perception is involved.

COGNITIVE MAPS AND SOCIAL WORLDS

Our own viewpoint is strongly influenced both by the 'action frame of reference', associated with the earlier work of Talcott Parsons (1959) and by more recent work in cognitive psychology (Miller *et al.,* 1960; Neisser 1967). Perception is not a simple, iconic, direct apprehension of external reality, but a process involving the interpretation and encoding of information. We do not respond directly to the social, or even the external physical world, but to our *image* of it. This 'internal representation', 'cognitive map', 'mental configuration', or 'schema' includes the person himself, and the social structure of which he is a part. It is thought of as being distinct from the outside world and hence acts as a boundary to what can be recognised in, and abstracted from, the environment (Neisser 1967: 286 *et seq.;* Transgaard 1972 : 138). [11] In the sociological context many of these ideas have been transmitted, at least partially, by means of concepts such as 'learned and shared meanings', 'self images', sociotypes' and 'role maps'. Thomas Kuhn (1970) has placed one particular sort of 'shared cognitive construct' — the paradigm — at the centre of the account which he gives of what 'doing science' consists of. It is illuminating to put the processed of 'interpreting science' and 'interpreting occupation' side by side in order to see the common features, and this provides useful insights into the present analysis.

The ability to see a variety of situations as like each other and equally to recognise a particular situation as like some and unlike others not previously encountered arises as a result of common problems and experiences. In the case of of organised scientific disciplines — and for many occupations — the student

> views the situations that confront him . . . in the same gestalt as other members of his specialists' group. For him they are no longer the same situations he had encountered when his training began. He has meanwhile assimilated a time-tested and group-licensed way of seeing (189).

Kuhn's 'situations' refer, of course, to the subject matter of a science, but the points he makes are no less true when applied to occupations themselves. Elizabeth Bott, in her study of family social networks (1971), reports that (sociological received wisdom notwithstanding) her repsondents do not agree either in their descriptions of stratification or in the criteria for describing it. She continues:

> Our data suggest, on the contrary, that people disagree profoundly in their views on class, so much so that we sometimes wondered if they were talking about the same society. Our conclusion is that in certain important respects they are not . . . [but] . . . live in different worlds; they have different jobs, different neighbours, and different family trees. Each bases his ideas of class on his own experience, so that it is hardly surprising that each had a different conception of the class structure as a whole (159-60).

This quotation makes it clear how much similarity there is between Kuhn's account and Bott's. Such anecdotal evidence might be taken to imply that there exist competing coherent, radically different conceptions and accounts of social stratification, but this cannot be sustained on any rigorous basis, for appropriate information is simply not available. But whilst the 'postulate of cognitive consensus' (compare Gross' (1958) 'postulate of role consensus') on the nature of the status structure may well be untenable, we simply do not yet know sufficient about the nature and form of the dissensus which clearly exists to offer any competing explanation. Once again, the most plausible hypotheses arise from the 'images of society' tradition. In an early, but neglected paper on 'Subjective aspects of social stratification', Martin (1954) discusses differential status perpectives. He concludes:

> The great majority of our subjects thought in terms of a three-class system and most of them described these classes by the same set of names — upper, middle and working. But could we assume that these names have the same significance to all who use them ? To speak of these classes was to refer implicity to a *mental map of the social scene.* But was it substantially the same map? Were the boundary lines separating the regions always drawn with the same degree of clarity and precision, or were they sometimes — either among a particular group of respondents or in respect of a particular division — vague and uncertain? Might it not be the case that for some of

our informants the boundaries had been shifted so as to increase or diminish the territory of a particular region? Would all subjects whatever their
own vantage point think of all the regions primarily in terms of the same
attributes? (1954: 58-9) (emphasis added).

Martin suggests the possibility that most people can agree upon a fairly
simple description about their society — that it can be divided into three
classes, labelled Upper, Middle and Working respectively — but that they
do not entirely agree about the allocation of such important symbols as
the names of occupations to those three classes. Furthermore Martin
asserts that disagreement of this kind is not purely idiosyncratic, but is
related to the respondent's social position.

We shall return to the work of continental sociologists such as Willener
and Ossowski in a moment; but, preserving the order of publication, the
next piece of evidence comes again from Elizabeth Bott.

Bott's work introduces several important points. First, she used material
from her unstructured interviews to argue that classes are what she terms
'constructed reference groups' and were used as such by nearly all her
respondents. However, she stresses that apart from an almost universal
tendency to use class terminology when discussing society as a whole (and
when placing strangers) the couples she studied varied greatly in the extent
to which they used reference groups in ordinary conversation:

> . . . everyone operates a model of the class structure, but the models
> are fluid and variable, and are used differently in different social
> contexts (169).

Bott says that people talk about society being divided into layers which
differ either in power or in prestige or in both. Here she is more or less
restating the point made by Martin. Second, and this is most important,
Bott talks about her respondents as 'operating a model of the class structure', but she *also* holds that these 'models' which people 'operate' (for
all of their seeming precision) — these models are only partly susceptible
of observation by the social scientist.

Perhaps there is more than a trace of Bott's psychoanalytic background
in this notion that the actor's underlying model of his society is in principle only partly observable. Bott stresses that in ordinary conversation,
people tend to use only part of their model, that responses to questions
are very strongly influenced by the immediate social situation, and by the
respondent' s relationship with the interviewer. She even says that
several of her subjects were *hardly aware* that they were operating a model
of the class structure, and that some of these experienced 'pain' in the
course of making their 'model' explicit, and realising its inconsistencies.
Clearly Bott is of the opinion that to investigate models of the class
structure is to delve at least partly into the unconscious. Furthermore she
thinks it perfectly justifiable for the interviewer to act as midwife in the
delivery of such models into consciousness, for at several points she uses

as evidence the fact that a respondent 'agreed with the fieldworker's suggestion', that such and such connections existed in his head. For example, a plumber

> ... was not aware of the precise contribution of each of his group memberships, even though he had talked about each of them separately, and he agreed with the fieldworker's suggestion that his experience in them provided the basis for his own view of the class structure (163).

Bearing in mind Bott's view that highly skilled and insightful interviewing is required to draw out an individual's model of the class structure, we can turn to her ideas about the different possible models.

As is well known, Bott describes four models of the total class structure:

(a) Two-valued power models
(b) Three-valued prestige models
(c) Many-valued prestige models
(d) Mixed power and prestige models

We do not propose to repeat Bott's description of the nature of these models. Rather we focus upon the logic which she uses to assign an individual's model to one or other of these four categories. Careful reading of what Bott says indicates that such allocation takes place through analysis of the *content* of what the interviewee says, and that her use of 'logic' is peculiar. Thus:

> ... the use of two basic classes is a *logical consequence* of using the ideas of power, conflict and opposition, since two units represent the smallest number required for a conflict. However many classes are actually mentioned, these models are *basically* two-valued (175, emphasis added).

And similarly:

> ... the use of a three-valued model is a *logical consequence* of thinking in terms of prestige. In order to conceptualize prestige ... one must represent one's equals, one's superiors and one's inferiors. Three groups is the natural number for such a representation (176 emphasis added).

It is hard to see how these conclusions follow from their premises. Ossowski holds similar notions that imagery of three or more classes is universally linked to consensus models and contrariwise that imagery of the two-class variety necessarily implies a conflict model.

But our purpose here is not to get into an argument about the validity of special kinds of 'socio-logic'. The really important point about Bott's work is that she appears to believe that her subjects' 'models of society' can only be described as the result of a very long-drawn-out process of discussion, probing, and suggestion, and that even then, the investigator has the right to engage in special pleading in order to separate out an hypothesised 'basic' model from its counterfeit manifestations.

We devote considerable space to Bott because even if her work is some-

times puzzling, it has been profoundly influential. Her conjecture that
the *content* of an individual's belief system gives information from which
the structure of that system may be deduced, runs through the work of
Lockwood and the *Affluent Worker* group, and has also influenced more
recent research (Bulmer 1975). A quotation from Runciman may give
some of the flavour of the way in which her work, together with that of
others, becomes incorporated into the body of sociological knowledge:

> . . . the pictures of Western industrial society which its inhabitants
> have, can in principle be classified in terms of class, status and power
> models (or mixed models incorporating elements of all three) . . .
> A pure power model is not found very often: it is the type of model
> used by people who see society in terms of 'us' and 'them', where
> 'them' means those seen to be in authority, such as the government
> and the bosses, rather then the rich or socially esteemed. A status model
> is the type where society is seen as arranged in a graded hierarchy of
> prestige; users of status models tend to see the social hierarchy as
> composed of more numerous and overlapping 'classes' (that is, status-
> strata) than the users of power or class models. A class model, finally,
> is a model based on distinctions of job or income, and particularly on
> the economic aspects of a person's job (44).

Runciman continues by elaborating upon the relationship between jobs and
occupations on the one hand, and their representation in different models
(or 'pictures') of society on the other:

> In a status model also, occupations may play an important role. But
> in a status model, the social aspect is more significant than the economic.
> The prestige of a job, or the style of life that goes with it, or the
> educational qualifications which it requires, are what matter for the
> hierarchy of status. In a power model, by contrast, the authority
> vested in certain occupational positions is their most important feature;
> and in a class model, the significance of occupations is the wealth or
> security of tenure which will accrue from them (44).

Bott says much the same thing more tersely, when making the point that
her respondents generally thought that occupation was the most important criterion of class membership, but that they mean different things by
the term:

> . . . some thought of occupation as a source of power, others were
> thinking of its general prestige, others of the income attached to it (172).

To summarise then, Bott and Runciman say that one important consequence of an individual's using one of these models of society rather than
another is that he will tend to pay special attention to certain attributes
of jobs and work situations. Rather as people operating a Freudian model
of personality dynamics are sensitive to the presence or absence of phallic

symbols (among other types) in dreams or in conversation, so people who operate a power model of social dynamics should be sensitive to the presence or absence of relations such as authority, exploitation and confrontation between different social groups. Similarly, of course, a special sensitivity to other types of relations between social groups might be a consequence of the operation of some other model or models: it will be one purpose of this study to investigate such 'differential sensitivity' and the implicit theories which people have about social stratification.

The main burden of argument so far has been that, despite the persistent tendency of sociologists of differing persuasions to reify the status structure, and strongly counterpose the 'objective' and the 'subjective' aspects, this has been neither satisfactory not successful. People's conceptions of the social structure in part determine it, and in part are reports upon it; to ignore either part of this proposition is to distort the nature of social reality.

What is the sociologist's role in analysing the multiple conceptions of social structure? John Rex (1973: 218-19) expresses what we think is an acceptable and workable viewpoint by saying that:

> What the sociologist does is to construct his own ideal types (a) of an actor's perception of the world of social relations which surround him and through this (b) of the pattern of mutual expectancies involved in thse social relations.

In the terms we have outlined, this certainly involves 'taking account of the concepts used by actors within social relations, or actors living in a world in which social relations appear as objects' (ibid p. 224) – but treating them neither as derivative distortions of an independently establishable structure, nor as final accounts all of co-equal validity. Certainly we may, and will, inquire about the adequacy, and at times about the accuracy, of people's conceptions, and we shall inquire whether differing conceptions bear any consistent relationships with each other. But we shall not imply that subjects only operate with one such structure or model, independently of the social situation.

2 Prestige Hierarchies

2.1 PRESTIGE AND DEFERENCE–ENTITLEMENT

One might suppose that people in our culture can buy a lifestyle with money and get most of their money through having a full-time job. However, the essence of a *sociological* approach to the use of occupation as an index of social status has been a belief held by sociologists that it is misleading to concentrate solely upon the economic aspects of occupation. On this view, a refuse collector might be better paid than a school-teacher, but because of cultural values subscribed to by a large majority of the population, the teacher might well enjoy higher social standing. There is no accounting for tastes. People just happen to think that handling other people's rubbish is less pleasant or of lower status than teaching other people's children. One can perhaps imagine societies where the carrying out of rectal examinations was an extremely low-status activity, even though in our culture it is part of the duties of rather high-status medical practitioners. Precisely because there is no accounting for tastes in these matters, a considerable number of extensive surveys have been carried out in order to find out how people evaluate occupations. The point is that only empirical investigation can tell us about the way in which people evaluate those bundles of activities we call occupations. Hence all the opinion surveys, whose results are usually discussed under the heading of 'occupational prestige rankings'.

Empirical surveys of this kind are of interest to students of social mobility. For though one might choose to study the mobility of individuals in 'social space' solely in economic terms, comparing, shall we say, gross wealth at one point in time with gross wealth at another, the objection usually raised to this is that people are motivated by factors other than money. In particular people are known to trade salary for prestige, respectability or deference.

Goldthorpe and Hope (1972, 1974) have recently contributed thoughtful analyses of the uses sociologists have made of the concept 'occupational prestige'. Following Shils (1968) and Mills (1951), they argue that 'prestige, in its classical sociological usage, is essentially to do with the honouring of "deference-entitlements" ' (a term used by Shils). To paraphrase their argument, a prestige hierarchy is one in which some people acknowledge that they are socially inferior to others (though they try to imitate and associate with these superiors, imitation of course being a sincere form of flattery). Superior people, on the other hand, avoid being in company with their social inferiors (except, as Goldthorpe and Hope point out, in situations where their own superiority is continually re-affirmed by routines of deference). At all levels of the hierarchy, people have notions about who are neither their superiors nor their inferiors, and it is with them that non-instrumental [1] social interaction (mutual entertainment, inter marriage, etc.) takes place. To summarise, in a prestige hierarchy, people *defer* to their superiors, *derogate* their inferiors, and *accept* their equals.

Goldthorpe and Hope emphasise that so far as prestige hierarchy is concerned, the bases of deference, derogation and acceptance are part of a socially constructed reality, and need not derive from economic or political inequalities. To quote them:

> ... prestige can be 'converted' into advantage and power of an economic or political kind — just as the latter may of course in turn be utilised in order to gain increased prestige. However it is still important to recognise that advantage and power in the form of prestige remain distinctive in that they *entirely depend upon* the existence of some shared universe of meaning and value among the actors concerned ... If the symbolic significance of roles and collectivities is not recognised, or if what is symbolized is subject to divergent evaluations, then no consistent basis for deference, differential social acceptance or derogation is present (1972: 25).

In a number of places, Goldthorpe and Hope indicate that their notion of prestige is essentially one of *traditional* beliefs and values about which there is massive agreement. They cite such problems as 'by what means does an aristo-cracy maintain its economic and political dominance?', and conversely they mention the status discrepancy dilemmas of *nouveaux-riches, parvenues* and C.P. Snow's 'new men' of power. Citing evidence of what they call 'status dissent' from the *Affluent Worker* study, Goldthorpe and Hope conclude that (given the definition which ties 'prestige' to behaviour of deference, derogation and acceptance), the demanding conditions necessary for the existence of a prestige order will be satisfied 'only locally transiently or imperfectly', in modern industrial societies (1972: 33). One thinks of Newby's study of the relationships between farmers and agricultural workers in Suffolk, or of the interactions between officers and other ranks in the British army. But apart from specific situations such as these (the general attitude to medical and religious personnel may be an exception), occupational titles do *not* entitle their bearers to deference. What then is occupational prestige? Goldthorpe and Hope review what other writers have called the prestige of an occupational title:

(1) A descriptive judgement of how desirable it would be to pursue that occupation (mostly in terms of material rewards offered by the occupation);

(2) Another kind of descriptive judgement about a typical person follow-ing that occupation, this time in terms of his statistical probability of being able able (by virtue of his occupational title), to extract deference from others and to gain acceptance from those commonly agreed to be of high prestige;

(3) A normative and moralistic judgement about the social and human worth of the work involved in that occupation.

The first of the three interpretations (occupational prestige as the material well-being associated with pursuing an occupation) seems to be over-conservative in its treatment of what people take into consideration when thinking about occupations. Their second interpretation of 'occupational prestige' is more sociologically interesting. It seems to be desirable to distinguish between deference received 'on the job' because of the occupational title from deference of this kind which is received 'off the job'. There is, of course, a social psychology of the face-to-face processes by which two people eventually reach an agreed-upon 'pecking order'. Michael Argyle has published the results of a number of experiments which show how age, type of accent, style of dress, the wearing of glasses, etc., all affect judgements of other people. In this book, however, we are concerned about the inferences drawn from occupational titles. As they are commonly used, the titles of occupations usually convey two kinds of information. In the first place they convey information about the general field of activity engaged in, e.g., agriculture, mining, transport, social services. Such a field is sometimes called a 'situs'. Secondly, they convey information about rank within the hierarchy of the field of work concerned, and of course rank is usually related to age. In hospital medicine, for example, there are house surgeons, registrars and consultants, while in general practice there are assistants, junior partners and senior partners, and among nurses there are staff nurses, sisters and matrons. Within each hierarchy, lower ranks are expected to show deference to higher ranks. Between hierarchies, however, matters are not always so clear. A house surgeon would be well advised to show deference to a matron, especially in the hospital context. In the presence of patients a general practitioner shows considerable deference to a consultant. A registrar and a general practitioner might very well disagree about who shows deference to whom. Occupational titles also have an important dimension — institutional affiliation — which is not normally recorded on sociologists' questionnaires. To be a college professor at one of the top-rated professional schools in the USA is markedly better than having the same occupational title, but being employed in a low-status institution. Since technocrats and members of the erstwhile 'free professions' increasingly carry out their work in large organisations, this is an important point.

Brown and Ford (1961) point out that an easily observable sign of deference being claimed and given in a relationship occurs in forms of address. A deference relationship exists when the superior person addresses his inferior by his first name, but receives in return the polite 'title with last name' form of address. There is evidence that a large age-difference between two people usually brings about deference of this kind. Its occurrence is also a function of relative occupational position for which Brown and Ford suggest the following varieties:

(1) a direct and enduring deference relationship between organisational superior and organisational inferior;

(2) a direct but temporary deference relationship as occurs in personal service occupations between a practitioner and his client;

(3) an enduring deference relationship not involving organisational subordination. This would be 'pure' deference based upon occupation, and as Brown says, it is difficult to think of modern examples where such 'pure' deference based upon occupational position would work. In a mid-nineteenth-century context, perhaps, clergymen may have been the recipients of 'pure' deference of this kind.

One rather interesting point made by Brown and Ford is that while a difference of age can bring about the non-reciprocal pattern of address which indicates a deference relationship, and a difference of occupational status can do the same, it seems empirically to be the case (in the USA at least) that when the age-difference and the occupational difference go in different directions (in pairs of people where the elder has the humbler occupation), then address is usually patterned in accordance with occupational status. In more traditional societies, one might perhaps expect a reverse ordering of precedence.[2]

It is true that certain types of service occupation are distinguished by the fact that practitioners meet their clients in situations where the practitioner's occupational skill is highly esoteric and at the same time vital for the client's well-being. Medicine and law are obvious examples of occupations of this kind where the practitioner is in a good tactical position to extract deference. We may also conjecture that people with the habit of command get more deference than people with the habit of obedience, and it seems obvious that some occupations involve giving orders to other adults while others involve taking orders. If the extraction of deference depends upon the possession of the conventional upper-class social skills and appearance (dress, accent, poise) then it seems likely that those occupations which recruit from the dominant class will tend to be seen as having practitioners of the kind that receive deference in interpersonal situations. But apart from such cases as these, the only reason that man's occupation (once revealed by him) should influence his standing in the eyes of others would appear to be the moral valuation that is placed on it by them. There seems little reason to suppose that people show deference to high income levels *per se*. We must ask about the different moral bases that exist for claims to high prestige. This gets us to the widely held view that occupations differ in their social usefulness.

Social usefulness is a slippery concept, but none the less important for that. Indeed its very slipperiness allows different versions to be included in the various 'functionalist' accounts of social stratification. We may ask, 'Socially useful to whom? – to the ruling elite, to the mass of the people or to some sectional interest?' The answer may come back, 'Socially useful in maintaining the existence of society, in which *everyone* has a share'.

Along the lines of this definition, it can be predicted that the perceived social usefulness of occupations will vary from one historical
circumstance to another. In time of war, members of the armed forces
(especially when victorious) are thought of as being socially useful. In times
of plague, doctors (when bringing about cures) are similarly thought of as
being socially useful. Perhaps nursing is the archetypal socially useful
occupation, in that its members can very easily and plausibly be described
as dedicated and self-sacrificing, working long hours for low pay at a
readily understandable and culturally valued task (but consider the cultural
valuation of pre-Nightingale nursing). Furthermore, nurses have very rarely
withdrawn their labour.

This brings us to a second approach to defining an occupation's social
usefulness: the degree to which society as currently understood could
continue to exist without the given occupation's specialised tasks being
carried out at all. On such a definition, occupations such as novelist or actor
might be considered less useful than occupations such as farmer or coal-
miner. George Orwell (1937) provides a good example of such sentiments:

> . . . Our civilization . . . is founded on coal . . . In the metabolism of the
> Western world, the coal miner is second in importance only to the man
> who ploughs the soil. He is a sort of grimy caryatid upon whose shoulders
> nearly everything that is *not* grimy is supported.

2.2 THE QUESTIONS THAT SOCIOLOGISTS HAVE ASKED ABOUT OCCUPATIONS

Although considerable information is available in the form of official
statistics on the average income levels and educational levels of most
officially recognised and legal occupations (and also on their age-composi-
tion, sex-composition and racial composition), sociologists persist in carrying out public opinion surveys to find out about their 'prestige' or 'general
standing' or their 'social usefulness'. One reason for this is that the possibility
of occupations which give high economic status, though relatively low social
esteem, to their incumbents is thought to be theoretically interesting.
Another reason might be to calibrate a prestige scale on which to measure
occupational mobility. The method typically used for obtaining the status
scores of occupational titles has been to conduct a door-to-door opinion poll,
each person surveyed being asked to make judgements about the relative
'prestige', 'social standing' or whatever, of a selection of occupational titles.
After the survey is completed, the data gathered are averaged, so that each
occupational title has a score reflecting what most people thought of it in
the door-to-door poll. Such a score is often called a 'prestige score' and is
used in later surveys to indicate the status situation of incumbents of the
relevant occupation. From a technical point of view, a man's occupation is

being used as an index of his status situation. There is also an implication that sociologists who use occupational prestige scores in this way believe that a man's occupation is the entire basis of his status situation. This seems to be implausible since deference relationships surely arise from ethnicities, personalities or situations and not simply from the occupations that people happen to follow.

The kind of judgement that is obtained in an interview situation presumably depends upon the form of the question asked of the respondent. Therefore it is necessary to examine the methods by which various 'occupational prestige' studies have gathered their basic data. The method of investigation most frequently used has been to obtain judgements about each of a number of occupations from each of a sample of respondents. The precise instructions given to the respondents vary from study to study, and a selection from those that have been used appears below.

1. Sarapata and Wesolowski (1966), in a Polish study.
    (a) In your own opinion, what material rewards, in our country today, are given in each of the following occupations?
        [five categories from 'very high material reward' to 'very small material reward']
    (b) A guarantee of having a stable job in the occupation. In your opinion which of the following occupations in our country today are:
        [four categories from 'very secure', to 'relatively insecure']
    (c) So far you rated the occupations by material rewards and security. But occupations are judged also by social prestige, that is, the respect which the people give to the occupations. Thinking of their social prestige, how do you rate these occupations?
2. Hammel (1970) in a Yugoslavian study.
    'If you had had all the opportunities in your life to become whatever you wanted, how would you have evaluated these [following] occupations? Would you have thought that *this* occupation [interviewer presents a card bearing the title of one occupation] was *best, good, middling* or *worst?* Take into account all characteristics of occupations that are important in your view.'
3   Haller *et al.* (1972) in a Brazilian study.
    'Respondents were shown a sheet of paper picturing a ladder with five steps or rungs. Occupations were read aloud by the interviewer and respondents were asked to indicate the prestige [*prestigio,* a word in common usage in Brazil] which people 'attribute to' the occupation, by pointing to the appropriate rung on the prestige ladder.'
4. Smith (1943), in a North American study.
    'The entire procedure consisted of two main parts. (1) Preliminary ranking of the occupations from high to low prestige status on the basis of the order of rank at a dinner honouring a celebrity, with an average member of each occupational class being seated at a formal distance

nearer to or farther from the celebrity than the average member of another, the distinction between occupations to be made entirely on the basis of occupational prestige; and (2) rating each occupation on a scale of 100 points . . .'

5. North and Hatt (1947) in a later North American study.
    Respondents were asked to rate each of 90 occupational titles in terms of 'General standing in the community'. More precisely, a door-to-door survey was carried out in the USA, in which each respondent was handed a card printed as follows:
    'For each job mentioned, please pick out the statement that best gives your own personal opinion of the general standing that such a job has:
    1. *Excellent* standing
    2. *Good* standing
    3. *Average* standing
    4. *Somewhat below average* standing
    5. *Poor* standing
    x. I don't know where to place that one.'

6. Siegel (1971) in yet another North American study asked respondents to rate each of a large number of occupational titles according to a number of different criteria:
    (a) social standing
    (b) perceived income
    (c) perceived skills
    (d) benefit to society
    (e) hard work v. easy work
    (f) interesting work
    (g) interesting context
    (h) freedom and independence
    (i) desirability
    (j) number of people affected in the day's work.

7. Vodzinskaia (1970) carried out a study in the USSR which also examined ratings of occupations on a number of different criteria:
    (a) possibilities for creativity
    (b) possibilities for [personal] growth: raising skills in the broadest sense of the word
    (c) level of wages
    (d) social prestige: the authority of an occupation in public opinion.

8. Goldthorpe and Hope (1972) in an English study.
    'Subjects were presented with a list of 27 occupations and were asked to rate each of them in two ways:
    (a) own rating ('subjective scale')
    (b) evaluations of public's rating ('subjective' scale)
    [Four response categories provided.]

9. Duncan *et al.* (1972) refer to a study carried out in the early 1920s by

F.E. Barr. Thirty judges were asked to rate each of 200 selected occupations (with brief descriptions supplied) according to the number of units of intelligence . . . the occupation demands for ordinary success'.

10.   Chun *et al.* (1975) report an investigation in which subjects were asked to rank (and also to rate) nineteen occupations in terms of 'their relative trustworthiness . . . that is, your comparison of the extent to which you trust what the members of these occupational groups do and say, and how they act in the course of their jobs'.

11.   Pineo and Porter (1967) had respondents sort 204 occupations into nine ordered categories, under the following instructions:
      'Now let's talk about jobs. Here is a ladder with nine boxes on it, and a card with the name of an occupation on each [sic]. Please put the card in the box at the *top* of the ladder if you think that occupation has the highest possible social standing. Put it in the box at the *bottom* of the ladder if you think it has the lowest possible social standing. If it belongs somewhere in between, just put it in the box that matches the social standing of that occupation.'

The various question-wordings exhibit considerable variety and some occupations indeed seem to be judged high in response to one wording, yet low in response to another. Yet sociologists who have reviewed the literature have been impressed by the marked tendency for occupations judged high in response to one question, also to be judged *high* in response to another. Linguistic analysis of the various question wordings may suggest that a set of occupations should be ordered very differently in response to them, but the empirical evidence is that people seem to give much the same rank ordering, no matter what question is asked. Goldthorpe and Hope conclude:

> Prestige ratings may be taken as indicating popular evaluations of the relative 'goodness' of occupations in terms of the entire range of prevailing criteria (36-7).

Coupling this position with the 'structuralist' view on the cross-national similarity of occupational prestige hierarchies, we seem to arrive at the situation where no matter who is questioned, or what they are questioned about, much the same rank order of occupations ensues. This seems very strange, and one suspects that there must be some methodological reason for sociologists' obtaining results which lead to such a view. It may be that in a doorstep interview the respondents seek an easy way of responding to a boring task, and react to the occupations in terms of some general evaluative feeling, no matter what the rubric of the question. People may react in one way to an occupational title which is encountered in the middle of a long and rather abstract task, but in quite another way when they meet someone whose job is covered by that same occupational title. (We expand on this point in section 4.3.)

This suggestion may seem a little far-fetched (surely respondents do all they can to help the sociologist!). However, the reader may care to reflect on how he or she would react when arbitrarily confronted with the task of ranking two hundred occupations (as happened to the respondents selected by Pineo and Porter in Canada).

2.3   CROSS-CULTURAL AND HISTORICAL ASPECTS OF OCCUPATIONS

The sociological literature of the last twenty years has managed to accomodate two contrasting threads of argument on the subject of how people esteem the different occupations in society. At one extreme, a sociologist whom we consulted in 1971 was able to write, 'There is not a single shred of convincing, systematic evidence which indicates that one can isolate meaningful social groups which hold widely divergent views of the structure of occupational evaluations, despite the attempt by many students of social stratification to isolate such groups', a position similar to that held by Treiman, Hodge and other Chicago-trained sociologists. The opposing view (that such differences do indeed exist) is held by sociologists such as Kahl and Haller and over the past decade proponents of these two viewpoints have talked past each other in the learned journals. One of the most curious features of the literature on this topic is the extent to which contrary evidence is simply ignored. For example, in the course of an authoritative review of conceptualisation and measurement in the study of stratification, Jackson and Curtis (1968) conclude that:

> 'Despite certain technical inadequacies, the North-Hatt study provides empirical justification for a unidimensional prestige ranking of occupations' (123).

This is just not true. The only investigation of the dimensionality of North-Hatt data (often referred to as the NORC data) was carried out by A.J. Reiss and his colleagues and is reported in the book *Occupations and Social Status*. Reiss (here the primary source) concludes:

> Since there is considerable variation in individual evaluations of the general standing of all occupations rated in the NORC study, and since it appears that occupational status is a multidimensional phenomenon, one wonders whether the assumption that there is a single value system in American society governing status evaluations is a tenable one. Both the variation in individual ratings for any occupation and the failure to achieve a uni-dimensional scale appear to be due to systematic variation in ratings among sub-groups in the American population as well as to error (107).

Reviewers of the sociological literature have commonly identified the Chicago position with a 'structuralist' point of view on occupational status and opposed it to a 'culturalist' perspective. As will become apparent later, one can discern a further perspective in the literature which, since it has been favoured by social psychologists, we might call the 'psychophysical' perspective (see Lewis 1964; Alexander 1972). In fact, the structuralist position has more and less general forms. The more general form holds that all large-scale societies have essentially the same occupational status hierarchy. Thus Britain in the mid-nineteenth century might be compared with Britain at the present time, and the occupational status hierarchy should be essentially unchanged (and this appears to be believed by some sociologists, despite the virtual disappearance of some occupations, e.g. 'farrier', the development of other occupations, e.g., computer programmer, the well- documented decline in status of clerks (Lockwood 1958) and the Anglican clergy (Coxon 1967), the rise in status of surgeons (Elliott 1972; Parry and Parry 1976), the shrinking of domestic service and agriculture, and the enormous change in the structure of the labour market in Britain over the last hundred years). Or the USA might be compared with Yugoslavia, and again there should, according to this theory, be no essential difference between the occupational status system of these two countries. In this more general form, the structualist view of occupational status is closely related to the so-called 'functional theory of social stratification' — that in any society, there are some occupational positions which 'need' to be filled by individuals of ability and energy, and that societies survive only where such occupational positions are associated with the enjoyment of material benefits such as financial reward, and of less tangible but no less important benefits such as high social prestige, a privileged position in community rituals, or an honoured place in the society's ideology of stratification. According to the theory, members of the society work hard and compete with one another in order to receive the material and symbolic rewards associated with positions culturally defined as being high on the ladder of success, and the fruits of this hard work benefit everyone in the society, and help it to survive against Nature, or in the face of attack from other societies.

Indeed one might argue that so far as the functional theory of stratification is concerned, it is not vitally important precisely *which* occupational positions have the greatest amount of material or symbolic reward, so long as those occupations which happen to be 'really' functionally important for the society are somewhere towards the upper end of the success ladder. On this view, a society might be allowed to indulge a 'taste' for giving high rewards to some occupation which was not in this sense functionally important. As examples, one might take film stars, or even the clergy (though of course, it is almost always possible to discern *some* function for any occupation or institution). The functional theory of stratification predicts some inter-societal agreement in terms of occupational status hierarchies, since there are no doubt some tasks which are universally functionally necessary. However, it also allows for some degree of inter-societal disagreement, since different societies may very well have different 'tastes' for honouring or rewarding occupations which do not relate to universally necessary tasks.

A less general, but stronger form of the structuralist position maintains that industrialisation and urbanisation lead to the establishment of dense populations with a considerable degree of occupational specialisation, institutionally regulated entry to occupational positions, and an appropriately organised system of formal education. Because of an 'internal logic' in the processes of urbanisation (or perhaps more simply because of cultural and institutional borrowing, to say nothing of the effects of imperialism), the systems of specialised occupations which emerge tend to have the same status hierarchy, the same educational hierarchy and the same hierarchy of material reward no matter what modern societies are under discussion. On this view, then, only industrialised and urbanised societies are considered, and among these, the occupational status hierarchies should be of precisely the same form.

The keenest upholders of the so-called 'structuralist' theory have been Robert Hodge and his co-workers, e.g. Hodge, Treiman and Rossi (1966), who suggest that all industrialised societies share a common occupational status hierarchy. Against this, there is the 'culturalist' view that different societies, and even different subcultures within the same society, may have quite dissimilar opinions about the nature of social stratification in general and of the occupational hierarchy in particular. This sort of view tends to be supported by anthropologists, and by those sociologists who have studied the images of society held by members of socially isolated and internally cohesive communities (Young and Willmott 1956; Brown and Brannen 1970). As one reads through the literature, one easily gains the impression that evidence in favour of the culturalist point of view tends to be impressionistic and informal, even verging upon the anecdotal. By contrast, the evidence in favour of between-society consensus on occupational evaluations appears to be thoroughly quantitative and by implication therefore, scientific.

From a sociological point of view, it is important to note that a system of beliefs about the relative worth of occupations can be viewed as an ideology even if (and perhaps especially if) it is held to be 'scientific' and 'true' by culturally dominant groups such as the Chicago sociologists.

The 'extreme culturalist' position (something of a straw man perhaps), first articulated by Inkeles and Rossi (1956) proceeds from the assumption that different societies have different traditional value systems, and that these are so potent that modern occupations such as hospital nurse, garage mechanic, lorry driver, etc., are each evaluated in the same way as some roughly corresponding occupation in the traditional economy of the society. There should then be some differences between countries though it should be emphasised that these differences need not be large ones. The culturalist view on occupational prestige might be seen simply as a residual of the structuralist position; that is, it might be considered as the proposition that there *are* differences between the occupational prestige hierarchies of different nations or of different sub-cultures. Most writers go a little further, and suggest locally specific reasons as to why the prestige hierarchy of occupations in one nation should be different from that obtained in, say, the USA. In general, however, there is no simple coherent 'culturalist' position (see Hunter 1977).

The empirically based argument which has most frequently been put forward in support of the 'consensus about occupational rankings' theory uses data in the following way. Average scores for each of the same (or closely matching) set of occupational titles are obtained in two or more societies, or among two or more sub-groups in the same society. For example, it might be found in both France and Germany that the occupation of surgeon scores very high, the occupation of plumber scores in the middle of the range, and the occupation of labourer scores very low. There is thus a high degree of similarity or correlation between the judged occupational hierarchies in France and Germany. Many studies using such 'profile correlations' have been carried out, usually based upon 20 or more occupational titles (sometimes as many as 80). Since they typically report correlation coefficients with values in excess of + 0.80 (considered 'very high' by the sociological community), it is generally concluded that massive inter-societal consensus exists about occupational hierarchies.[3] The high positive values of the profile correlations between the averaged prestige judgements of people from different countries seem to undergo a sort of distorted translation into a mental picture of two representative people deciding that they are in agreement. It is this elision between impressive-sounding numbers and their sociological interpretation that has made for confusion in cross-national comparisons of occupational prestige. Such comparisons almost always use the Pearson correlation co-efficient (or its square, the 'coefficient of determination'). Either of these will reach the value of unity when the prestige scores of a set of occupations in one country can be plotted on a graph as a perfect straight line against prestige scores for the corresponding occupations in another country.

Inkeles and Rossi (1956) were very struck by the existence of high profile correlations between averaged prestige judgements of occupations in six different countries. For example, averaged prestige ratings from Japan were correlated at a value of 0.93 (over 25 selected occupational titles) with average prestige ratings in the USA. The comparison between Japanese prestige ratings and Russian prestige ratings was less satisfactory, partly because the Russian sample was composed of 'displaced persons' after the Second World War, and partly because only seven occupational titles in the list judged by Russians could be matched with comparable occupational titles judged by Japanese. Nevertheless, the correlation coefficient between Japanese and Russian ratings was as high as 0.74 over these seven occupational titles. The between-country correlations found by workers such as Inkeles and Rossi, and later by Treiman (1976) have been high but by no means perfect. The discrepancies in the relative positions of occupations between different countries are reported as involving agricultural or personal service occupations, and are explained away on the argument that (in the case of farming) the same occupational title can refer to quite different types of activity in two different countries or (in the case of personal service) that there is a special tendency for low-status ethnic groups to become engaged in personal service occupations so that ethnic evaluations become mixed with occupational evaluations.

Hodge and his colleagues (1966) collected together the results from studies of occupational prestige in 24 countries. Their first and most widely cited conclusion was that the high correlations that could be calculated between countries indicated that their occupational structures had essentially similar prestige hierarchies. They qualified this conclusion in two important ways. First, they noted that when attention is focused upon blue-collar jobs alone, the correlations between societies are smaller than when white-collar jobs are used (we have mentioned elsewhere that sociologists usually over-sample professional and white-collar jobs when selecting a list of occupational titles for an opinion poll on occupational prestige). This squares with Kahl's proposition that 'People agree more about the top of the [prestige] range than the bottom, and make more distinctions about the top than about the bottom.' The conclusion is strongly confirmed in a later empirical study by Hunter (1977).

Hodge *et al.* illustrate their second qualification by an impressive scatter-plot. Countries with relatively low levels of economic development have occupational prestige hierarchies which are correlated positively with the prestige hierarchy in the USA, but are not correlated so highly as countries having high economic development. In order for this second conclusion to stand, it seems logically necessary that all societies do *not* have the same occupational prestige hierarchy (since one needs variation before one can have co-variation).

At this point in the argument it is necessary, though perhaps rather tedious, to discuss some of the 'methodology' of cross-cultural correlations between occupational prestige hierarchies. What seems to have happened over the last quarter-century is that sociologists in different countries have each selected between 30 and 100 occupational titles the selection being carried out with no explicit rationale (see Coxon and Jones 1974b), and have used some sort of opinion poll to estimate average prestige scores. The usual reason for doing this is so as to provide some 'public opinion' validation for a scale of occupational status to be used in studies of stratification and mobility. Other sociologists have wished to compare the occupational prestige hierarchies in different countries. In order to make such comparisons, it is necessary to throw away part of the data. Attention must be restricted to the prestige scores of those occupations which were included in the lists selected by sociologists in different countries. Subjective elements can creep into the data analysis, as when it must be decided whether the occupational title 'Pharmacist' in North America has the same sociological meaning as 'Pharmacien' in France, or whether 'Truck Driver' in an advanced society is in some sense equivalent to 'Carter' in a backward one.

When assessing the similarity between the occupational prestige hierarchies of two countries, the occupations whose prestige scores are to enter the calculations are always a *selected* subset. For example Hodge *et al.* (1966) report the correlations between the occupational prestige hierarchy in the USA (NORC scores on 88 distinct occupations) and those in 23 other

countries. The average (median) number of occupations over which the 23
profile correlations were calculated is only 19. The basis for statements about
similarity between occupational prestige hierarchies in the USA and the USSR
(data collected from emigrés) is a calculation based on as few as seven comparable occupational titles (of which all except one were white-collar jobs). Even
the profile correlation that is most reliable (being based on the greatest
number of matched occupations) is suspect. The correlation between Danish
and NORC scores is based on 35 occupations, but these have been selected
for comparability from the original 75 occupations rated by Danes and the
original 88 occupations rated by Americans.

Because of this problem of 'matching' occupational titles from a study
in one country to a study in another, most of the high correlations that are
quoted as evidence of what Coleman (1964) calls 'the striking uniformity
of occupational prestige from country to country' (27), are based upon small
numbers of highly selected occupations.

One notable exception to this criticism is the comparison between Anglophone and Francophone Canadians made possible by the careful study of
196 occupational titles carried out by Pineo and Porter (1967). The possibility of such a comparison had been built into the design of ths study, (with
care being taken about such matters as the idiomatic translation of occupational titles between English and French) and therefore no occupational
titles were excluded from comparison because of failure to 'match' them
cross-culturally. This study reported a very high profile correlation between
averaged judgements of Anglophone and Francophone respondents, and so
might be taken as supporting the structuralist position. However recent re-
analyses of the same data by Hunter (1977) show that when attention is
restricted to the 52 occupations classified as semi-skilled or unskilled, the
Anglophone-Francophone profile correlation is much lower ($r = 0.71$) than
when one uses the 21 professions ($r = 0.81$) or the 23 occupations classified
as clerical and sales (where $r = 0.92$).

Studies from Eastern Europe provide a number of empirically based
counter-examples to the doctrine of the invariance of occupational prestige
hierarchies. Penn (1975) has reported a comparison between rankings of
occupations according to their 'esteem and honour' in Czechoslovakia and
in the USA, between which he finds the relatively low profile correlation of
0.56, (which falls to the even lower value of 0.30 when the Czech rankings
are correlated with the 'social standing' scores of the corresponding occupations from the 1947 NORC study). Penn finds that the Czech respondents
have a far more favourable evaluation of skilled manual workers than is the
case in the USA. This might be ascribed to socialist propaganda in the
Czechoslovak mass media, but an explanation of this kind would hardly
explain a second difference reported by Penn: that the Czechoslovak
respondents evaluated judges much lower than did Americans.

But even if all correlations between the average occupational prestige
scores of different countries and cultures were very high (higher than, say,

$r = 0.90$, and this is by no means the case), there would still be two major problems associated with this kind of evidence. These are:

  (a) In what way can the technique hide or reveal significant disagreement about the occupational hierarchy;

  (b) In what ways are the results of the technique affected by the selection of occupational titles to be judged, or by the sampling of survey respondents to judge them?

Taking point *(a)* first, we would argue that the computation of profile correlations over the average scores given to occupations by different groups or societies is insensitive to real differences that exist. This is because such differences as occur are swamped in the massive agreement that also exists. For example there is a marked difference between the status of the medical profession (occupation of 'physician') in the USSR as compared with the USA. Field (1960) reports that most Russian physicians are women (76 per cent), and that medicine commands low salaries when compared with other technical specialities. In the USA, by contrast, the NORC social standing score of 'physician' is very high indeed and a recent analysis of data from the 1970 US Census showed that only 9 per cent of physicians were women (DiCesare 1975). The median annual earnings of men physicians in the USA were the highest of any occupational category of the Census (Sommers 1974). Hollander (1973) provides supporting evidence when he notes that the 'restratification' of Soviet society which took place in the 1930s gave the highest material rewards (and through the use of mass media the highest status) to the experts in science, engineering and administration (and also to the military). Both absolutely and relatively the material and social status of the medical profession is lower in the USSR than in the USA. The same is true for the legal profession for the very good reason that legal institutions are not very important in Russia. Perhaps we may labour this point about the difference between the occupational status structures in the USA and the USSR by quoting one more source. Berliner (1961) says:

> The young American already not dedicated to some particular field, but motivated by a roughly equal desire for prestige and money, might select some field such as law, medicine, business, or engineering. He would decidedly not go into education or science. An equivalent young Soviet person would make a somewhat different choice. He would certainly not select law, which has been assigned a most humble role in Soviet society. Nor would he select medicine, for while the prestige is high, the income is low. On the other hand, higher education or science would be an excellent choice. The very title of Professor or Scientific Worker would assure him of one of the highest places of honour in the society. And an outstanding career in either of those fields would assure him of an income ranking in the upper ten per cent of perhaps even five per cent (data are hard to come by) of the population. The difference in the economic and social position of the scientist and teacher in the two countries is of fundamental importance in the matter of career recruitment (1961: 364).

And yet if the conventional survey data upon occupational prestige were available for the USSR, it is practically certain that empirical sociologists could find the usual high 'profile correlation' over occupation scores between Russia and the USA. This is because the between country differences that exist for Medicine and some other occupations are swamped by the between country *agreement* that exists about such things as skilled jobs being better than unskilled jobs.

In order to illustrate further the absurdity of using correlation coefficients in this way, let us consider an hypothetical example of judgements concerning eleven deviant acts. Suppose that we wish to compare two individuals or two subcultures, one of which subscribes to traditional morality and the other of which is more modern.

	Rank	Per cent rating as 'very serious'		Rank
		Old %	Young %	
Grevious bodily harm	2	90	90	2
Murder	1	99	99	1
Rape	3	89	89	3
Embezzlement	6	80	80	5
Arson	4	85	85	4
Marijuana possession	5	84	5	10
Drunk and incapable	9	22	50	6
Vagrancy	7	50	2	11
Shoplifting	10	20	20	8
Income tax evasion	8	25	35	7
Littering	11	15	15	9

There is agreement between these two subgroups on the seriousness of most of the deviant acts itemised, and there is a high correlation (Spearman's rho is 0.73) between the two profiles. But disagreement there is (e.g. about marijuana possession), and we know from other sources that this disagreement has considerable cultural significance.

Secondly, we can ask how the technique of correlating the various scores assigned to occupations is affected by the sampling of occupations, and of survey respondents to judge them. A number of writers have tried to account for the high intercorrelations between prestige rankings of occupations in different societies in terms of biased sampling of 'western-style' occupations as stimuli to be judged, or in terms of biased sampling of respondents to make the judgements. In many studies, the respondents have been students who were ready to hand and who might be supposed to be already on the road to being Westernised. Certainly they would be unlikely to be typical of up-country peasants in their countries.

However this may be, the problem of obtaining a representative sample

of people from a large population is so well understood that it can be
regarded as a technical detail. In considerable contrast, the task of sampling
a set of occupational titles to be judged raises very thorny problems which
are not only technical, but also involve considerations of theory. It is not
difficult to suggest a scheme for the selection of occupation titles which
would show low profile correlations between the scores assigned in different
societies. One would try to focus the sampling towards those occupations
that were towards the middle of the range on a number of obvious criteria
such as income, or their required educational level. One would also try to
make the occupational titles as non-stereotyped as possible. Supposing on
the other hand that one wished to have occupational titles sampled in such
a way that high profile correlations could be produced between societies.
In this case, the appropriate strategy would be to over-sample both very
high-status occupations and very low-status occupations. Whatever the
variations on cognition and evaluation of occupations, it is not likely
that members of any subculture are going to rank-order such occupations
as 'Physician' lower than such occupations as 'Janitor'. Therefore the
greater the degree to which such 'very high' compared to 'very low'
comparisons can be implied by the sampling scheme used for selecting
occupational titles, the more likely it is that spuriously high 'agreement'
will be shown between societies. Perhaps the fairest sampling scheme would
be for occupational titles to be selected proportionately to the numbers
of people in those occupations. This would give titles such as 'Physician'
a relatively low probability of being selected, and would be quite different
from currently used sampling schemes, which seem to favour the selection
of 'visible' and even stereotyped occupational titles.

    While all these objections to cross-national prestige studies are solid, our
first point seems most basic. The important disagreements are hidden by
such agreement as there is. Nosanchuk (1972) has elaborated upon this
idea in a rather interested way. He suggests as a plausible simplifying hypothesis that people perceive occupations partly in terms of the stratum
membership they imply and partly in terms of the occupational area or
speciality they imply. The strata might be thought of as being perceived
social classes or, more psychologically, they might be thought of as the
semantic categories marked by such terms as 'professional', 'manual worker'
and so forth. Examples of occupational areas might be the categories of
business, health, government, education. Nosanchuk's suggestion is that all
socialised members of modern societies agree about the assignment of
occupations to strata and about the prestige orderings of those strata.
Where individual and group differences are hypothesised as arising is in
the prestige ordering of the occupational specialities. One community might
value education above business while another might invert that ordering.
Operating with this model, Nosanchuk is able to contruct sets of hypothetical data where the disagreements about the prestige ordering of
occupational specialities (though not of the social classes) are as great as

they could possibly be. The data for pairs of raters were made up so as to be as unlike each other as possible in terms of prestige orderings of situses, but with the condition that there was a shared perception of the ordered strata. Rank correlations of 0.88, 0.79 and 0.87 were produced with this sort of hypothetical experiment: clear evidence that high profile correlations are not necessarily indicative of agreement about occupational prestige hierarchies.

The Pineo-Porter data on occupational prestige rankings by Canadians provide a substantive example. Re-analysing these data, Nosanchuk showed that French-speaking Canadians ranked occupations in the medical and construction situses consistently more highly than they were ranked by English-speakers. On the average, these differences were 1.7 ranks for medical occupations and 1.1 ranks for contruction workers. Also, the French-speakers ranked occupations in the educational and government situses consistently lower than English-speakers ranked them (on the average, 2.2 and 1.8 ranks respectively). Nosanchuk's approach shows up these interesting and significant differences even in the Pineo-Porter data, where the profile correlation between Anglophone and Francophone occupational prestige heirarchies is as high as 0.95. (Interestingly, this is the same as the value of the profile correlation between White and Black occupational prestige hierarchies, as reported by Siegel (1970.) In line with the Nosanchuk model, there was considerable agreement between the two language communities about the assignment of occupations to strata. However, even this agreement was not perfect.

If the profile correlation is considered as an index of the similarity between occupational hierarchies (as is conventionally done), the Nosanchuk model factors the original correlation of 0.97 into a 'between-stratum-within-situs' correlation of 0.99, with a within-stratum-between situs' correlation of 0.77 (both of these have been increased by a 'correction for attenuation'). The correlations between the occupational prestige hierarchies of different societies that have been reported by many sociologists might likewise be factored into 'between-stratum' and 'within-stratum' correlations. Where the 'between stratum' correlation tends to unity, this may be taken as supportive of the structuralist point of view. Where the 'within stratum' correlation tends to zero, or even becomes negative, the 'culturalist' viewpoint gains increased credence. Both of these events may occur in the same data (though they need not), so that in Nosanchuk's formulation of the problem, both structuralist' and 'culturalist' theories about occupational prestige hierarchies might be supported by the same data.

By accident or design, it seems that Nosanchuk gives rather little attention to the cognitive implications of his model. He assumes that different people in various societies agree about the number of strata that exist (and that different societies have the same number of strata). He also assumes that people agree about the assignment of occupations to strata (though this second assumption seems partly to be tested as a matter of routine, in the

computation of the 'between-stratum correlation). The crucial assumption
in Nosanchuk's model is a cognitive one. He says,

> Let us assume that there exists a set of strata which are perceived by the
> raters to be disjoint, i.e., that *all* elements of any stratum are ranked more
> highly than any element of any lower stratum, where a stratum is defined
> as an aggregate of like-status occupations . . . [and] . . . in each stratum
> there exists precisely one representative from each situs . . . (1972: 358).

It is not clear that his model could work in the case where disagreements
existed between people as to the number of strata and the assignment of
of occupations to them. While people often talk about their societies in
metaphors which imply the existence of discrete strata (social classes) it is
not at all clear that they agree about their number and nature. Indeed
much argument about the status of certain occupations is to do with the
correctness of their assignment to a particular stratum. Consider Howard
Becker 1970: 90) on the use made of the term 'profession':

> Members of some occupations use it to describe themselves. Members
> of other occupations would like to use it to describe themselves, but
> find that no one else takes their claim seriously. Laymen habitually
> use it to refer to certain kinds of work and not to others, which they
> describe variously as 'businesses', 'sciences', 'trades', 'rackets', and the
> like . . . It is a term of invidious comparison and moral evaluation; in
> applying it to a particular occupation, people mean to say that the
> occupation is morally praiseworthy just as, in refusing to apply it to
> another occupation, they mean to say that it is not worthy of the
> honour . . . Because the title of profession expresses a postive moral
> evaluation, many work groups seek it. The arguments over definition
> also express disagreement between members of different occupations
> and within the general public over whether particular groups have
> achieved this honoured state.

Nosanchuk's own data analyses were far removed from consideration of the
data provided by individual subjects. Like many investigators in this area, he
performed secondary analyses of data which had already been partially
summarised by the primary researchers (Pineo and Porter). Notwithstanding
his claim that the re-analysis of the Pineo-Porter data was merely illustrative,
his inference that the set of occupations ought to be divided into four strata
(rather then, say, two, or perhaps seven) is nowhere systematically justified.
Noasnchuk's formulation of the structuralist—culturalist controversy concerning occupational prestige hierarchies is interesting and creative, but as we see,
it raises and fails to answer a problem about the perception and cognition of
occupations.

2.4   WHAT DETERMINES EVALUATIONS OF OCCUPATIONS?

Textbooks usually define occupations as collections of tasks; perhaps with the comment that some tasks are more central and some less so. For example the British Department of Employment gives each of the occupations it considers a list of prescribed activities followed by a second list of activities that incumbents of the occupations 'may' undertake. For example, in order to be a university professor a person must teach and engage in research, though he may or may not become involved in administration. But occupations also refer to collections of people with typical skills, training, social class background, income level, style of life and age structure. Furthermore many occupations (and all professional occupations) are social organisations with associations, trade unions or guilds acting so as to control the conduct of practitioners and the admission of recruits. Associations, unions and guilds also attempt to develop and maintain a sense of common feeling of solidarity among their members, and of course they bargain on behalf of members about levels of remuneration, types of job-specification and job structure, fringe benefits and conditions of service.

Office-holders in such associations, unions and guilds are concerned about the favourability of the 'image' of their profession in the public consciousness. This concern is not merely a matter of conceit, for there is a close relationship between current ideas about the status of an occupation, the duties which should be performed by its practitioners and the contribution the occupation makes to society on the one hand, and the level of remuneration and style of life which should be enjoyed by its members on the other. As a concrete example, we may quote an attempt by British engineers in 1975 to set up a new professional organisation to be called the Institute of Engineers. This was proposed as a replacement to the existing Council of Engineers (a federation of some 15 chartered institutions). The *Financial Times* reported that this move was the result of widespread feeling among young engineers that their status in the community was not sufficiently high, and that this was damaging to recruitment. Engineers wished to establish a status comparable to that of doctors or solicitors, and the proposed Institute of Engineers was to take steps to attain this through public relations activities and the defence of the professional engineer's code of conduct.[4] Occupations are not passive objects of perception then. In many cases they are self-conscious and self-publicising organisations, each striving to maintain its public image.

To judge from the current literature on prestige studies, the evidence of temporal stability in occupational prestige hierarchies (Plata 1975) seems to be regarded as unproblematical, (even while books and learned papers are being written about 'professionalisation' and 'deprofessionalisation'). But given the possibility that occupations as a whole can gain or lose status, the methods by which they manage to maintain their postions become sociologically interesting. It is not difficult to show that occupational wage differentials, for example, exhibit considerable variation in response to immigration, trade unionism or the fluctuation of the business cycle. Ozanne (1962) showed that the wage rate for skilled workers at a single manufacturing plant in Chicago has sometimes been more than twice the rate for common labourers and sometimes less than one-and-a-half the labourer rate. One supposes that the social distance between the two categories of worker bears some relationship to the economic distance, and therefore that social distances are not fixed over time.

Lockwood' s classic discussion of the rise of the black-coated worker in the ninteeenth-century Britain is another case in point. To quote him:

> Economic advantage does not simply confer social status; in many cases, traditional social status is a ground for the perpetuation of economic differences . . . The differential in the reward of black coated (clerical) and manual work, which was established in those decades of the counting house era when literate workers were scarce and manual labour plentiful, gave substance to the general claim of the clerk to a superior social standing. The status and advantage that had been won through scarcity was perpetuated by tradition and proved extremely resistant to change (100).

As an economist might put it, the status of an occupation is 'sticky downwards', perhaps 'stickier' (i.e. more resistant to being reduced), than wage or salary levels. The time-course for the equilibration of wage or salary levels is shorter than that for social status, though the two are of course connected with one another.

It is often the case in sociology that there are important differences between micro- and macro-levels of analysis. This is certainly true when we consider the relationship between earnings and social status. At the micro-level, trade-offs can be made between status and earnings. In terms of career lines, white-collar workers in Europe and North America often attempt to accumulate status (via prestigious qualifications or prestigious institutional affiliations or both) when young, and then encash it in later life. Sometimes a decrease in prestige is traded for an increase in earnings, and sometimes vice versa. (It may be among the common dilemmas of Oxbridge academic life to decide upon the best time to exchange the prestige of college life for the emoluments of a provincial chair.) At the macro-level, however, different processes operate. There will always exist basic supply and demand tendencies, so that an increase in the prestige of any occupation will attract greater numbers of recruits to it, and so that this augmented supply will (if unregulated) tend to depress the earnings of practitioners of that occupation (see Cain 1974). Sociologically inclined writers such as Lockwood (1958) or Johnson (1972) would argue that should an occupation become seen as more prestigious for one reason or another (one thinks of the rise of medicine for example), this socially established fact will be used as an additional resource by those who are leaders and organisers in the occupational association, trade union, guild or whatever. As Lockwood puts it:

> The fact that an occupation recruits its members from higher social strata . . . is at once an index and a cause of its social standing (106).

A Johnson-Lockwood analysis would argue that the major interest of such an occupational association and its officers is an increasing of the occupation's autonomy. This concerns partly its control over recruitment levels (and entry qualifications) and partly its ability to obtain higher remuneration for its members, as well as exerting control over them through some licensing arrangement. In summary, this view conceives of occupational associations as having the habit of attempting (not necessarily successfully) to 'bootstrap' themselves into greater autonomy, greater remuneration and greater prestige. These are aimed at partly for themselves, and partly since, once obtained, they are useful as resources for further bootstrapping.

The previous argument leads to an intuitive feeling for the way in which the relative positions of occupations and professions are maintained over time. Nevertheless change does take place. Vance Packard's popular book *The Status Seekers* (1959) contains perhaps the clearest and certainly the best-written account of occupational prestige in the USA. He points out that the rank order of average earnings between physicians, lawyers and professional engineers has shifted from a pattern with lawyers on the top and physicians at the bottom (with engineers in between) in the twenties to one with physicians at the top and lawyers in third place.

The countries of Eastern Europe have undergone major economic, political and social changes since the beginning of the twentieth century. It would be odd indeed if the experience of two major wars, military occupations by various forces, communist takeovers and industrialisation had left the hierarchy of occupational evaluations as a single fixed and unchanging reality while all else was in flux. Sociologists in Poland have been active in studying the changes in class structure of their society over this period (see Sarapata 1966; Wesolowski 1966; Szczepanski 1970; Vaughan 1971). Prior to 1945, white-collar employment in general (mental work), and the status of being a university graduate in particular, seem to have been very highly prestigious – relatively more so than in other countries. Hertz (1951) explained as follows:

> [In Anglo-Saxon countries] a college graduate may be a member of an intellectual group – a faculty, a learned society, a professional association, the bar, etc., but by no means does education make him regard himself as a member of a separate class or caste, bound to lead the nation to its destiny. In most cases, he defines his social status as that of the middle class. Matters are different in Poland . . . formal education acquired in an institution of higher learning meant, and still means, more than personal success, but rather a permanent asset which sets the individual apart and gives him access to a higher social sphere. The diploma from an institution of higher learning not only entitles a person to follow a particular profession. It gives more than that, it bestows a title, a dignity that will remain forever associated with its bearer (quoted by Szczepanski 1970: 120).

Sarapata and Wesolowski (1961) carried out a study of the opinions held about occupations by people in Warsaw in 1958. Comparison with occupational prestige scores collected by Bolte in West Germany showed the usual high profile correlation (0.90) between the two countries. However, the authors use their sociological intuition, and still maintain, 'we think that these figures are not correct indicators of the public image in the compared countries' and they point to the relatively higher prestige positions in Poland of skilled manual workers and the intellectual occupations. This study also showed systematic differences in evaluations of occupations, depending on the evaluator's own occupational position.

> The private entrepreneurs evaluate their own jobs higher than do others the skilled and unskilled workers about the same as do others; and the engineers, teachers and office clerks lower than do others . . . engineers and physicians tend to evaluate their own professions lower than do others because they feel that their profession is understeemed by both government and people (589).

Sarapata (1962) asked a sample of Polish men whether each of a list of 21 occupations had a higher position in society than before the war, a lower position, or an unchanged position. So far as we are aware, this is the only investigation where this sort of direct question about the movement of occupations has been asked. The question of temporal stability in occupational prestige hierarchies has almost always been attacked by comparing survey data from different time-points (e.g. Plata 1972). Sarapata's direct question approach is open to the criticism that the memories of the informants might be biased. But even if this were so, these biased opinions would constitute a 'social reality' and should therefore be conceded some existence Needless to say, there was some disagreement between the informants. However there was some fair consensus that the social positions of journalists, small farmers (peasants) and of skilled and unskilled workers had improved, while the social positions of private businessmen, priests and clerks had declined compared with the period before the war.

It seems to be established that occupations do indeed move up and down some kind of social scale. This raises questions about the determinants of such movements and gets us back to the problem of what characteristics of occupations give them higher or lower amounts of public esteem.

The arrow diagrams or flow graphs which are isomorphic with structural equations models are quite common in the sociological journals nowadays, and it was to be expected that they would make their appearance in papers on the determinants of the prestige of occupations. Siegel (1970) produced the first application in this field. Structural equations models are exceptionally simple (one might say simplistic) accounts of social phenomena, though this simplicity is sometimes concealed by the debates which take place about the efficiency of procedures for estimating their parameters.

The classic papers by Blishen and Duncan are concerned with the prediction of an occupation's prestige score from knowledge of the income levels of people in that occupation and also of the educational attainment of people in that occupation. In the usual regression equation formulation:

$$
\begin{array}{l}
\text{average person's} \\
\text{judgement of the} \\
\text{prestige of the} \\
\text{occupation}
\end{array}
= b_1
\begin{bmatrix}
\text{income level} \\
\text{of people in} \\
\text{that occupation}
\end{bmatrix}
+ b_2
\begin{bmatrix}
\text{educational level} \\
\text{of people in} \\
\text{that occupation}
\end{bmatrix}
$$

where b_1 and b_2 are the partial regression coefficients. (There may also be a constant term (or 'intercept' though this is always zero if the variables are considered in standard score form, and anyway has no interesting substantive interpretation.)

While Duncan and Blishen sometimes talk as if their use of the previously described regression equation was purely a technical matter with no substantive implications whatever (recall the title of Duncan's paper — 'a socio-economic index for all occupations'), both they and other writers have written as if they interpreted the regression equation model as if it was in fact meant to be a substantively relevant statement about the social and psychological processes by which people assign prestige to occupational titles. In the case of the Duncan/Blishen model, the assertion is made that there are no systematic differences between people as judges of the prestige of occupational titles, and that on the average the only important factors influencing the prestige judgement for any given occupation are the average income level and the average educational level for people in the occupation.

Econometricians have been the clearest-headed users of structural equation models, and among other considerations they have stressed the importance of the social scientist's setting up a correctly specified model before estimating it. Putting the matter very simply, it is of the first importance that the social scientist should include all the relevant predictor variables. If, for example, it should happen that the proportion of Blacks in an occupation systematically influences the prestige judgements that are made of that occupation in a way that is independent of the effects of income levels and educational levels, then the Blishen/Duncan model which is expressed in the regression equation under discussion would be 'mis-specified', since it leaves out the 'proportion of Blacks' predictor. The same might be said for such properties of occupations that might possibly influence their prestige as the percentage of women in the occupation; or whether or not the occupation is classified as a profession (which might be bound with the presence of an occupational association or organisation).

The notion that Blacks in the USA have a different subculture from Whites led some sociologists to suggest that the occupational prestige hierarchy among Blacks is different from its White counterpart (see Glenn 1963). Paul Siegel tried to test this notion in 1970, using aggregate-level data on the prestige ratings of occupational titles made by white and black males. He postulated two structural equations.

$$\begin{bmatrix}\text{average white} \\ \text{person's judge-} \\ \text{ment of the} \\ \text{prestige of the} \\ \text{occupation}\end{bmatrix} = b_1 \begin{bmatrix}\text{income of} \\ \text{Whites in the} \\ \text{occupation}\end{bmatrix} + b_2 \begin{bmatrix}\text{education of} \\ \text{Whites in the} \\ \text{occupation}\end{bmatrix} + b_3 \begin{bmatrix}\text{proportion of} \\ \text{Blacks in the} \\ \text{occupation}\end{bmatrix}$$

(and on no other systematic factors)

$$\begin{bmatrix}\text{average black} \\ \text{person's judge-} \\ \text{ment of the}\end{bmatrix} = b_4 \begin{bmatrix}\text{income of} \\ \text{Blacks in the} \\ \text{occupation}\end{bmatrix} + b_5 \begin{bmatrix}\text{education of} \\ \text{Blacks in the} \\ \text{occupation}\end{bmatrix} + b_6 \begin{bmatrix}\text{proportion of} \\ \text{Blacks in the} \\ \text{occupation}\end{bmatrix}$$

(and on no other systematic factors)

This was Siegel's first model, and is perhaps more than a little absurd (at least in the context in which Siegel chose to estimate the coefficients). The culture of Blacks in the US is hypothesised to be so separate from that of Whites that the judgements of occupational prestige made by Blacks are unaffected by the income levels of Whites in those occupations. (This general approach might, of course, be useful with other pairs of social groups, such as Men and Women; or (in Canada), Canadians of Francophone or Anglophone origin, or with any pair of nations.)

After exploring a number of intermediate models, Siegel concluded that neither the prestige ratings of Whites nor those of Blacks are significantly influenced by the following two occupational characteristics;

(a) The educational attainment of Blacks in the occupation whose prestige is being judged.

(b) The income level of Blacks in the occupation whose prestige is being judged.

Siegel also concluded more positively that the prestige ratings made by Whites and also by Blacks *are* influenced by;

(i) The educational attainment of Whites in the occupation whose prestige is being judged.

(ii) The income level of Whites in the occupation whose prestige is being judged.[5]

The conclusion drawn by Siegel is that when Blacks are asked about the prestige of occupations, the factors they bear in mind when making their judgements are only three in number and that they give these factors roughly the same importance as do Whites. The standardised partial regression coefficients for the prediction of Black and White average prestige scores, can be shown in tabular form.

		Black	*White*
(i)	The educational level of people in the job	0.37	0.44
(ii)	The income level of people in the job	0.41	0.37
(iii)	The proportion of Blacks in the job	−0.24	−0.27

This analysis of the correlations between census characteristics of occupations and the averaged prestige scores of those occupations is abstract to say the least. It takes a certain heroism to believe that valid conclusions about perceptual processes could emerge from this sort of work.

One possible line of criticism that may be made of Siegel's study is that the prestige ratings made by Blacks were made in response to the standard NORC question about occupational prestige. Subjects were asked to make a rating of the 'general standing in the community' of each of a set of occupations. The Blacks in the study may have been reporting about the general (numerically dominated by Whites) view of occupational status rather than about the views of fellow-blacks. Another line of criticism is that Blacks are more likely to be unemployed, or in illegal occupations and one might expect any distinctive Black culture to have views on activities that were different from those of the White majority. Siegel's study cannot address this objection, since the list of occupational titles that he used does not contain 'unemployment' as a stimulus to be judged, [5] nor does it contain any illegal occupations. Both of these criticisms are essentially to do with the fact that Siegel[7] was engaged in secondary analysis. We may put it less kindly by saying that he was unable to collect fresh data of a kind that might have borne more directly on his substantive problem.

It seems strange that empirical sociologists have been prepared to accept the proposition that an occupation's prestige level is determined by only two or three factors (its income level, its educational requirements and the proportion of Blacks in it). In his unpublished thesis, Siegel (1971) has proposed quite a complex model of the determinants of an occupational category's prestige rating. His model is closely oriented to the data on occupations that are available in the US Census publications and suggests that an occupational category's prestige level depends on ten other characteristics, which are (for each occupational category):

	Occupational Characteristics	*Correlation with average prestige ratings*
E	Educational level*	0.85
L	Degree of self-employment*	0.14
M	Per cent employed in manufacturing*	−0.13
S	Per cent employed in the South ('Southness')*	−0.16
C	Per cent employed in urban areas (urban-ness')*	−0.18
H	Hours worked per week*	0.38
W	Weeks worked per year*	0.50
I	Income level*	0.81
N	Per cent non-white*	−0.53
F	Per cent women in the occupation	−0.13

* Among men in the occupation category

As part of this same model, Siegel proposed an interesting dynamic mechanism of circular causation, which is specified as follows:

(a) An occupation's prestige depends on all the factors mentioned above one of which is the annual income level of the occupation.

(b) The average hourly pay in an occupation is conceptually and empirically distinct from the average annual income level (though in Siegel's data, they were correlated at about $r = 0.85$).

[Average hourly pay depends on most of the same factors as does prestige level, but it also depends on prestige level. Siegel's notion seems to have been that one of the consequences of high prestige is an increment in hourly pay over what might have been predicted from the standard list of occupational characteristics, (such as educational level etc.). We would presume that an effect of this kind in Siegel's statistical model arises from social processes in which attention is paid to an occupation's prestige level during negotiations about hours of work or levels of pay.]

(c) The circle of causation is closed with the proposal that annual income depends in part upon hourly pay.

. . . while the twin rewards of income and prestige are attached to occupations in sufficient quantity to insure that the occupations get filled, the relative temporal stability of occupational prestige would seem to mark it as a constraint against which the more vivacious [sic] rewards, i.e. wages, are adjusted, at least in the short and intermediate runs. In this view, prestige could be a cause for wage rates, at least in the short run, for wages need only be adjusted to fine-tune the supply generated by prestige to match the current levels of demand. Yet . . . the income levels of incumbents must provide some clue, at least in a general way, to an aspect of the desirability of particular occupations for the general populace. Thus income should appear as a cause of prestige. (1971: 304).

Siegel's model here is clearly a homoeostatic one, in which the prestige level of an occupation functions as a kind of flywheel. Temporary situations of supply and demand may shift occupations from their long-run 'equilibrium' rank order, but the social consciousness of the society carries a memory about what this long-run occupational structure 'should' be. (All that is meant by terms like 'flywheel', 'memory' and 'should' is that the prestige level of an occupation is some kind of integration over the span of a generation or so — perhaps fifty years — of the income in an occupation: more simply perhaps, a society carries in its group memory a blurred notion of the fifty-year moving average of the typical income level for each occupation, and this is a major contributor to the public notion of that occupation's general desirability or prestige level.) Since Siegel's model is a homoeostatic one, it is not particularly useful in explaining why some occupations manage to hold on to the status gained in periods when they have a sellers' market for their services, while others do not. There must be stabilising factors which tend to maintain the hierarchy of occupations. Professional and occupational associations try to exert control over the supply-demand situation of their members by exerting influence upon recruitment, seniority, hours of work and retirement. Obviously, some occupations are more successful than others in this task. In tranquil times, perhaps there is a general feeling that the pre-vailing order of society is satisfactory and should be handed on to the next generation. The hierarchy of occupations may change slowly in response to such factors as population shifts to the cities, industrialisation or an increase in the general level of education. Rapid change seems to take place only in response to some pretty major stimulus, such as a period of rapid inflation, or a period of strong government direction of the kind that comes only in war, or in the wake of revolution. Waites (1976) suggests that the artisan stratum of the British working class failed to maintain their economic advan-tage over the remainder of the workers over the period of the 1914-18 war.

> Artisan families which before the war had figured on the 'slavey or skivvy line' and 'single indoor domestic servant level' of the social scale of res-pectability were among the first to feel the rising cost and shortage of service. While it is true that the differentials between skilled and unskilled earnings tended to rise after the slump of 1921, they were never to be of the same order as before the war, nor the phenomenon of social im-mobility between distinct working class strata to be so marked. The very term 'artisan class' tended to disappear from the language of social observation (1976: 35).

We can conclude that the best-known structural equations models which have been put forward in order to account for occupational status have mostly been mis-specified. Such mis-specification has taken the form of failure to include important determinants of occupational status, and failure to consider the positive and negative feedback effects which would become susceptible to modelling activity if the time dimension was properly taken into account.[8]

2.5   DIFFERENCES IN EVALUATION

UPSIDE-DOWNERS?

The argument so far has been that such high profile correlations as can be found between the prestige scores of occupations in different societies do *not* necessarily provide supporting evidence for 'structuralist' theories. Sociolog-ists and intellectuals seem to have been mesmerised by the high values of such profile correlations, and appear to have forgotten the principle that disagree-ments which may be very important are necessarily accompanied by num-erous basic agreements. The mere fact that a crude count shows more agree-ments than disagreements does not mean that there is overall agreement. The sociological literature also contains a curious counterpoint to the dogma about similarity of occupational prestige hierarchies. This counterpoint

becomes apparent as a kind of 'Lord of Misrule' image, in the form of references to subcultures who supposedly invert the status order accepted by the
middle classes. A paper frequently cited in this context is by Young and
Willmott (1956), who reported that workers from London's East End ranked
garbage collectors (dustmen) as more important than many middle-class
occupations. One way to deal with evidence which disconfirms a theory is to
give it a label which defines it as being in some sense a lawful exception. The
Young-Willmott phenomenon has been dealt with in this way by calling it
'status dissent', or borrowing a word from Geiger, *proletarierstolz* (Lockwood
1958: 209). The structuralist argument now becomes something like: there
is broad agreement between and within modern societies about the occupational prestige hierarchy, but in so far as class conflict exists, there will never
be complete unanimity about the criteria of status, and therefore even in
modern societies, class-conscious members of the working class may reject
the dominant bourgeois values. Another way to maintain belief in a theory
is to be rather vague about what evidence would count in support of it, and
at the same time, to make very strong requirements in terms of the kind of
evidence which would go against it. Part of the reason that the 'culturalist'
argument is so weak against the 'structuralist' argument is that the supporter
of the 'culturalist' view is in danger of being required to find societies or
subcultures which have a rank order of occupational prestige which is precisely the mirror-image of the conventional Western European or North
American one – mirror-image in the sense that the last shall be first, the first
last and so on. Because of the ambiguity about what constitutes a 'high'
correlation (anything, it seems, from 0.7 up) the structuralist is on much
easier ground. Our point of view is that although it would be sociologically
interesting to find complete disagreement about prestige orders, we do not
expect to find any instances of it. Systematic differences in occupational
evaluation are quite compatible with the high profile correlations reported
in the literature.

It is possible that there are societies or subcultures which have precisely
the same prestige rank order of occuparions, but even if there were, this would
not necessarily consitute support for a 'structuralist' theory. It is plausible
to suppose that people evaluate occupations on at least an 'ordered metric'
scale, so that there could well be sociologically significant disagreement about
the order of the *separations* between pairs of occupations on the same unidimensional scale. For example, two persons might agree upon the social
prestige order of (*a*) physician, (*b*) butcher, *(c)* typist – and yet one of them
(Jones) might hold that the separation in prestige between physician and
butcher is larger than the separation between butcher and typist. The other
(Smith) might as passionately believe that physicians are quite close to
butchers in terms of social prestige, and that both are a long way above
typists. If it could be shown that Jones and Smith differed in this way
because of systematic and sociologically relevant factors, then findings like
this would be relevant in such areas as the study of class consciousness and

social mobility. Of course the example is hypothetical. Its purpose is to show that even perfect agreement on rank order would not preclude the existence of sociologically significant disagreement.

OCCUPATIONAL EGOISM

At one point in his early writings, Goffman casually mentions the 'well-known phenomenon' that people always tend to have a better opinion of their own occupation than the opinion which other people, not pursuing that occupation, hold of it. Thus garbage collectors may dwell upon the fact that their job, though it requires no particular skills, is one that the community cannot well dispense with: sewage workers as they splash through their catacombs may reflect that for all their contact with filth they too provide a needed service to the community. In the same way, prostitutes, abortionists, and university lecturers in sociology may feel that ill-informed members of the community do not know the details of how hard they work, or of the essential nature of the services they provide. There is then a fairly widely held hypothesis of *egoism* in the opinions that people have of the relative worth of occupations (e.g. Gerstl and Cohen 1964; Goode 1969; Pavalko 1971). The 1947 NORC study of occupational prestige in the USA concluded:

> . . . when a person rated his own job, or one closely related to it, his evaluation was almost always considerably *higher* than the average evaluation of the position (Bendix and Lipset 1953: 415 — emphasis in original).

Alexander (1972) showed that it is useful to examine individuals' judgements of the status of others in the light of well-established social-psychological theories about the perception of evaluatively laden concepts. He argues that the perceptions people have about *any* status system of which they are members are systematically influenced by their own positions in that system. In particular, he suggests that the lower a perceiver's actual, imagined or aspired-to status, the closer together he puts the status categories. Those of lower status diminish the distance between persons or positions in the system by raising the status of those who are (like themselves) in the lower regions.' Alexander carried out a re-analysis of the data from the 1947 NORC survey on the general standing of occupations in order to test these ideas. He found that respondents from high and low statuses differed markedly in their judgements of occupations in the lower two thirds of the prestige hierarchy. This difference was clearly the result of a reluctance on the part of low-status respondents to describe the general standing of low status occupations as 'poor' (the label of the lowest of the four evaluative categories used in the NORC study). High-status respondents did not share this reluctance. A similar pattern of findings has been shown to exist when people make judgements of the social standing of ethnic groups (Pineo 1977).[9]

There are certain points in the occupational system at which dissensus of an 'egoistic' variety is particularly marked. The dividing line between manual and non-manual work is a good example. Social historians of the later nineteenth and early twentieth centuries have often discussed the 'status rivalry' between clerical workers and the 'labour aristocracy'[10] of skilled manual workers. The clerk would emphasise his clean hands, and his educational attainments, while the skilled worker would stress his skill and strength, and the indispensability of manual labour. Depending on the point of view, dirty hands represented self-evidently honest and immediately useful work, or brute toil: clean hands represented a claim to the status of a gentleman, or on the other hand a lack of manliness.

Moving back to the present century, Campbell (1952) reports a survey in which interviewees were asked about the general difficulty of moving from a lower occupational level to a higher one. He found systematic differences between respondents of higher and lower status groups, the higher-status respondents being significantly more likely to use terms indicating relatively easy upward social movement (236). If one can generalise this, one might say that higher-status people are more likely than lower-status people to believe in the availability of upward mobility routes. Campbell's (1952: 133) findings are consistent with the 'egoism' hypothesis; individuals tended to rank jobs that were similar to their own higher then they were ranked by others. He also reports that his higher-status group of respondents tended to rank governmental and political occupations less favourably than they were ranked by the lower-status group. On the argument that higher-status people are in favour of less government while lower-status people are in favour of more, Campbell subsumes this difference under an 'egoism' hypothesis as well. This now becomes a proposition something like: 'People tend to be especially favourable in judging occupations that are similar to their own, or occupations of whose function they approve.'

A little thought will enable us to make even further deductions. If people generally rate their present occupations especially favourably (this is a well-established empirical generalisation) it seems highly likely that they also make especially favourable ratings of the occupations which are auxiliary to their own (and perhaps also of the occupations that they themselves have previously worked in).

On this argument, the pattern of differences in evaluations of occupations is necessarily related to different ideas about similarities between occupations, which are in turn determined by career histories and perhaps also by patterns of social interaction between members of different occupations.

The occupational egoism phenomenon may be regarded as a special case of general cognitive manoeuvrings that people engage in as a means of retaining as high an opinion of themselves as possible. Barkow puts it well:

Reference-group tactics involve shifting from one individual-oriented group-membership strategy to another. Particular groups tend to have particular group membership criteria associated with them. Under certain circumstances, individuals may discover that their relative standing is higher in terms of one set of evaluation criteria than another, and shift reference groups to their own advantage. For example, a pious Hausa in Maradi, Niger Republic, judges himself not in terms of his Western sophistication, but in terms of his knowledge of Islam; this allows himself to evaluate himself as of higher rank than the powerful government functionaries, who in turn rank themselves as superior on the basis of their European-style knowledge (1975: 557).

As Barkow argues it, individuals engage in tactics of cognitive distortion (shifting the frames of reference for evaluation and so forth) in a continuing attempt to maximise their individual prestige. But groups do the same, and occupational groups often have representatives to argue on their behalf.[11] Naturally this is important at the time of negotiations about salaries. Goldthorpe points out in the context of a discussion of Britain:

> Given the diversity of moral opinion, virtually any occupational group seeking a pay increase is likely to be able to find some legitimation for pressing its case (1974).

2.6 SOCIAL MOBILITY AND SOCIAL SPACE

Students of social mobility have usually been content to use occupations as empirical indicators of social categories. The crudest measurements of mobility focus attention upon obvious boundaries such as those between rural and urban employment or between a manual (blue-collar) and a non-manual (white-collar) job.

Dichotomous classifications such as these have the virtue of simplicity. However, they conceal any mobility that happens not to cross rural/urban or non-manual/manual boundaries. The tendency therefore has been to increase the number of occupational categories between which the sociologist sees movement as taking place. In the classic British study of mobility for example, Glass and his colleagues used seven 'status categories' into which a man might be assigned by virtue of his occupation.

The investigator's choice of categories between which mobility will be recorded as taking place is clearly of crucial importance. If the investigator makes his system of categories too coarse, he will fail to record some of the mobility that really takes place. But finer classification may result in mobility which is of no real significance, being counted equally with real social movement. How can the investigator judge whether a potential social boundary line is to be included in his system of operational categories? A number of points of view are possible here, but we would say that the basic criterion must be concerned with the perceptions of those people whose mobility is being researched. Macdonald argues (1973) that sociologists studying mobility are obliged (in so far as they are sociologists rather than statesticians) to show that their analytic categories match with the social categories seen as significant by the people whose movement they examine. To some extent, competent empiricists follow this prescription anyway. For example, in Katz's study of mobility in Hamilton, Ontario, the transition to home ownership is used as an index of mobility, on the grounds that *social* mobility involves consideration of property ownership as well as occupation.

While sociologists have typically confined their analysis to social movement on *one* vertical dimension of status, Katz (1975) makes use of *four* status dimensions: economic rank, occupational rank, property status and number of servants employed. His study of social mobility in nineteenth century Ontario shows that movement on these four dimensions of status is by no means highly correlated: Katz talks (153) of 'relative independence' of movement on these four mobility scales. Indeed, he points out (115) that the measurement of social class by occupation is a dubious procedure with historical (nineteenth-century) data.

Many sociologists tailor the classification of occupations to be used in each study to the local conditions. Oldman and Illsley (1966) carried out a study of intermarriage patterns in Aberdeen, where fish-workers are a numerically important and socially distinct local occupational group. Because of this social distinctiveness Oldham and Illsley analysed their data with a category system having fish-workers as a separate occupational group, even though a more conventional analysis at that time would have lumped them in with semi-skilled or unskilled workers in the Registrar-General's Social Class classification of occupations. In the empirical studies carried out by Warner and his colleagues, a serious attempt was made to estimate the status situation of each person in the small community being studied. Studies carried out since Warner's time have been less painstaking, for although they have claimed to be concerned with the status situations of individuals and social groups, they have typically shied away from the effort involved in emulating Warner's example. Instead, they have used an individual's occupation as an empirical index of his social status. This involves the dubious assumption that all people with the same occupational title are in much the same status situation, but few sociologists seem to have been very worried by that.[12]

Beginning with the work of Blishen and Duncan in the 1950s and sixties, the popular tendency has been to consider social mobility as that movement (of men) which occurs between the detailed occupational categories of the census authorities. Such categories are sometimes quite fine, though as Pamela Oliver points out (1974), they make finer discriminations among occupations at the level of professions, and tend to lump working-class occupations together into heterogeneous categories. The mass of the working population is concentrated in these unskilled and semi-skilled jobs and the vast majority of all social movements take place between such occupations (and not between professional occupations nor between working-class occupations and the professions). But it is precisely these unskilled and semi-skilled jobs about whose relative prestige there is least agreement (see Hodge *et al*. 1966; Hunter 1977).

As we have seen sociologists have been persuaded of the virtues of 'occupational prestige' scales of social status by the high values of profile correlations between different societies. But these high correlations come about because of the implicit comparisons between very high-status occupations and very low- status occupations that are involved in their computation. There is indeed agreement about *some* possible occupational movements, but these are precisely the movements which do not take place very frequently. The sleight of hand in the 'structuralist' argument on occupational prestige is to quote the high agreement about those movements which occur infrequently in support of the (false) proposition that there is similarly high agreement about the size and direction of the 'step-by-step' occupational movements between various kinds of working-class jobs.

Census classification of occupations are often inappropriate for sociological purposes. Treiman mentions (1975) that some national census classifications of occupations represent the armed forces, the police or the educational system by single categories with no distinction made between the different ranks or positions (197). Clearly, such classification systems are useless for the study of career mobility, and sub-optimal for the comparison of the occupational achievements of fathers and sons. Along with the work of Blishen and Duncan has come a theoretical tendency to restrict the subject-matter of 'social mobility' to the study of movements 'up' or 'down' in a one-dimensional hierarchy of occupational prestige. Each occupational category of the census is given a score on a prestige dimension. Mobility from one occupational position to another (but only if it occurs so as to cross the boundary separating census categories) is treated mathematically as upward or downward movement between the numerical scores corresponding to those occupational categories. Treiman (1977) has provided a technical advance in this tradition by publishing an International Occupational Prestige Scale. This has the advantage that the problems of comparability between different national census classifications are circumvented, and the further advantage that its categories make distinctions by rank as well as by industry. However it makes the same assumptions about the cognitive and evaluative inferences that people make from knowledge of occupational titles as do the scales it supersedes. Before taking up the use of a scale such as Treiman's, sociologists ought perhaps to review these assumptions, which may be outlined as follows:

(1) We need to be able to assume that a person's occupation is an adequate index of his position in the social hierarchy. If people are prepared to use occupation by itself as a major item of information from which to draw inferences about status, then this assumption will be valid. On the other hand, if people are only confident in drawing inferences about status when given information about occupation in conjunction with information about other characteristics, such as age, ethnicity, nationality, religion, family

name or linguistic group, then the widespread use of occupation *by itself* as an index of status, will surely be ill-founded. (See Beshers and Reiter 1963: 7; Triandis and Triandis 1960).

(2) If the first assumption is considered reasonable, we still need to be prepared to assume that people have the same *cognition* of the domain of occupations. We must assume consensus as to the fineness or coarseness of the distinctions it is reasonable to make between occupational categories, and we must also assume consensus about the semantic nature of the dimensions that may be used to distinguish occupations.

(3) The two previous assumptions being granted, there is the final require-ment that there be consensus as to the *evaluation* of occupations. It may be objected that the inferences people are prepared to draw from know-ledge of occupation need not enter any consideration of the use of occupation as an index of socio-economic status. It might be the case as a matter of entirely contingent fact, that occupation is an accurate index of a person's income and educational level. This objection might be allowed to stand, but only at the price (which most theorists have been entirely unwilling to pay) of removing the subjective element (thoughts in the head of the social actor) from any explanation of his reasons for desiring upward mobility or his reacting in whatever way he does to downward mobility.

SOCIAL SPACE

The idea of 'social space' has a long and honourable history in sociology generally, as well as in the field of social mobility. It is used to particular effect by Durkheim and Simmel among the classics, and features as an important unifying theme in the writings of Park, Burgess and others of the 1920s Chicago school. McFarland (in Laumann 1966: 23 *et seq.*) provides a useful overview of the development of this concept.

The core meaning of the term, common to all variants of its use, is that individuals (or other social entities) are depicted as points in a space, in such a way that the relationships among the points represent a particular property of interest. Within this framework, 'social space' is used to serve two rather different purposes. Sorokin (1959: 5 *et seq.*) used it primarily as a *locational* device. The position of a man − or any other social entity − is defined by his relations to other reference points, which will normally be other individuals or groups. In Sorokin's account, to say 'X is a White, Catholic, Liberal Democrat, cabdriver' is equivalent to listing the coordinates of his social position. Each descriptor successively narrows down his social location, leading in the end to a set of equivalence classes in each of which individuals share the same attributes, in much the same way as Lazarsfeld uses 'property space' to define different types of individual. Sorokin did not go so far beyond this in his metaphorical thinking but more recent work in status consistency (also termed status crystallisation or rank equilibration) has adopted a very similar use. Beginning with the assumption that status is multi-faceted, sociologists distinguish several component attributes (occupation, race, income, etc.) locate a given individual on each scale, and then look at the pattern of his ranks on each attribute. Their focus of interest is in the pattern and degree of consistency in his location, in the belief that the extent of inconsistency between the ranks is in itself a factor producing such social effects as political radicalism. (A simple index of status like Warner's, which is summarily aggregated over the various 'dimensions', would, of course, mask such status inconsistency.)

In contrast to this 'locational' use, writers such as Bogardus used social space — or rather, in this case, social distance — primarily to represent relative proximity. Whether couched in behavioural terms (resting upon actual patterns of interaction) or in terms of attitudes (depending upon expressed interaction preferences), the attraction and repulsion between individuals or groups is represented by closeness and distance in the space. In this case, the values of the component attributes of the space are largely irrelevant, and substantive interest focuses simply on relative distance (usually between ethnic groups), upon movement in the space, and upon related phenomena, such as the geographical zoning of cities.[13]

Perhaps because Sorokin collapsed all significant dimensions of variation to two 'principal varieties' — the vertical and horizontal dimensions of the social universe' (7), and largely restricted attention to movement along the latter, both social and ethnic mobility studies have searched for a single dimension of variation. In the case of social mobility, 'popular evaluation of occupations' was used in the attempt to define it. But it turned out to be a hazardous enterprise, for several reasons (discussed in detail in Coxon and Jones 1974b). In particular:

(1) the possible number of occupations which could enter such judgements is huge, and most people are familiar with only a small proportion of them;

(2) the number of occupational titles which is practical terms can be judged in a systematic manner depends upon the method of data collection used. Unfortunately it is also the case that those methods best adapted to collect information about the social standing of large numbers of occupations yield the least information about the relational aspects of occupations;

(3) virtually all tests of the unidimensionality of prestige ratings (and of other related properties) indicate that several dimensions are necessary to represent the data.

Yet if the use of people's judgements about the occupational structure is intended to be anything other than a convenient (and anti-theoretical) means of quantification, then these results should not be surprising. As Mayer (1972: 92) expresses it:

A generalised one-dimensional concept of social mobility pre-supposes either common value-orientations in the population to which it is to be applied or a stratification system which is organised according to one specific dimension of social inequality and has such a great impact that people have no other choice than to define their life goals and concerns in terms of this structure.

To the degree that there are systematic individual differences in subjective definitions of social inequality, it might seem reasonable for sociologists to take them into account in their theory and practice. An approach of this kind would take the things to be represented in a scaling study as being the constructions which men use to comprehend their world.

Such a 'constructional' approach also involves a rather different way of looking at 'social space', for the basis of this space is the socially shared cognitive map. The research enterprise starts with the attempt to guess at how the subject contrues the occupational world, and to infer the principles of organisation involved. As a starting hypothesis – and nothing more– it seems reasonable to interpret the idea of the map fairly literally – a representation of the location of a set of 'objects' (e.g. occupations) in a continuous space such that the relative proximity between the objects reflects and represents their relative similarity. The cognitive space is spanned by (an unknown number of) dimensions, each of which represents a general attribute or characteristic of the occupations. In fact, we do not perceive unique attributes of occupations (or of anything else), but rather attributes which they have *in common* with other occupations. It should therefore be possible to infer the common bases of attribution in the judgements which people make about occupations. In this case this may be done by interpreting the judgements of similarity which subjects make as providing information on the relative proximity of occupations in his occupational map, and then using scaling procedures to obtain a spatial representation of it.

Even in this apparently innocent interpretation there lurk a number of strong and questionable assumptions which we shall have occasion to examine at a later point; suffice it to say that the spatial analogy can be treacherous as well as illuminating. But a cognitive structure is not simply a map, nor is it necessarily best represented spatially. Cognition also involves classification, categorisation – we 'give attention to similar differences and different similarities' as Bohm (Shanin: 254) put it – as well as the operation of rules. It may well be that several important properties of this system can be depicted spatially, but other aspects we shall be concerned with may well have no natural quantitative or spatial representation.[14]

In this volume we are concerned with subjective models of the occupational structure, with how people judge the relationships between occupations. In making such a study, we assume that occupational cognition may vary, that the conceptions which people have of the world of occupations differ according to who they are, and in terms of the occupations actually referred to. But we cannot, of course, inspect people's conceptions directly, and any information we gain must be inferred from what people do and what they say.

Ideally, such behaviour and language should be observed in its natural social context, for then we should at least know that the information we obtain does not depend upon our intervention – in short, our data would then be non-reactive. This was not, however, the option we chose as our main research strategy, and such a decision needs justification.

We might begin by contrasting the full richness, complexity, subtlety (and inconsistency) of an individual's 'real' beliefs about occupations with the restricted and artificial simplicity of most survey-based questions on occupational prestige. But we resist such a characterisation as unhelpful and misleading. It is misleading because we never know in any natural context about the individual's beliefs in their full complexity. Rather, we build up an impression or account of them from a wide range of social interactions of differing complexity. Quite often the information transmitted in such an encounter takes the form of simple and self-contained predications ('doctors are very well-paid'). Moreover, the information is usually fragmentary, because explicit comparisons are infrequent in normal discourse. But when people do make comparative judgements (' . . . but, look, doctors don't go on strike nearly as much as the miners do') then the pieces of fragmentary information become linked together (or structured) into a rudimentary *system* of beliefs.

A more fundamental problem, inherent in any inquiry of this sort, is whether the meaning (both sense and reference) of occupational discourse is indexical. The contrast between 'objective' or 'literal' statements on the one hand and 'indexical' statements on the other is a well-established one in philosophy; in brief, the truth of an 'objective' statement is held to be context-independent and decidable in terms of specifiable features, whereas an 'indexical' statement is not (Bar Hillel 1954). Ethnomethodologists (following Garfinkel 1967: 425) have extended (and altered) this sense of indexicality by ignoring the question of the truths of such statements, and they have directed attention instead to the social processes whereby actors develop (or 'negotiate') the ground rules for establishing the meaning of words. They have also emphasised the point that the people interpret, and expand, utterances by reference to an extensive background of largely implicit and unspoken assumptions of 'what everyone knows' or takes for granted about the topic concerned (Cicourel 1971: 151)[15] Moreover, different situations can, and do, involve different assumptions being used to interpret the same utterance. And it is here that one of the chief interpretative rules of ethnomethodology is evident; to look *at,* rather than through, the taken-for-granted features of discourse:

> Though we ordinarily only see things with the economy of practical vision, we can look at them instead of through them, and then their suppressed forms and their unusual meanings emerge for us (Langer, cited in Manning 1971: 251).

The chief relevance of this debate for occupational cognition is our contention that occupational discourse, which we rely upon to infer occupational beliefs, is inherently indexical. Yet it is precisely this assumption which most studies of social stratification – whether 'subjectivist', 'structuralist' or marxist – implicitly or explicitly deny. A negative argument will make this clear. In the debate on indexicality in the context of natural science methodology, those who wish to preserve the non-indexicality of (some) scientific statements (i.e. as being independent of context and also intersubjectively verifiable) have had to hang their argument on the theses:

> . . . they must take it for granted that the following are enforceable criteria for the products of research activity.
> 1. A description of a phenomenon as an instance of a class specifies the particular features of the phenomenon that are sufficient conditions for counting it as belonging to that class.
> 2. The features on which the classification is based are demonstrably recognisable by any competent member of the relevant . . . community independently of the other members.

(Wilson, op cit.: 72; and see Barnes and Law, op. cit.: 228).

If this quotation is now re-read with 'social class' replacing 'class', the point will be immediately clear: for there to be an 'objective' specification of social class, both the referents (instances) and characteristics (features) must be explicit, and intersubjectively agreed – whether the community be sociologists or survey respondents. The weak form of refutation is simply that the highly restrictive conditions for such an 'objective' interpretations have simply been ignored, and the argument is made by assertion. Virtually no classic study investigates (let alone tests) either instantial reference or contextual significance on subjects' use of class terminology.[16] Nor is the argument saved by treating professional sociologists (rather then subjects) as the relevant community: as much dissensus is evident among sociologists as among their subjects on the features of class membership (Hartman 1975). To this extent, at least, the ethnomethodological critique of conventional sociology has cogency, and we must therefore adopt a methodology which takes the problems of indexicality expressly into account.

3 Occupational Cognition and Similarity

INTRODUCTION

Despite its sometimes elusive properties, cognition is central to any sociological account of meaningful behaviour, since it refers to the ways in which the actor relates to the world, how he defines the situation, and how the objects in the situation are construed and given meaning.

In his analysis of the basic features of social action, Parsons (Parsons and Shils 1962: 126 *et seq.*) draws particular attention to the mechanisms of cognitive learning. Under this heading he includes:

(i)   the cognition of the differences between different objects, and different attributes of the same objects in terms of the significance or meaning of these differences to the actor ('discrimination').

(ii) the process whereby different objects and groups of them are classed together in terms of the properties which they share ('generalisation').

Both discrimination and generalisation, he argues, are aspects of the 'cognitive mapping' of the situation, a mechanism which features in all systems of action.

When applied to occupations as symbolic objects, Parsons' formulation accurately describes our concern with occupational cognition. The second mechanism (generalisation) is dealt with in some detail in later books, but discrimination is the central focus of this one—cognition of the similarities and differences between different occupations, and cognition of different attributes of the same occupation.

How, then, shall the analysis of occupational cognition begin? The most basic cognitive operation is the recognition of *overall similarity* between objects, which functions as an ordering principle creating units and setting boundaries in both language and perception (Goldmeier 1972: 14). More complex cognitive tasks, such as classification, grouping and constructing analogies, all depend upon the prior recognition of the extent to which things are similar. Yet the recognition of similarity is not simply a psychological matter, for the units and boundaries which the judgement of similarity establishes are encoded in the language and culture of the group, and are transmitted in the socialisation process. Indeed, one of the most basic skills transmitted in socialisation is the ability to see new situations according to 'group-licensed ways of perceiving similarity', a capability which is fundamental in situations as diverse as learning shared scientific exemplars (Kuhn 1970: 192) or learning to behave appropriately in drug-addict subcultures (Agar 1973: 14 *et seq.*). The importance of learning to recognise 'different similarities and similar differences' among a range of reference groups has also been well documented for a wide range of occupations and professions (Elliott 1972), and it is here – in the processes of 'creating units and setting boundaries' – that the fundamental bases of subjective theories of stratification are based, and it is from this point that a study such as this must start.

Any judgement about occupations is bound to contain both cognitive and evaluative components, and there is clearly an important difference between a judgement which is a report on how the world is (or seems to be) and one which primarily expresses an opinion on how right, good, or desirable a state of affairs is. Whilst these two types of judgement often merge in practice, they are in many ways independent of each other; I may well agree with you that regime A is more left-wing than regime B, whilst disagreeing with you over the merits of both, and the fact that we may actually agree in evaluating regime C as better than regime D may well have quite different meaning and significance if we happen to construe the political world in different ways (Axelrod 1973). There is therefore no warrant for supposing either that similar evaluation presupposes similar cognition, or that common cognition leads to common evaluation; this argument has been covered in Chapter 1. We adopt a position similar to that of Reiss (1961: 106-7) that it is logical to enquire first about the cognitive component before attempting to assess the significance of the evaluations.

3.1 METHODS

The major problem in investigating occupational cognition is how to begin eliciting information, since any decision is bound to involve a certain degree of arbitrariness. If a very general similarity relation is taken as the basis for data collection, it can rightly be objected that the significance of the similarity differs from person to person, and that these bases may be incommensurable. If, on the other hand, the subject is provided with specific bases for making his similarity judgement then one forgoes the knowledge about how salient these bases really are in subjects' thinking. Moreover, the less specific the criterion for judgement is, the more likely it is that the subjects are trying, in turn, to work out what the researcher is 'really after' and even the choice of a particular set of occupational titles may give the subject what he thinks are valuable clues. There seem to be several ways to combat this (see Coxon and Jones 1974b): to vary the set of titles (and in particular their specificity and range), to employ a wide range of methods of data collection, to replace occupational names with extensional definitions (Osipow 1962) and to define an explicit social situation as the context for judgement. Each of these strategies has been adopted at some point in this study, as we explain in our third volume. In this instance we decided:

(i)   to use two methods of data collection in order to compare judgements of 'absolute' similarity ('How similar are x and y?') and 'relative' similarity ('Which two of the three are the most similar?');

(ii)   to make the basis of the similarity judgement deliberately general, but to ask the subjects in a systematic way about the basis (or bases) on which they were making their judgements;

(iii)   to identify those factors known to influence cognitive representations of the occupational structure, and create a corresponding typology of occupations;

(iv)   to select both the occupational titles to be used, and the subjects to make the judgements in terms of this typology.

Definitive information on how the subjects and occupational titles were selected is presented in the third volume, but it is appropriate to comment briefly on the way in which the decisions were implemented.

COLLECTING SIMILARITIES DATA

The most commonly used technique for collecting direct similarities data is to ask subjects to make a rating judgement of 'overall similarity' between every *pair* of objects.[1]

The instructions given to the subject were:

Below you will find pairs of names of occupations, separated by nine numbers. We would like you to judge how similar, in your opinion, each of these pairs of occupations is. Will you please do this by circling the number which best expresses the amount of similarity you think there is — a 9 means totally similar, and a 1 means totally dissimilar.

I realize that this sometimes is a difficult task, and you may find it hard to decide in some cases. Please make a judgement nonetheless, but mark that pair with an 'X'.

Since it is the subject's own opinion of similarity that is being requested, no *basis* for the similarity is provided. For this reason it is sometimes termed a 'dimensionless' task, and it becomes a task of analysis to infer the bases of general similarity from the judgements made. In practice, subjects were asked several times during the task what basis they had used to make the immediately preceding judgement, and their sponaneous comments and observations were recorded. Since the task is constructed to throw on the subject the onus of defining 'similarity', it is not surprising that they sometimes tried to elicit clues from the interviewer. The questions asked were deflected back to the subject, and it was insisted that it was *his* interpretation alone that was acceptable. It was found that 120 judgements of similarity (i.e. between all pairs of 16 occupational titles) was the maximum that was feasible for most subjects.

The second technique used, to elicit *relative* similarity judgements, was the method of triads. In this task, the subject is presented with sets of three occupational titles, and is then asked to suggest for each set an important way in which two of the three occupations are alike, and at the same time different from the third: that is —

which two of the three occupations is the most similar one, and
which two are least alike?

They are also asked to state the way (or ways) in which the pairs are alike or different, and information is hence obtained on the basis of the judgement.[2] Such a task is valuable in providing information on relative similarity — even if a subject says that he thinks x and z are most similar *relative to y*, it may well be that when he is presented with the triad (x, z, a) he judges that x and z are now *least* similar when compared to a (on the same, or some other, criterion).

The method of triads thus provides a 'fine-grain' method of data collection, ideally suited to eliciting occupational predicates on a systematic basis, without the investigator imposing his preconceptions about what that basis is. It also provides valuable information on the comparative similarity of occupations. Unfortunately it also suffers from severe shortcomings. Since the number of triads increases approximately as the cube of the number of objects, it rapidly becomes an unfeasible method — eight objects involves the subject in making judgements on 56 triads, 10 objects involves 120, and 16 involves a virtually impossible 560 triads. To a large extent, this labour can be reduced and a good deal of information retained by the use of incomplete designs, which have been well documented by Burton and Nerlove (1976). A design which ensured that each pair occurred twice was adapted for our purposes, and this involved the subject in making judgements on 52 triads, based upon a set of 13 occupational titles (see Technical Appendix 3.1).[3] But, despite its methodological acceptability, even this turned out to be too taxing for many subjects, and the goal of obtaining such data from a group of subjects drawn from the full range of occupations had to be abandoned. This means that the triadic similarities data cannot provide information for a full analysis of occupational similarity, such as that based upon the pairwise similarities. Consequently the triadic data are used in a subsidiary role, and in a much more restrictive fashion than was originally intended.

SELECTION OF SUBJECTS AND OCCUPATIONAL TITLES

In defining the typology of occupations, the two factors chosen as most important in affecting occupational cognition were:

I   the formal educational qualification of a job;

II the degree to which a job requires its incumbents to work directly with
people (rather than with data or machines).

The resulting fourfold typology, used to select both the subject groups and
the occupational titles used in the similarities task, has the form:

I EDUCATIONAL REQUIREMENTS	II JOB REQUIREMENTS: Work predominantly with	
	People	Data
Relatively high	(Quadrant A)	(Quadrant B)
Relatively low	(Quadrant C)	(Quadrant D)

(See the third book for a fuller specification.)

The occupations which typify each quadrant share a range of common
characteristics, and the members of these occupations could be expected to
have similar social experiences and share broadly similar occupational life
histories.

The selection of a standard set of occupational titles to be judged by all
subjects is a particularly important problem in a study such as this, since
subjects' judgements can change with apparently innocuous changes of
occupation name, and both the range of titles chosen and the degree to which
they are specified can systematically affect the judgemental process (Coxon
and Jones 1972). We we have argued elsewhere (Coxon and Jones 1974b), the
main problems encountered in the selection of occupational titles are those of
comparability, representativeness and operational feasibility. Comparability
and representativeness were sought in this case by selecting a set of eight
titles from the Hall-Jones (1950) set, and augmenting it by a further eight
titles, two from each quadrant, which referred to the occupations of the
subjects we wished to investigate. This basic set of 16 titles was reduced to
13 for the triadic similarities task, and is specified in Table 3.1.

From time to time, questions were asked by the subjects about particular
titles. Two special instances merit especial comment. The title 'Civil Servant
(Executive)', was inherited from Moser and Hall (1954), and was itself an
unexplained contraction of Hall and Jones' (1951) 'Civil Servant (Executive
grade)', but the epithet 'executive' was very widely misinterpreted to refer to
what in fact is the Civil Service Administrative grade; it is interesting evidence
of occupational misinformation. Secondly, the title 'Qualified Actuary'
showed that there was fairly widespread ignorance of what it was, and what
the job involved, and that, as in the NORC study (Reiss 1961: 12-18), such

TABLE 3.1   Occupational title sets used in similarities tasks

| | | *Similarities task:* | |
Occupation title	*Abbreviation*	*Pairwise*	*Triadic*
Church of Scotland Minister	MIN	X	X
Comprehensive School Teacher	CST	X	X
Qualified Actuary	QA	X	X
Chartered Accountant	CA	X	X
Male Psychiatric Nurse	MPN	X	X
Ambulance Driver	AD	X	X
Building Site Labourer	BSL	X	X
Machine Tool Operator	MTO	X	X
Country Solicitor	SOL	X	–
Civil Servant (Executive)	CSE	X	–
Commercial Traveller	CT	X	X
Policeman	PM	X	X
Carpenter	C	X	X
Lorry Driver	LD	X	X
Railway Porter	RP	X	–
Barman	BM	X	X
		N = 16	13

(See third volume for further details.)

occupational ignorance varied with educational level to a considerable extent. Since this title is not well known, it might have been preferable to remove it, but as a group of actuaries formed an integral part of the subject sample, this was not done. Instead, a standard brief job description was given to the subject if he requested it. As it turned out this was a perfectly reasonable compromise, for other procedures were developed at a later stage for systematically investigating the content and bases of subjects' occupational judgements.

When selecting subjects, the intention was that they should mainly be drawn from occupations which examplify the occupational typology. The composition of the set of subjects who provided pairwise similarities data is given in Table 3.2 and is further described in the third volume.

3.2 PRELIMINARY ANALYSIS: SIMILARITY RATINGS[4]

Perhaps the most striking characteristic of the subjects' rating procedure was what might in other contexts be termed a 'response set' (Cronbach 1946) or, perhaps more accurately, a 'response style' (Rorer 1965) — namely the tendency to respond to items in a systematic way which appears to be virtually independent of the content of the items. In this task, a common response set consisted of a subject going down the pair-comparisons schedule indicating a 1 ('totally dissimilar') to an apparently excessive number of pairs; indeed, almost 10 per cent of subjects place two-thirds of their pairwise

TABLE 3.2   Occupational composition of respondents' sample (pairwise similarities task)

FACTOR II:

JOB REQUIREMENTS: Work Predominantly with

FACTOR I:
EDUCATIONAL
REQUIREMENTS:

	People	*Data and Machines*
Relatively high	**QUADRANT A** (N = 90) *Core:* Clergymen (22) Teachers (19) *Supplementary:* Education students (33) Theological students (10) Journalists (6)	**QUADRANT B** (N = 66) *Core:* Qualified Actuaries (17) Chartered Accountants (11) *Supplementary:* Chemical Engineering students (16), Electrical Engineering students (22)
Relatively low	**QUADRANT C** (N = 48) *Core:* Ambulance Drivers (16) Policemen (13) *Supplementary:* Nurses (19)	**QUADRANT D** (N = 60 *Core:* Engineers (18) Joiners – Fitters (12) *Supplementary:* Builders and related trades (25), Printers (5)

Additional Supplementary groups: Law Students (6),   (264)
Business Administration students (17)   (23)

N = 287

Notes: 'Clergymen' covers Church of Scotland ministers (13) and Scottish Episcopalian priests (9)
ii)   All the subjects in Quadrant D, with the exception of Printers, are day-release apprentices
iii)   The core occupations which include female subjects are Police (2), and in the Supplementary occupations: Education (27) and Nurses (12)

judgements in this category. The tendency to respond to this pole of the
rating scale is the most striking feature of the distribution of individual
judgements, and the response of 'totally dissimilar' is given in a total of one-
third of the pairwise judgements, as can be seen from Figure 3.1 and T3.2.

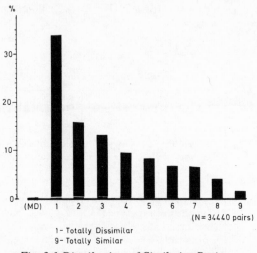

1- Totally Dissimilar
9- Totally Similar

Fig. 3.1 Distribution of Similarity Ratings

Moreover, this response style is not simply an individual characteristic, for
the proportion of such judgements is lowest among occupations in Quadrants
A and B and the occupations with the heaviest concentration are without
exception in Quadrants C and D (T3.3). It would seem, therefore, that
education systematically affects the propensity to respond in this way, but it
is not clear whether it is because it familiarises people with such pencil-and-
paper cognitive tasks or for some more profound reason. Explanations for
this phenomenon are not easy to find in professional literature, but Flavell
and Johnson (1961: 345) state that in their studies of the meaning of
similarity judgement that subjects generally took longer to make a judgement
of high dissimilarity, and suggest that:

> when a subject judges a pair of words on a similarity – dissimilarity scale,
> he tends to find it easy to rate them at the similar end if some *one*
> similarity comes quickly and easily to mind. It may be that the very fact
> of having to *search* for a similarity in itself disposes him to rate the words
> as dissimilar. The paradigm may be: 'I judge these words to be dissimilar
> *because* I cannot readily (with brief latency) see a similarity between them.'

Comments made by our subjects tend to confirm this interpretation, and they
also used phrases like 'very far removed' of highly dissimilar pairs. This spatial
imagery is revealing and suggests a more interesting interpretation; may it not
be that 'total dissimilarity' can simply be understood as signifying maximum

social distance? If this were so, then we should expect that the number of persons judging a particular *pair* of occupations as totally dissimilar will vary according to how 'far distant' they are in people's conceptions of social space.

When the distribution of similarity ratings is examined *within* each pair of occupations, the differences are dramatic (T3.4) and are far greater and more systematic than any considered so far. Moreover, the number of 'totally dissimilar' judgements varies more from pair to pair than is the case for any other rating category. These differences reflect our intuitions about occupational differences, 'totally dissimilar' could well feature as a measure of social distance in its own right. But see Hoijer (1970a: 18 *et seq.*), who discusses problems in the definition of null similarity.)

3.3 REPRESENTING OCCUPATIONAL SIMILARITIES

The similarity ratings are presumably the outcome of a cognitive process involving subjective experiences of the relationships between occupations. but we know little either about how these experiences are subjectively organised or about how information is combined in arriving at such an overall numerical judgement (see Hoijer 1971; and Gregson 1975).

Several models have been suggested for representing similarity, each making rather different assumptions about the nature of the underlying cognitive processes and about the internal representation of the information. Spatial models, which correspond to the paradigmatic analysis of descriptive semantics, assume that the cognitive space can be defined by a number of dimensions, each representing an attribute or feature which is common to all the objects (e.g. occupational titles), and each object is then located in the space in terms of the extent to which it possesses each attribute. The two most commonly used spatial models of similarity are the *distance* model, and the *vector* model. In the distance model, each object is represented as a point located in the attribute space, and a similarity judgement between two objects is interpreted as a report on the relative closeness (proximity) of the two points. In the vector (or factor) model, each object is represented by a directed line (vector) from the origin of the space to the point giving the location of the object, and the similarity judgement is interpreted as referring to the extent to which the two vectors are separated, measured in terms of the size of the angle between them. In either case, the models assume a continuous and homogeneous subjective space, whose constituent axes correspond to subjective dimensions which are descriptive of the objects, and the cognitive process involved is thought of as a set of rules for combining the dimensional information into an overall judgement: see T3.5 and McFarland and Brown (1973) for a more detailed discussion.

A rather different model, generally known as the 'content model' (Ekman and Sjöberg 1965; Waern 1971; Eisler and Roskam 1973) postulates that a similarity judgement informs us of the number of elements or properties common to two objects, as a fraction of the total number of elements. The content model does not make the strong assumptions of the spatial model, since the properties are thought of as discrete categories rather than as dimensions. As a result, there is no need to assume either that the attributes which underlie occupational judgement vary continuously, or that all attributes apply to every object. In the content model the subjective occupational space is not thought of as necessarily being continuous and homogeneous, but rather as consisting of discontinuous, differentiated regions, and it is perfectly consistent with this model to assert that a change of position in one region may not have the same subjective meaning as it does in another (Sjöberg 1972). Despite these differences between the spatial and content model, Eisler and Roskam (1973) have shown that both may be interpreted in terms of a vector space. Moreover experimental studies have so far been unable to distinguish between the models, and it is certainly the case that our similarities rating data are not sufficiently subtle to enable such a test to be made. Despite this empirical inconclusiveness the simple and intuitively appealing properties of the content model merit especial attention when analysing these data.

Similarity data have also been represented non-quantitatively. Since the data from the analysis of social and cognitive objects often fail manifestly to exhibit consistent and regular variation, it is perhaps not surprising that clustering procedures, which attempt to discover a number of more or less dense or highly similar 'clumps' of objects, have been commonly used (Cormack 1971). In cognitive studies, hierarchical stratified clustering procedures (Hartigan 1967; Johnson 1967) have been especially popular (Miller 1969; Anglin 1970; Fillenbaum and Rapoport 1971; Coxon 1971; Burton 1972), since they correspond exactly to taxonomic models of descriptive semantics, where a set of clusters at one level are subsumed under others of greater generality at higher levels, and are further specified into more homogeneous clusters at lower levels. The natural representation for such a system is the dendrogram or tree (see Figure 3.7 for an example) where the similarity between two nodes is represented by the level ('height') of their lowest common ancestor. The actual objects are mapped on to the highest single-end branches of the tree, and the clusters at lower levels are taken to represent superordinate concepts, markers or attributes describing objects above them. (Note that, unlike the spatial model, a particular attribute need not, and usually will not, describe every object, and that the attributes or markers are ordered.) Although the dimensional and taxonomic representations are often combined (Shepard 1972) they are not generally compatible, from a formal point of view (T3.6). Although it will not be possible to decide between the spatial and hierarchical models with data which include error, it is known that there are likely to be systematic deviations from one model rather than the other (Holman 1972: 419; and see T3.7).

3.4 AGGREGATE ANALYSIS: AVERAGED SIMILARITIES

Problems of aggregation appear as soon as the analysis of occupational similarities begins. As we have seen above, there is every reason to suppose that different social groups will hold somewhat different representations of the occupational structure (see also Form 1946; Holland 1963; Wiggins and Fishbein 1969). It would be foolhardy, therefore, to assume, as many conventional sociological studies do, that cognitions of social structures are directly comparable, and that any individual differences are purely idiosyncratic. On the other hand, it is equally misleading and asociological to adopt the opposite ideographic extreme, and insist that each representation is unique and incomparable. As Durkheim (1938: 106) reminds us, collective representations, involving as they do an individual's ideas concerning his social environment, are caused 'not by certain states of the consciousness of individuals, but by the conditions in which the social group in its totality is placed'. Yet the social and cultural factors involved must exercise very considerable and homogeneous force if cognitive structures are to be common to whole groups of individuals (cf. Coombs 1964: 331). If this is so, then the analysis must be sensitive both to common bases of judgement and to systematic differences. To this end, the sequence of analysis will be:

(i)   to investigate the grosser, aggregate, characteristics of the data in order to arrive at an initial approximation to an acceptable collective representation;

(ii)   to invoke a model which is especially sensitive to individual differences, in order to examine their extent and see whether it is systematic in terms of sociological factors;

(iii) to return to individual sets of data to exemplify the logic of the interrelations in the aggregate data, or where it appears that they are sufficiently deviant to warrant separate inspection.

COGNITIVE MAPS OF OCCUPATIONS

(i) Based on averaged similarities data
The similarity judgements made between pairs of occupations were averaged across subjects to produce a single similarity matrix. In fact, two sorts of average were calculated — the arithmetic mean and the root mean square (RMS), the latter because it corresponds more precisely to the assumptions of one of the models to be used at a later stage. This information, together with the standard deviations and number of judgements involved is presented in T3.8.

The spread of average ratings is large, from 1.5 to almost seven, and it is encouraging to note that the most extreme values correspond fairly closely to what would be expected in terms of social distance. The occupational pairs which are judged the most similar, on average, are Chartered Accountant with

Qualified Actuary, Country Solicitor with Civil Servant (Executive) and Lorry Driver with Ambulance Driver. At the other extreme, the most socially distant pairs, on average, are Building Site Labourer with Qualified Actuary, Chartered Accountant and Civil Servant (Executive), and Railway Porter with Qualified Actuary.

It is quite impossible to take in all the information just by inspecting the averages, and multidimensional scaling (MDS) or 'smallest space' models have been developed to represent the totality of the information as faithfully as possible. The distance model assumes that the pairwise similarity judgements are a function of how close the two points are in (subjective) occupational space; the more dissimilar a pair of occupations are judged to be, the more distant they must be in that space. The scaling procedures which are used to obtain a geometrical representation of the data require that the researcher stipulate both the number of dimensions of this space (with the proviso that any information on n points can be represented in $n - 2$ dimensions), and the type of function which is supposed to relate the data to the dissimilarities. Here, we shall seek spaces of one to five dimensions, and adopt a cautious approach by first allowing the data to be ordinally related to the solution (non-metric analysis) and then investigating the effect of requiring the more stringent linear function (metric analysis). The technical results are presented in T3.9 (newcomers to the model are referred to Shepard *et al.* 1972; McFarland and Brown 1973; and Coxon 1975), and the two-dimensional maps are portrayed in Figure 3.2

The orientation of the points is entirely arbitrary, and since non-metric analysis is intended to concentrate attention on the configuration itself rather than on the dimensions involved, the defining dimensions are not presented in the figure. (It is of interest to note, however, that the one-dimensional 'space' is very similar to the horizontal axis in both solutions.)

Two criteria are normally used in multidimensional scaling to determine the 'correct' underlying dimensionality of the data, the first concerned with acceptable levels of badness-of-fit (stress) and the second with interpretability. Since the sampling distribution of stress is not known, it is not possible to decide on statistical grounds what constitutes an 'acceptable level' of stress, or even whether the addition of a further dimension significantly increases the goodness of fit. More approximate models are therefore called for. Comparing this result with a wide range of other non-metric MDS solutions of data involving a similar number of points, the stress levels are noticeably lower. Even the value for the one-dimensional solution would be interpreted as 'fair' by Kruskal's evaluation (Wagenaar and Padmos 1971: 101). More recently developed methods for deciding on appropriate dimensionality have a more rational foundation, being based upon simulation studies where a large number of random configurations of n points in r dimensions are produced and scaled. The stress values of these configurations provide a base line – the random configuration – against which the extent of 'structuredness' of *non*-randomness of actual configurations can be assessed (see T3.10). The result of comparing the stress values for the scaling solutions of the mean similarities data in dimensions 1 to 5 to the stress values obtained from the simulation studies (Spence and Graef 1973) is both surprising and unexpected: by far the most acceptable fit is for the map of *one*, or possibly two, 'true' underlying dimensions (compare Stewart *et al.* 1973: 416). Moreover, this holds for both the metric and non-metric solutions, although not as well in the former case.

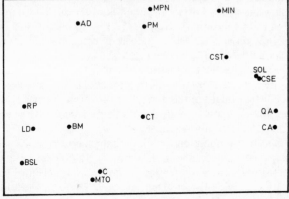

(METRIC)

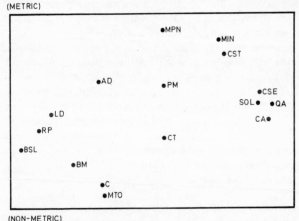

(NON-METRIC)

Fig. 3.2 Distance model analysis: averaged similarity ratings

The second criterion used to decide on the solution of the best dimensionality is parsimony: if a *r*-dimensional solution is interpretable, but the (*r* + 1)th dimensional structure yields no added information, then the *r*-dimensional solution should be used (Kruskal 1964: 16). In this case, it is fairly evident that the vertical dimension does at least involve a meaningful contrast, which opposes Nurse, Ambulance Driver, Policeman and Minister at one extreme to Machine Tool Operator, Carpenter, Labourer at the other. The dimension seems to represent what might be termed a 'People-orientation' quality or

'People/Things' distinction. For this, and other reasons which will become evident, the two-dimensional solution is accepted. There are slight variations in the location of particular points, depending on the numerical procedure used. In the non-metric case, the maps produced by different procedures are virtually identical, except for the fact that in some solutions the Carpenter and Machine Tool Operator pair of points are located equally closely, but in a position on a line with Church of Scotland Minister and Comprehensive School Teacher and above Lorry Driver and Barman. Such local instability is not unusual in MDS solutions (Coxon 1971: 352; Bailey 1974: 27) and in this case it simply reflects the fact that these two occupations are not thought of as fitting naturally into the 'People/Things' distinction.

The differences between the metric and non-metric solutions do not seem to be very systematic. The metric solution breaks up the more compact professional cluster evident in the non-metric solution, further separates the 'financial' occupations, and also dissociates the Ambulance Driver and Policeman titles from Male Psychiatric Nurse.

At this juncture it is common is sociological analysis to embark upon a dimension-labelling exercise, and in the case of data on occupations a socioeconomic status or 'prestige' dimension is almost always claimed to be present (see for example Blau and Duncan 1967: 71; Laumann and Guttmann 1966: 177). Macdonald (1972: 227) has dismissed as 'nonsense' the attempt to identify one dimension of an MDS solution with 'prestige' and then use it to calibrate a scale for international studies; our objection is based upon somewhat different grounds. The shift from aggregate behavioural data (such as associational and mobility probabilities) to references involving subjects' cognitions and evaluations (how they conceive the social structure and why they so behave) is illegitimate in the absence of additional information which relates the two. It cannot simply be assumed that subjects share the same predilections as their investigators, and if such cognitive inferences are to be made they must be based on the subjects' own accounts. This was one reason why subjects' verbalisations were obtained at the time they were making similarity judgements, and these data will be used to interpret the aggregate cognitive maps in a later section.

(ii) Aggregate triads scaling
Analysis of the aggregate triadic data provides an alternative view of the similarities structure of the set of occupations, although it is based on a more limited and unsystematised subject set. The 47 subjects who completed the triads task provided similarities judgements on a total of 1866 triads. These triadic judgements were analysed directly, using a special non-metric scaling program known as TRISOSCAL which obtains an optimum fit between the rank order of the distances in the output map and all the separate triadic rank orders (see T3.11). Since in the case of triadic scaling, there is no direct parallel to the averaged similarities matrix, we therefore go directly to the scaling solution.

The cognitive map corresponding to the triadic data is presented in Figure 3.3 Although the triads refer to only 13 occupations, it is instructive to compare it to the averaged similarities map of Figure 3.2 in order to see whether the absolute and relative similarities tasks are tapping the same kind of information.

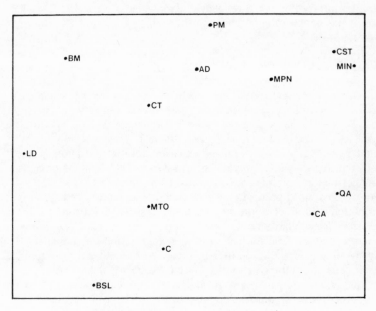

Fig. 3.3 Configuration from aggregate triads data

Unfortunately neither the interpretation of stress values nor the criteria for deciding upon the 'true dimensionality' of a solution are as well founded for triadic data as for the more conventional procedures used in the last section, and it is therefore necessary to rely upon more informal methods. (A fuller technical discussion is contained in T3.11.) None the less, the indications are that a two-dimensional solution is acceptable, despite a fairly high 'local' stress value.

When the aggregate maps are compared, it is clear that there is a broad correspondence, if the three titles which are present only in the pairwise task — the Railway Porter, Civil Servant (Executive) and Country Solicitor — are ignored. The clusters: Qualified Actuary — Chartered Accountant; Church of Scotland Minister — Comprehensive School Teacher; Policeman — Ambulance Driver — Male Psychiatric Nurse and Carpenter — Machine Tool

Operator — Building Site Labourer all maintain their relative position, but the internal orientation of the clusters is not maintained. The points Commercial Traveller, Barman and Lorry Driver have moved along roughly parallel lines obliquely towards the 'people-oriented' side of the map. The reasons for the instability of their positioning will be better understood after the more detailed analysis. Now it is sufficient to note the general congruence of the cognitive maps, and the fact that the earlier interpretation of similarities space is reinforced by the movement of Barman and Commercial Traveller towards the 'people-orientation' end of the map.

3.5 AGGREGATION AND INDIVIDUAL DIFFERENCES

Although sociologists have argued forcefully for many years that shared cognitive orientations are a functional prerequisite of society (Aberle *et al.* 1950; Parsons 1971), it has been challenged equally forcefully by others, such as Wallace (1961: 39 *et seq.*) who goes so far as to argue not only that societies *can* contain cognitive maps which are not uniform among participants, but that they invariably *do* contain systems which rely upon mutual misunderstanding, or are based upon distinct cognitive maps.

In the analysis of occupational cognition just presented, we have assumed, in common with other workers in this field (Reeb 1959; Burton, 1972) that the *aggregated* similarity ratings are a function of a common, uniformly-perceived, occupational configuration. But what if subjects' similarity judgements actually refer to different subjective occupational structures? The answer depends on the type of difference envisaged. If the individual structures are entirely different, if they refer to quite different 'collective representations', then it is hard to see how their data can be compared at all, and the notion of a single consensual occupational structure becomes meaningless. Such an eventuality is not usually considered in sociological studies.

Two problems arise in a sociological interpretation of cognitive maps of the occupational structure — how individual maps relate one to another, and how they relate to some 'actual' stratification system. Let us take the second problem first. The notion of one 'objective' occupational system which is established independently of individual cognitions is one we find it hard to give unambiguous meaning to, as we have argued in Chapter 1. To be sure, occupations can be characterised by such things as requiring particular skills, or as having a certain range of incomes. Both of these properties are capable, in principle, of being checked, and an individual's cognition could be said to be right or wrong by reference to them. But this is not at issue. The usage which seems objectionable is one which implies the existence of an external occupational structure, of which individual cognitions are necessarily derivative distortions. On the other hand, if occupational structure is viewed as being a constructed entity, in which individual cognitions play a crucial role, then the sociologist's description or conception of the structure will not differ *in kind* from that of his subject, although it may very well be more descriptively accurate.

Excluding this crude notion of objective social structure does not imply the acceptance of a purely relativist account. One way of reformulating many of the problems is to refer to a common cultural basis for individual cognitions. This is turn can be given at least two distinct interpretations. First, it can be given a 'generative' interpretation (see Wallace, 1961b; Fararo, 1970: 93-101) by analogy with linguistic usage, where a grammar is said to 'generate' the sentences of a language — i.e., an infinitely large number of possible utterances (sentences) can be produced from a finite, restricted, set of basic elements. A generative interpretation of the relationship between the actors' cognitive maps is to say that they are produced from a single, common basis, called the 'objective system'. This 'deep structure' is thought of as generating the individual maps by means of a further set of 'transformational rules' which takes one individual map into another. The attractiveness of such an interpretation is that is preserves the 'objective/subjective' contrast intact, and is explicitly concerned with how new outcomes can be produced from a small basis of information or knowledge. Its shortcoming in the present instance is that it is not at all clear how the sociologist's 'deep structure' or 'actual stratification system' could be established, unless it were construed as a purely theoretical entity.

Alternatively, the 'common basis' could be understood to refer to a modal 'collective representation', describing simply what is common to the differing maps. The advantage of the 'commonality' approach of multidimensional scaling procedures is that it produces a plausible and easily understandable representation of the extent and form of cultural commonality in different maps, and avoids the need to postulate one single, authentic, 'objective' structure. Yet the very fact that subjects are able, with great facility, to use their occupational information to perform cognitive tasks and respond to questions which they had probably never before encountered strongly suggests that subjects do possess the ability to produce information in a generative manner. This property, which is singularly lacking in spatial models (cf. D'Andrade, 1971) means that any representation of cognitive maps which does not include a generative capacity is bound to be deficient in the long run.

But the 'generative' and 'commonality' interpretations are not necessarily exclusive. The commonality approach, concerned with the extent of cognitive sharing by inferring what is culturally fundamental to individual cognitive maps is presupposed by the generative approach. Yet we do not know *a priori* the extent of commonality between subjects' conceptions of the occupational structure, and the conventional MDS analysis of aggregated data imposes a consensual solution by *fiat*, whilst the separate analysis of each individual's set of data gives up the notion that there is any commonality. Put this way, the question of how to infer the 'common basis' can be seen as an instance of the aggregation problem, and the answer to the question hinges upon how individual maps are conceived to differ.

The INDSCAL model

The aggregate distance model we have used above on page 75 interprets the notion of 'map' literally. According to this model, individual occupational structures could differ in that

(i)   subjects could either use different attributes (or dimensions);

or (ii)   could have maps which cannot be related by any regular mathematical function;

or (iii)   could use different rules when combining attributes into overall judgements of similarity.

Several recent writers have dealt with the first two types of difference. One approach to the problem is Horan's (1960: 140) proposal to introduce the idea of what he terms a 'normal attribute space', defined by *all* the attributes which subjects use in differentiating between a set of cultural objects or stimuli. Any particular individual's 'private' cognitive space could then be interpreted as a special case of this culturally common 'Group Map',[5] and those dimensions which a subject did not 'use' could be thought of as being given a zero weight by him. It is only a simple extension of this idea to think of each subject as attaching differential 'importance', 'salience', or weight to each dimension of the Group Space. Put slightly differently, each subject can be conceived as applying his own 'subjective metric' (in the form of differential stretching or shrinking of the axes) to the Group Map. A multidimensional scaling model which implements these ideas is known by the acronym INDSCAL (for *In*dividual *D*ifferences *Scal*ing) and was developed by Carroll and Chang (1969). It is described in greater detail in T3.12.

The main difference between the INDSCAL model and the simple distance model is that in the INDSCAL model the subject's (dis)similarity judgement is represented as a *weighted* distance in the Group Space. INDSCAL thus involves a simple generalisation of the simple distance model. The dissimilarity between occupation j and occupation k for individual i is assumed to be a function of distances between the occupations in his own private space, but these 'private distances' can equally well be thought of as being modified, weighted distances in the Group Space.

Certain properties of the INDSCAL model are particularly relevant to the questions we have raised. Unlike the usual MDS and factor analysis solutions, the orientation of the dimensions of the Group Attribute Space are not arbitrary, for any rotation of the reference axes will destroy the least squares properties of the solution (see T3.12, section B(iv)). In the ordinary distance model, only the *uniform* stretching or shrinking of axes preserves distances, whereas the INDSCAL model allows subjects to stretch the dimensions differentially.

The purpose of the INDSCAL model is to use the judgements of a number of subjects to estimate these fixed dimensions, and the coordinates of the stimuli on those dimensions. This it does by taking advantage of whatever communality exists in the subjects' judgements, and using this information to locate the dimensions uniquely. It offers, therefore, an especially strong procedure for identifying the salient dimensions in subjects' cognitions, in a way that does not depend upon the arbitrary rotations of axes which have brought certain types of factor analysis into disrepute.

In this section, attention will be concentrated on using the INDSCAL model to identify a properly oriented Group Cognitive Map, or 'Group Space' which conforms to the greatest extent with the individual data of our subjects. So long as major, systematic differences between individuals are not revealed by this analysis, it will be possible to take the INDSCAL Group Space as a best estimate of the 'common cultural basis' of 'collective representation' of the occupational cognition of our subjects. The analysis of patterns of communality and difference among and between subjects will be left until section 3.6.

DATA INPUT AND THE GROUP MAP

The data input to INDSCAL consists of a 'three-way matrix' of a number of individual sets of pairwise similarity judgements. In this case, if all the data of all the subjects were to be used, there would be 287 sets of 120 pairwise similarity judgements — 34,440 data in all. For obvious reasons, there are considerable problems of computer storage and analysis of such large amounts of data, and whilst it would have been possible to modify the program to accommodate the data, we chose a different strategy. This consisted, first, in isolating a balanced set of 'core subjects' (drawn in equal numbers from our subject typology presented in Table 3.2), and using their data to obtain a representative estimate of the INDSCAL Group Space. This configuration was then used as a basis for estimating the dimensional weights (saliences) of all the subjects.

The procedure actually followed consisted of first defining the 'population' of eligible subjects, removing those whose data were unacceptably defective, and then sampling in order to obtain a smaller, 'balanced set'.

Several factors affected our decisions about what the composition of the 'population' and the characteristics of the sample ought to be:

(1) Only 70 cases can be scaled simultaneously by the INDSCAL program, and if equal numbers were to be drawn from each quadrant (to ensure representativeness), the effective sample size was limited to 68 — i.e. 17 subjects from each quadrant.

(2) Current procedures for estimating INDSCAL parameters when there are missing data are far from satisfactory, and it was therefore necessary to exclude a subject from consideration who had more than one missing datum.

(3) Cases with excessively high numbers of 'totally dissimilar' judgements
    were not considered for inclusion in the population (although their
    data *were* scaled in the second stage).

Further details of the selection of the 'balanced set' of 68 subjects are given
in T3.13.

The similarities data of these subjects were analysed by the INDSCAL
model, using a number of starting configurations, different numbers of
dimensions and other options (see T3.14) to estimate the overall Group Space.
The best three-dimensional solution is presented in Figure 3.4, and technical
details are given in T3.14 and T3.15.

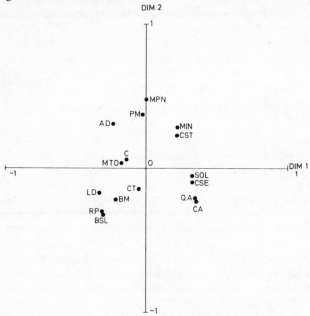

Fig. 3.4 INDSCAL analysis: group space

Despite the attractive properties claimed for the INDSCAL model,
relatively little is known about how well the INDSCAL model is able to
recover a known Group Space or pattern of subject weights in the presence of
error and departures from the assumptions of the model. It is encouraging,
therefore, to learn from a recent study (Jones and Wadington 1975) that, at
least with regard to the Group Stimulus Space, recovery is generally excellent
even in the presence of very severe error:

(1) Even if only a few subjects use a dimension, it is recovered with
    moderate to high accuracy;
(2) Orientation of dimension is generally accurately recovered;
(3) Scale values along the component dimensions are well recovered.

For these and other reasons discussed in T3.15 we may conclude that the three-dimensional Group Space configuration corresponds very closely to an optimal solution.

INTERPRETATION OF THE GROUP MAP

A number of approaches will now be used to interpret this configuration, using both our own insights and the verbal material elicited from groups of subjects whilst making their similarity judgements. Before beginning such an interpretation, one point should be stressed: the INDSCAL Group Space, like the average similarities solution, is also an aggregate solution, in the sense that it does not directly represent the data of any single subject, except one who weights the dimensions identically. But the INDSCAL solution provides a rather different answer to the problem of aggregation. Instead of taking the average judgement as the unique representative of the subjects' data, it provides a Group Map to which all individual 'private spaces' directly refer, and in terms of which they may be compared to each other. The INDSCAL Group Space is therefore a 'collective representation' of the subjects' judgements in this special sense.

When compared to the average similarities maps (and especially the metric version) in Figure 3.2, the resemblance is striking. Taking into account the greater dispersion along the second dimension of the INDSCAL solution, the relative positioning of occupations is very similar, except for Railway Porter and for the Machine Tool Operator and Carpenter pair, whose location has already been found to be fairly unstable. (The similar orientations of the two solutions are not however accidental — the original solution was rotated rigidly through 200° into closest conformity to the INDSCAL solution in order to make comparison easier.) Yet the INDSCAL solution is certainly more clustered, pulling the Accountant and Actuary, the Minister and the Teacher, and the Porter and the Lorry Driver into closer proximity, and making the configuration a good deal easier to interpret.

The first dimension involves a contrast between the group of Chartered Accountant, Qualified Actuary, Civil Servant (Executive) and Country Solicitor on the one hand, and Building Site Labourer, Railway Porter and Lorry Driver on the other; and there is also a fairly large discontinuity between Male Psychiatric Nurse and Comprehensive School Teacher. The contrast is a familiar one, although a variety of attributes are employed to describe it. Subjects used the terms 'Work conditions', 'Qualifications', 'Income', 'Skills required', 'Status', 'Education', 'Power' and 'Training' to describe it. One of the most concise statements of this multi-faceted contrast was made by a Church of Scotland Minister when judging the similarity of the Civil Servant (Executive) and Building Site Labourer:

> They're dissimilar in the type of work they do . . . their social standing is not similar in the eyes of society — one [Civil Servant (Executive)] is paid so much more. Their outlooks, the way they respond to people in

general, are different. Again, their habits, hobbies, newspapers, type of
friend, will contrast . . .

These occupations are, in the words of a printer, 'worlds apart':

> I can't see them [Country Solicitor and Building Site Labourer] in the
> same social groupings, or having the same friends . . . Not intermarrying.
> Worlds apart — totally different social groups.

Perhaps the most interesting insights provided by these quotations are that
the descriptions used by subjects include both attributes (e.g. status of a job,
degree of responsibility) *and* relational or interactional terms (intermarriage,
type of friend). It is also interesting that high dissimilarity of this sort is
naturally interpreted in terms of social distance, reflecting Laumann's 'like-
me hypothesis' — 'persons prefer to establish intimate social relationships
with other persons of comparable occupational status' (Laumann 1966: 53).
The common core of the descriptions is a contrast referring to skills,
qualifications and educational requirements, and it does not seem unreason-
able to use the label of *Educational Qualifications* to describe this dimension,
recognising that other connotations including income and status are also
involved.

Because the occupational titles are less clustered on the second dimension,
it is not clear which titles should be involved in the contrast used to name it.
Moreover, the predicates used to distinguish Male Psychiatric Nurse and
Postman from Railway Porter and Building Site Labourer on the one hand are
not generally the same as those used to distinguish them from Qualified
Actuary and Chartered Accountant. Apart from differences in skill and
training, which are recognised in both contrasts (and which can be taken to
refer to differences on the first dimension), the (Male Psychiatric Nurse,
Postman) v. (Railway Porter, Building Site Labourer) contrast does elicit
from subjects fairly frequent references to 'dealing with people' and 'helping
the public' as opposed to physical work, and a similar contrast is seen in the
(Male Psychiatric Nurse, Postman) *v.* (Qualified Actuary, Chartered Accountant) comparison, namely involvement with persons and 'subjective' aspects
as opposed to concern with finance, or 'things':

> Actuaries are ivory-tower people, withdrawn, who shut themselves off . . .
> engaged just in objective paperwork, whereas the nurse is subjective and
> goes to people.
>
> (Chartered Accountant)

and

> A good male psychiatric nurse is not doing computing in his head, but
> doing a real job on insight and care for people. An accountant is a person
> largely dealing with figures . . .
>
> (Episcopalian priest)

The second dimension reflects a service or succourant orientation related to
judgements about 'contribution to society' and also the 'dedicated-selfish'

aspects of occupations. (It is also not dissimilar to the 'people v. data and things' contrast used to define the stimuli and select the subjects.) The dimension may tentatively be labelled '*Service Orientation*' to reflect these characteristics.

The third dimension separates Carpenter and Machine Tool Operator from the other occupations, and contrasts them most with Ambulance Driver and Commercial Traveller. There is virtual unanimity that the distinguishing characteristic of Machine Tool Operator and Carpenter is that they are 'time-served' skilled crafts or trades, as opposed both to professions and to manual occupations not involving apprenticeships. An insubstantial 'static v. mobile' contrast also appears, but this third dimension may reasonably be labelled a '*Skill*' or '*Trades*' dimension.

GRAPHIC ANALYSIS

After exploring the dimensional aspects of the spatial representation of occupational similarities, it is instructive to turn to other ways of inferring structure. Rapoport and Fillenbaum (1971) and Waern (1971) have found, in different ways, that the analysis of cognitive structures can be considerably aided by treating similarities data as a graph, with links drawn between points to represent high pairwise similarity.

It has been claimed (Moss 1967: 182) that a graphic approach lends itself to the analysis of important structural aspects of the data, such as establishing the presence and limits of groupings, which are easily overlooked or lost in a dimensional representation. Waern (*ibid* 18-20) views the graphical analysis of similarities data both as a way of inferring the existence of particularly dense, highly similar, clusters of points, and as a way of revealing a basis of variation which is perceived as common only to a relatively small, 'local', group of points, but which is not necessarily present in all points. She reports (p. 20) that the application of graph-theoretic analysis to cognitive structures frequently brought to light aspects of the stimuli which were common to only some of them.

OCCUPATIONAL SEQUENCE

In a rather different context, Kendall (1971) was interested in the problem of whether it is possible to 'seriate' (i.e. infer the correct temporal sequence) of a set of cultural artefacts from information on the extent of their similarity. (His particular interest was inferring the correct historical sequence of the famous La Tène graves at Müssingen-Rain from information on the number of artefacts — pottery, jewellery etc. — common to each pair of graves.) The procedure he suggested was to scale the data in two dimensions, and then map highly similar links into the MDS configuration to see whether there is anything approximating a path (or sequence of links) through the points which reduces them to a 'true' linear order. Even if such a path exists there is,

of course, no guarantee that it will form a *straight* line in the MDS solution.
Indeed, Kendall shows that when the distance of a true linear (unidimensional)
sequence are grouped into ranked categories, such as the nine-step rating
scale of our data, the points of the 'recovered' sequence are not arranged
linearly but have become contorted into the form of a horseshoe (i.e. a two-
dimensional sequence)

> from which one could not possibly derive a meaningful one-dimensional
> seriation by projection on the (first) principal component − indeed . . . we
> should wind up with a projection of the diagram on some rather arbitrary
> diameter of it, which would be utterly useless. (p. 231)

What structure is revealed by the application of these graphic methods to the
occupational similarities data? The results are quite striking, and are presented
in Figure 3.5. The highest quartile of the average similarities (see T3.8) were
mapped into the two-dimensional INDSCAL Group Space configuration.

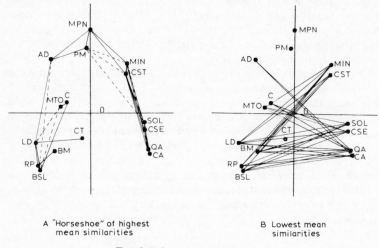

| A "Horseshoe" of highest | B Lowest mean |
| mean similarities | similarities |

Fig. 3.5 Occupational Sequence

After the highest 23 links had been drawn in, the configuration becomes
connected (i.e. a path exists between every point, and no occupational title is
isolated), and the subsequent seven links are denoted by a pecked line. Whilst
a goodly number of links occur within the professional group of occupations,
the 'horseshoe' sequence is very evident, and is oriented in the direction of
the main axes.

But the sequence is not straightforwardly linear − it is not at all clear, for
instance, at what point the Carpenter − Machine Tool Operator pair, Barman
and Commercial Traveller should appear in the occupational series.

Before passing on to the interpretation of the sequence, a further point should be made. If the dispersions (standard deviations) rather than averages are mapped in the same way into the Group Stimulus Space, virtually the same patterns result. Why is this? A possible reason springs from interpreting the standard deviations as a measure of consensus in cognitive judgement, in much the same way as Gross *et al.* (1958: 167-9) treat variance as a measure of role consensus. The pattern of standard deviations reflects the fact that the occupations which are closest to each other are characterised by low consensus, but there is high consensus on those occupations most socially distant from each other. People agree strongly about occupations which are highly dissimilar, but differ considerably over the most similar ones. This phenomenon has been commented on by other sociologists in the context of prestige judgements (Gerstl and Cohen, 1964; Bolte, 1959). Very appositely Stehr (1974: 413) has pointed out that since conventional prestige measurement procedures concentrate on widely disparate occupational titles, and since it is easier to communicate and objectify extreme occupational differences than less extreme ones, this gives rise to an entirely spurious impression of consensus in occupational judgements.

If a fairly regular sequence is discernible in the occupational titles of the Group Space, why does it take on the characteristic horseshoe shape? A similar situation arises in the analysis of subjective judgements of colour, when the physical continuum (wavelength) becomes transformed into a circle when the pairwise similarity judgements are scaled (Shepard and Carroll 1966). The reasons for such transformations is not fully understood, but a fairly convincing topological interpretation can be given (see T3.16). In brief, subjects appear to make judgements according to a kind of 'local Euclidean metric' — that is, the usual distance axioms hold for judgements which they make between occupations that are sufficiently close subjectively, but beyond a certain threshold *all* pairs are judged as equally far distant. As a possible explanation of the abundance of 'totally dissimilar' judgements in our data, it is too appealing to miss.

It remains to be seen whether this structure of occupational titles is anything more than an artefact of the aggregation procedure, and whether it is a peculiarity of the pairwise similarities data. In later sections, different sets of data will be analysed to see whether this characteristic structure can be discerned in individual cognitive judgements, and in a variety of data-types.

The most useful way of integrating the quantitative and verbal information is to select the occupations which were judged to be the most similar, inspect the available information on the verbal bases given by the subjects for the judgement concerned, and then systematically lower the average similarity value, and see which constructs persist and which new ones emerge. This will be done for the first quartile (30) of pairwise judgements which make up the 'horseshoe' (Figure 3.5A). The results are summarised in Figure 3.6.

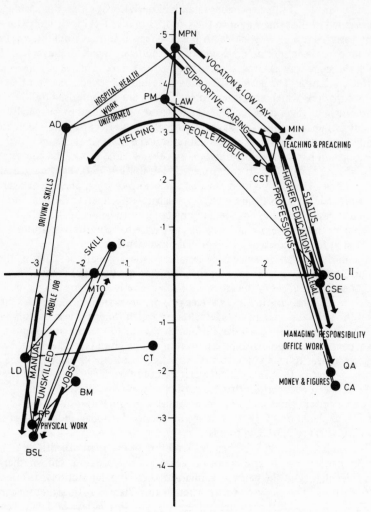

Fig. 3.6 Horseshoe sequence and range of predicates

1. The highest average similarity links Qualified Actuary and Chartered Accountant, and this forms the basis for a cluster centred on Chartered Accountant:

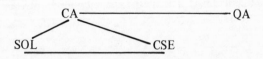

The Chartered Accountant – Qualified Actuary link is described
repeatedly as 'dealing with money or figures'. All the occupations in
this cluster are also described as being professions, being highly qualified
academically, and as working in an office. The Civil Servant
(Executive) – Country Solicitor link also evokes the conception of
manipulation (managing or 'juggling' with both individuals and things).
In addition, dyadic links occur which form the basis of clusters at lower
levels of similarity:

(*a*) *Ambulance Driver, Lorry Driver*: this is an important, but somewhat tenuous, link based on the common reference to driving skills,
but it also involves the connotations of jobs which are not tied to
offices and buildings.

(b) Carpenter, Machine Tool Operator: this pair of occupations are the
most salient in defining the third dimension of the INDSCAL
solution in contrast to Railway Porter, Building Site Labourer and
Lorry Driver. This link is overwhelmingly described in terms of the
skilled craft or trade status of Carpenter, Machine Tool Operator,
compared to the unskilled work of Railway Porter, Building Site
Labourer and Lorry Driver.

(c) Railway Porter, Building Site Labourer: these are 'relatively
unskilled jobs – hauling stuff around', as an accountant describes
them: physical, unskilled jobs are the salient characteristics.

2. The next set of links serve to connect the original clusters:

(a) Two links, centring on Church of Scotland Minister, serve first to
cluster this title to Comprehensive School Teacher, largely on the basis
of their common teaching and service role:

> 'They deal directly with people in a capacity in which one person is
> *receiving* something from another, either by way of learning or by
> receiving counsel. . . . Similarity is on the basis of the relationship
> of the person providing the service with the person receiving it'
> (Church of Scotland minister);   .

and to link with the 'Legal-Financial' professional group (Church of
Scotland Minister to Country Solicitor), in terms of the common
service and counselling role, and by the more general professional,
university education.

(b) Two links, centred on Ambulance Driver, form the basis of a
uniformed public service group (Ambulance Driver, Policeman and
Ambulance Driver, Male Psychiatric Nurse) involving the predicates of
'working in hospitals', 'care of the sick', 'dealing with casualties',
'work for the social services' and 'wear uniform'.

(c) Two links centred on Lorry Driver (Lorry Driver, Railway Porter
and Lorry Driver, Building Site Labourer) which form the unskilled

manual group, and use the predicates of 'work outside', 'physical work', 'manual work'.

(d) A link connecting the skilled Carpenter, Machine Tool Operator dyad with the unskilled manual group (Carpenter, Building Site Labourer) in terms of their common 'manual work' status but also because of their involvement in construction. This contrast is nicely illustrated by a journalist:

> Obviously they have a great deal in common because they are both working in construction, aren't they? Though in fact, a carpenter would tend to look down on a building site labourer.

3. The next set of links further interrelates the professional group, connects the public service group (from Male Psychiatric Nurse to Comprehensive School Teacher) and attaches the Commercial Traveller into the 'driving' group. At this stage, the network becomes connected, except for Barman, which is only later attached to the manual groups.

HIERARCHICAL ANALYSIS

In the course of analysis it becomes clear, first, that the 'horseshoe' *in fact represents a linked set of clusters, rather than a strict linear sequence of occupations.* This impression is confirmed by the hierarchical clustering analysis (see T3.6) of the averaged similarities data (see Fig. 3.7).

Since the data do not perfectly satisfy the ultrametric inequality, there are discrepancies between the two solutions, (though they are fairly minor). Both solutions seem to agree that there is a mostly professional cluster and a mostly manual cluster. Both solutions put Qualified Actuary, Chartered Accountant, Civil Servant (Executive), and Country Solicitor into one major branch of the professional cluster, and both put Church of Scotland Minister and Comprehensive School Teacher into the other. So far as the manual occupations are concerned, both solutions agree that Lorry Driver and Ambulance Driver, Building Site Labourer and Railway Porter, Carpenter and Machine Tool Operator, and Commercial Traveller are in the same (left hand) cluster. The major discrepancy arises with the placement of Policeman and Male Psychiatric Nurse. This pair is placed with the people-oriented professions, (Church of Scotland Minister and Comprehensive School Teacher) by the diameter methods, but the connectedness solution splits them up, and attaches them to the 'mostly manual' cluster. A further discrepancy is that Barman and Commercial Traveller are paired together and linked to the manual cluster in the diameter method, but are simply attached at the least stable level of the clustering by the connectedness method. So we find once more that the location of these two occupations is ambiguous; – this may possibly be a consequence of the very wide range of possible reference for the terms, Barman and Commercial Traveller.

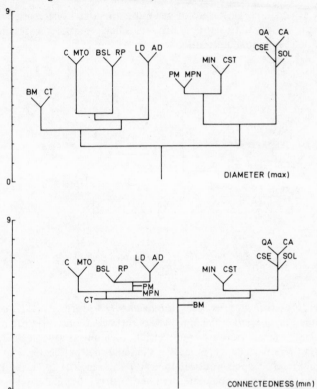

Fig. 3.7 Hierarchical clusterings of averaged similarities data

Despite the fact that hierarchical clustering is not a spatial model, it is interesting to note that the dendograms are easily drawn to follow the horseshoe sequence of occupations (except for Barman and Commercial Traveller, whose location is anyway uncertain) but they cannot be drawn to follow the order of the coordinates along any INDSCAL or average similarities scaling *dimension* without crossing stems.

Secondly *the semantic bases for judgement evidently exist at different levels of generality* (illustrated in Figure 3.6 by the length of the associated arrows). The hierarchical clustering, and especially the diameter solution, confirm this point: it seems a fairly simple matter to identify the level of generality of a predicate by inspecting the range of occupations to which it is typically applied, and then mapping it into the appropriate level of the dendrogram. A possible location of predicates is presented in Figure 3.8 for the Diameter solution, and it bears a strong resemblance to the interpretation which Burton (1972: 67-70) gives to the diameter solution of similarity measures between 60 occupations, although it was obtained by quite different procedures. In a later book we shall examine the level of generality at which predicates occur in a more direct and systematic way. At present it is sufficient to note that it seems likely that predicates are organised in a taxonomic fashion.

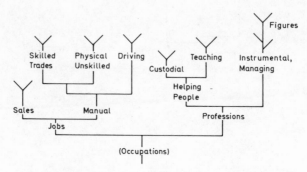

Fig 3.8 Diameter clustering and predicates

Thirdly, *the predicates (or bases of judgement) repeatedly change as one moves along the 'horseshoe',* making it very difficult to interpret the map as only involving a single contrast or dimension, even one as general as 'social status'. Yet there is sequence, at least in the sense that predicates tend to overlap, and rarely reappear outside their 'typical' range of applicability. Rather than representing one dimension or property, the predicates seem to be related to one another in many different sorts of ways. In moving from cluster to cluster along the sequence there are certainly many correspondences, but, equally, common features drop out and others appear;

> ... and the result of this examination is: we see a complicated network of similarities overlapping and criss-crossing: sometimes overall similarities, sometimes similarities of detail

as Wittgenstein (1958, section 66) appositely describes a similar phenomenon in developing his 'family resemblances' theory of meaning. Such an interpretation has some affinity with the 'content' model of similarity, which asserts that a judgement of general similarity of two objects represents a report on the ratio between the common and total amount of the properties perceived as relevant. This interpretation is occasionally borne out by subjects' comments:

> I find it very difficult relating the two — finding grounds for comparison. It is difficult to evaluate any elements which are common to the two
> (Male nurse, assessing Qualified Actuary and Church of Scotland Minister)

Fourthly, *the basis of similarity sometimes refers quite explicitly to a social or interactional context* — that is, the similarity of a pair of occupations is assessed not only in terms of common properties, but also in terms of how likely members of the occupations are to engage in some form of social interaction or 'substitute' for each other in some way. Examples of this, drawn from the subjects' unprompted verbalisations, are:

(Substitution)
One tends to wonder whether each bloke might have chosen the other occupation rather than the one he did choose.
> (Accountant, referring to Qualified Actuary and Church of Scotland Minister)

The Actuary can act as, or take the place of, a lay preacher.
> (Ambulance driver, referrring to Church of Scotland Minister and Qualified Actuary)

(Social interaction)
I can't see them in the same social groupings, or having the same friends. Not intermarrying. Worlds apart — totally different social groups.
> (Printer, referring to Country Solicitor and Building Site Labourer)

By the nature of events they are often thrown together.
> (Journalist, referring to Policeman and Ambulance Driver)

Both reponsible jobs dealing with complex machinery. They get similar wages. You could imagine them going to the same pub, or club, or a football match. Their politics will probably be similar, both likely to vote Labour.
> (Church of Scotland Minister, referring to Lorry Driver and Machine Tool Operator)

These quotations provide fairly naturalistic instances of 'contact situations' which lie between direct and indirect social experience which Schutz (1972: 171) sees as so important in the process of typification of social relationships.

INTERPRETATION OF THE AGGREGATE MAP ON THE BASIS OF TRIADIC SCALING AND CONSTRUCTS [6]

A subset of the subjects who provided triadic similarities data also gave the bases on which they made judgements of 'most similar' for two of the three occupations in the triad. This allows the simultaneous mapping of the similarities space and the semantic interpretation of the 13 occupations. Correspondence between the aggregate triadic map and the INDSCAL Group space map provides another method of interpretation.

The bases for triadic similarities judgements were elicited from 23 subjects — mainly student teachers, together with 4 policemen, 2 clergy and 1 accountant — giving a total of 1052 'construct triads' i.e. judged triads for which the basis of the 'most similar' judgement is known. They were scaled in exactly the same way as the total triadic data set and with similar results. (See T3.11 for details of the algorithm and relevant stress values.) The similarities configuration of the construct triads is presented in Figure 3.9.

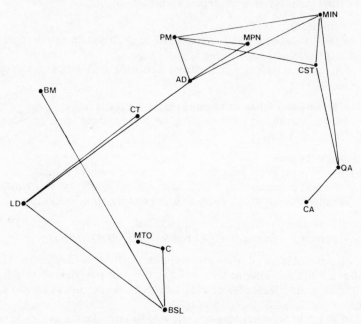

Fig. 3.9 Triadic similarities: highest linkages

Compared with the INDSCAL group space of Figure 3.4 or Figure 3.5A, the 'horseshoe' is still discernible, although in a flattened form. The main discrepancies again are in the relative positioning of Commercial Traveller, Barman and Lorry Driver.

The triadic similarities data set does not directly permit the computation of 'average similarities', which could enable a graphing to be made of the highest similarity linkages, as was done for the INDSCAL group space in Figure 3.5A. A possible alternative is to use the triadic similarity vote count for each pair of occupations. (The vote count is computed by averaging over all the triads in which a pair of occupations occurs, counting the value of 1 if they are judged most similar, 0 if least similar and 0.5 if neither.) Although the vote count method can be hazardous when scaling triadic data from incomplete designs (see T3.1), because its value depends to a great deal upon the identity of the third occupation in the particular triads judged, there is no danger in using it to separate out only the highest similarities, since occupations which are seen to be very similar will be judged as such irrespective of the identity of the third occupations.

The linkages mapped on to the map of Figure 3.9 are the 16 highest vote counts. Ignoring the occupations which are not present in the triads task, the two linkage patterns are quite similar (indeed, more so than the configurations themselves). The only major points of non-correspondence involve the links between the Church of Scotland Minister-Comprehensive School Teacher and Policeman-Ambulance Driver-Male Psychiatric Nurse clusters. The other vote-count links, even though they do not match the triads map very neatly, do match the INDSCAL linkages.

The most interesting correspondences are:

(a) in both cases, Ambulance Driver forms the bridge between the Policeman-Male Psychiatric Nurse and Lorry Driver;

(b) this chain is continued in exactly the same order—Lorry Driver, Building Site Labourer, Carpenter, Machine Tool Operator;

(c) in both cases, the Commercial Traveller is linked only to Lorry Driver.

In the case of the triads, Railway Porter is not available as a link for Barman, which substitutes Railway Porter's closest INDSCAL neighbour as its only link. Thus the triads and pairwise similarities tasks appear to be representing highest similarities in a similar manner.

The constructs were originally represented as lines on the map when more than six bases of similarity judgement referred to them as a pair. The resulting diagram was rather complex and the Venn diagram form of Figure 3.10 is a representative distillation of the line mapping. Each 'set' is defined by a single enclosed line, encompassing those occupations to which a particular construct was consistently applied.

The four most commonly occurring construct themes (mapped in heavy lines) are

(1) professional/high education (which can be considered as two themes co-extensive with regard to the set of occupations under consideration);

(2) working with, or coming into contact with, people;

(3) unskilled;

(4) manual.

Less frequent, and often more specific, bases are

(a) jobs involving driving;

(b) jobs involving skill (training);

(c) jobs connected with commerce.

These three cross-cut the 4 major themes. The remainder are subsets of the major themes:

(d) jobs involving dealing with figures (a subset of the professional/high education);

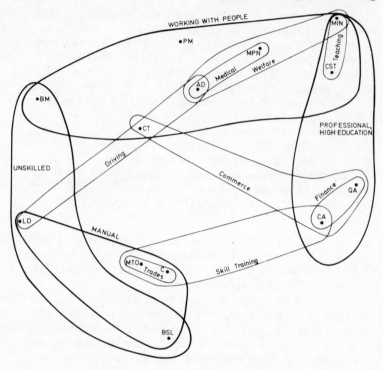

Fig. 3.10 Triads configuration interpreted by constructs

(e)   jobs involving teaching (this sub-theme is, in a sense, the intersect
of 'people contact' and 'professional/high education');
(f)   jobs involving welfare (a sub-theme of 'people');
(g)   jobs with a medical connection (a sub-theme of 'welfare');
(h)   jobs involving skill in the sense of a trade, which forms the
complement of unskilled within the manual category.

The advantage of the Venn diagram representation is that it allows overlap
to be shown. Overlapping constructs demonstrate the range of different job
attributes which can be invoked as grounds for making similarities judgements
about a particular occupation, when it depends upon the identities of the
other two occupations. For example, a Church of Scotland Minister can be
regarded as a professional with high education, working with people, teaching
and involved in welfare — this list derived only from the most commonly
used constructs.

A dimensional interpretation can of course be read into the mapping of the constructs — the 'working with people' set, for instance, covers one half of the configuration. The unskilled/manual sets are maximally differentiated from the professional, high education set. These major contrasts are interleaved however with much more specific grounds of similarity which would tend to overthrow any two-factor interpretation — the 'driving' construct is likely to be irrelevant to judgements involving occupations other than Ambulance Driver, Commercial Traveller and Lorry Driver.

The overlaps of constructs on occupations once again suggests an interpretation based on the content model of similarity and Wittgenstein's family theory of meaning cited earlier.

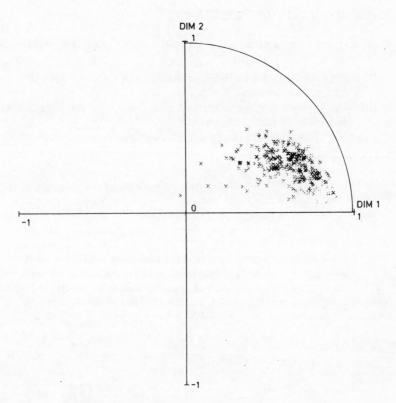

Fig. 3.11 INDSCAL analysis: subject space

3.6 INDIVIDUAL AND COLLECTIVE VARIATION

As we have seen above (page 80), the 'private map' is nothing but an idiosyncratic rescaling of the Group Space which is systematically modified or contorted into one more closely matching an individual's similarities data. A useful way of depicting the differences in subject's 'private maps' is to define a 'Subject Space' (having the same dimensions as the Group Map) and then represent each subject by a point which is located by the weights which he has on the several dimensions. The Subject Space corresponding to the first two dimensions of the INDSCAL solution is presented in Figure 3.11, and further technical details are presented in T3.17.

TYPES OF COLLECTIVE VARIATION

A considerable amount of variation is revealed by this analysis. It takes three basic forms:

(i)   the extent to which a subject's similarities data are reproduced or explained by this model;

(ii)   the differences in the importance or salience which each dimension has in the subject's judgements;

(iii)   the pattern of dimension usage which characterises each subject.

Let us examine each in turn.

Variation in the extent to which subjects' data are explained
The distance of a subject's point from the origin of the Subject Space indicates the extent to which his data are explained by the INDSCAL model ('indicates' because this relationship only holds approximately – strictly, the square of this distance corresponds to the proportion of individual variance accounted for when the coordinates of the stimulus coordinates in the Group Map are uncorrelated). A more accurate measure of goodness of fit is the simple correlation between the subject's original similarity ratings, and those predicted on the basis of the model. The distribution of these individual correlations is presented in Figure 3.12.

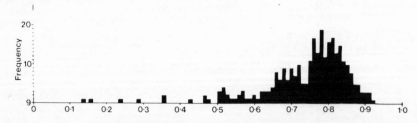

Fig. 3.12 INDSCAL model: goodness of fit

The distribution is obviously skew; the vast majority of cases are well fit, but there are a few individuals whose data are fit rather poorly (these same individuals appear as the points which fall close to the origin of the Subject Space in Figure 3.11). Almost without exception, the badly-fit subjects are drawn from the two groups who were interviewed in a communal data-collection session, and the poor fit may simply reflect this fact.

But does this considerable individual variation have any systematic social basis? One way of answering this question is to see whether the average correlations within the subject-group quadrants differ in any systematic fashion.

TABLE 3.3 INDSCAL averaged individual correlations, by quadrant and occupation

QUADRANT A:	0.763	QUADRANT B:	0.787
Clergy:	0.765	Qualified Actuaries:	0.802
Teachers:	0.763	Chartered Accountants:	0.770
		Chemical Engineers:	0.773
		Electrical Engineers:	0.765
QUADRANT C:	0.758	QUADRANT D:	0.685
Nurses	0.789	Engineers, Fitters:	0.683
Ambulance Drivers:	0.721		
Police	0.752		

(See also T3.18)

(Business Students: 0.787)

OVERALL AVERAGE CORRELATION: 0.789

Whilst the Occupation Group (averaged) correlations do not fluctuate widely, a clear pattern is evident, both for types of occupation (the quadrants) and for the constituent occupations.

An analysis of variance of these data (presented in T3.18) leads to the conclusion that the variation is not random fluctuation; the pattern of means is also consistent: goodness of fit is higher among the professional occupations, and lower in the skilled and unskilled working class groups. In part this may simply be due to the fact that tasks such as making systematic similarity judgements are more familiar to more highly educated people, but this in turn presupposes that they have more developed cognitive skills, so differential cognition is still involved (see also section 3.2 above).

What of the 'deviant cases', whose data are badly fit by the INDSCAL model? Are their conceptions generically different from the other subjects, or is it simply that their data are less consistent? Taking the twelve individuals whose correlations are lowest, there is only one case — a journalist — whose data are coherent in the sense that they do not include a very high proportion of 'totally dissimilar' judgements, conform fairly closely to the triangle inequality requirement for distance models, and yield a scaling solution which is interpretable. His data merit separate discussion. All the other cases display degeneracies or inadequacies of one sort or another (see T3.19); with this one exception, the data of the subjects who are badly fit by the INDSCAL model would not fit any obvious alternative model any better, and do not seem to have any coherence.

An ill-fitting, but coherent case – Case J271 (News sub-editor and Father of the Chapel, National Union of Journalists)
The subject performed the pairwise similarities task, followed by an early pre-test version of free-grouping, and finished by making a number of ranking and rating judgements.

The interviewer commented:
A long and empathic interview – he has a very coherent (and unusual) conception of jobs . . . most of his ideas come out in the [pairwise similarities] task . . . he was very articulate. He said several times that he was 'prejudiced' against policemen and ministers.

His distribution of similarity ratings is fairly regular, symmetric and is not skewed (*mean*: 4.8, *s.d.*: 2.1). The data conform much more closely to a spatial rather than a hierarchical model, and so were scaled by non-metric MDS to yield the following two-dimensional map (stress$_1$ = 0.16)

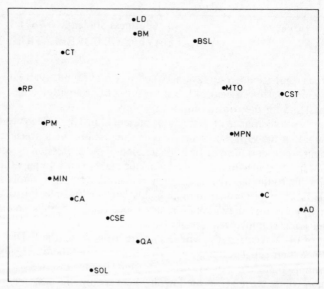

Fig. 3.13 Scaling of J271's similarities data

There are certain similarities with both the aggregate MDS (Figure 3.2) and
the INDSCAL Group Space (Figure 3.4) maps – the professional group
(Civil Servant (Executive), Country Solicitor, Qualified Actuary, Chartered
Accountant) and the unskilled cluster (Barman, Lorry Driver, Building Site
Labourer) of those maps are also discernible in J271's map. But here the
similarity ends. A graphic analysis of the highest similarities gives nothing
resembling the C-shaped serial order, but rather a criss-crossing pattern of
lines.

The verbal information is fortunately quite extensive, and is invaluable in
interpreting his data.

The key to interpretation lies in the very crucial distinction he makes
between what he calls the 'predictable' group of occupations at the left-hand
side (Church of Scotland Minister, Policeman, Commercial Traveller, Railway
Porter), and the 'unpredictable' group at the other side. By 'predictable
occupations' he means those that attract a certain type of people, who tend to
be rather similar and share the same outlook, whilst 'unpredictable occupations' are held to include a far greater variety of people, who come to the
job with a wider range of motivations, and are hence much less predictable in
outlook. His characterisation of the 'predictable' occupations centres on the
Minister and the Policeman. Both, he says, attract people who like to wear
uniform, and exert authority and power they would not otherwise have.
Together with the Commercial Traveller, they are engaged in 'selling the
product', manipulating people's real desires. Railway Porters share many of
these properties and have a low standard of intelligence – 'like the police',
he comments, ' – but then I'm prejudiced'.

The occupations most unlike these latter are the Carpenter and the
Ambulance Driver. In them, the individual 'can express his own personality
and talents', and can choose freely to be concerned with people or skills,
without any ulterior motives.

Are the contrasts used to name the INDSCAL Group Space discernible in
his judgements? The 'professional' group are not so described by him; indeed,
this term never appears in his comments, and educational qualifications and
status terminology appear only under the guise of 'talents'. Nor is 'people-
orientation' in jobs recognised as such. But he does recognise skill as an
important factor in certain cases: 'the Carpenter would reject the Machine
Tool Operator as not a craftsman, although he could become one'.

After 'predictableness', the types of property which he invokes are things
like job satisfaction, fulfilment, and the extent to which one has autonomy
or is under others' control. Perhaps the best illustration of these distinctions
(and the way in which he largely ignores status considerations) is provided by
the free-grouping he made of 35 occupations (which include the 16 used in the
similarities task, and which are italicised below).

Group A   *(Railway Porter, Building Site Labourer, Barman,* Routine Clerk,
              Shop Assistant, Bricklayer, Dock Labourer)

'Completely under the control of others; generally not inspiring; high staff turnover.'

Group B   *(Carpenter,* Chef, Farmer, Newsagent and Tobacconist)
            'The individual can express his own personality and talents (opposite of Group A).'

Group C   *(Machine Tool Operator, Lorry Driver, Chartered Accountant,*
            Tractor Driver, Fitter, Road Sweeper, Coal Hewer, Agricultural Labourer)
            'Job satisfaction and fulfilment. Demands a certain amount of talents. Half-way between A and B.'

Group D   *(Qualified Actuary, Civil Servant (Executive),* Jobbing Master
            Builder, Works Manager, Medical Officer, Company Director, Business Manager, Insurance Agent)
            'Jobs in which it is possible to *feel* you are fulfilling job-desires and using talents. But, in the end, you're still controlled by others.'

Group E   *(Country Solicitor, Commercial Traveller, Comprehensive
            School Teacher, Male Psychiatric Nurse, Ambulance Driver, News Reporter)*
            'Jobs that people do because they *want* to, although they may not be constantly satisfying.'

Group F   *(Church of Scotland Minister, Policeman)*
            'Jobs people are attracted to for reasons other than the job itself — especially because of the appeal of exercise of authority and power'

Several characteristics appear both here and in the pairwise similarity task. The centrality of Group F has already been commented upon, and the predictable/unpredictable contrast appears again here, in a somewhat more muted form. But control and autonomy have become especially salient.

Perhaps even more interesting than the construct system he uses is how often interchange, substitution or mobility-imagery appears as a basis for his similarity judgements:

High similarity judgements (8,7,6)

Comprehensive School Teacher 'may well have been' a Building Site Labourer. (8)
Male Psychiatric Nurse, Lorry Driver: 'both equally well fit into the other job'. (7)
Commercial Traveller 'could quite easily become' a Lorry Driver. (8)
Comprehensive School Teacher 'might well have been' a Machine Tool Operator. (7)
'Some Barmen would make excellent Policemen'. (6)

Low similarity judgements (1,2)

Ambulance Driver, Church of Scotland Minister are 'unlikely to change jobs satisfactorily'. (1)
Commercial Traveller, Male Psychiatric Nurse all 'entirely uninterested in each other's jobs'. (2)

An especially relevant example occurs when he describes the asymmetry of movement between Ambulance Driver and the Policeman (which are of course almost maximally distant in his cognitive map):

If an Ambulance Driver became a Policeman he would quickly get disillusioned with being one . . . but if a Policeman became an Ambulance Driver, he would find it hard to carry out the same community work without a policeman's authority and perks, and would resent the fact that he couldn't.

This extended description brings to life the similarity judgements of one man, and shows that whilst they may differ substantially from those made by most subjects, they do possess a readily understood inner coherence – they are entirely comprehensible, given that he adopts a rather different frame of reference from most. Yet he is fully aware of other viewpoints. When asked later to rank the occupations in terms of 'general standing in the community' (the traditional sociological operational form of 'prestige'), he provides a ranking very similar to other people's, whilst insisting that he is engaged in *interpreting* public opinion ('clichés' as he terms it), not giving his personal view.

Yet it is well not to stress these differences at the expense of the commonality which undoubtedly exists between his judgements and those of other subjects. Like him, other subjects often refer to types of people, rather than to attributes of jobs, and consider questions of involvement and personal fulfilment. Like them, he recognises several groups of occupations as having affinities which they describe in terms of 'educational qualifications' or 'training', but which he does not comment upon. Like them, he also uses substitution and mobility bases for assessing similarity, and recognises 'skill' as an important difference between some jobs. But when all this has been said, no other subject articulated such a well-defined frame of reference, which was clearly out of accord with that used by other subjects. Yet the frame of reference he uses is obviously evaluative to a large degree, and this merits comment. Whilst it is important to distinguish logically between cognition and evaluation, as we have done, it is equally important to recognise that people can, and do, operate in several modes. The usual effect of directing their attention to the similarity between things is to elicit a cognitively-based judgement, but others, such as this subject, undoubtedly interpret the task evaluatively.

Variation in the salience of the dimensions

One way of interpreting INDSCAL subject weights is to suppose that if a particular subject's weight is large, then the individual uses that dimension a lot in making discriminations between occupations; if it is a small one, then he tends to ignore that dimension. The extent to which individual differences exist, and can be accommodated by the INDSCAL model, is best illustrated by extracting two relatively extreme cases, and in each case constructing the 'private space' (which is the Group Map rescaled in the subjective metric of the individual concerned). The two subjects chosen are a qualified actuary and a policeman. The actuary's data are very well-fit ($r = .89$) by the INDSCAL model, and his judgements are determined virtually entirely in terms of the first dimension. By contrast, the policeman makes about equal use of the first and third dimension, but by reference to the whole group of subjects, his use of the 'Trades' dimension is considerable. His data are less well-fit ($r = .65$). The private spaces of these two individuals are plotted in Figure 3.14 and graphically illustrate these points.

Since the individual numerical weights are comparable between subjects, they can be used to test the hypothesis that the perception of relationships between occupations varies systematically according to the perceiver's position in the occupational structure. T3.20 shows the means and standard deviations of subject weights within each occupational group and quadrant. So far as the first dimension is concerned, the largest weights tend to occur among higher-status, highly-qualified occupations; not surprisingly, those in occupations which involve considerable investment in obtaining academic qualifications give somewhat greater weight to the dimension labelled 'Educational Qualifications' in making their similarity judgements. On the second and third dimensions ('Service orientation' and 'Trades/Skill' respectively) where the range of variation is a good deal less, the pattern of salience seems to be much the same: lower-status, skilled occupations attach greater importance to these facets in assessing similarity. It is worth noting that the Engineers and Fitters have a profile of average weights which is more extreme than that of any other group, and that the Nurses (who here include a number of mature university students) resemble the professions more than they do other service-oriented occupations.

The analysis of variance (presented in T3.20) largely confirm these impressions:

(i) the multivariate analysis of variance (taking the three INDSCAL weights conjointly) indicates that the occupational groups are centred at different locations in the INDSCAL subject space, and that a modest amount of variation (21 per cent) in subjects' weights lies between the 11 occupational groups;

(ii) corroborative evidence is provided by the univariate analysis — the differences in the salience of the first dimension contribute very predominately to the discrimination between the occupational groups.

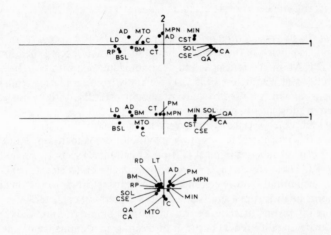

SUBJECT: Qualified Actuary

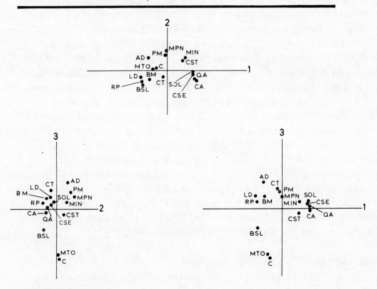

SUBJECT: Policeman

Fig. 3.14 INDSCAL analysis, private spaces

It may be reasonably concluded, therefore, that whilst individual differences are revealed by the INDSCAL analysis, systematic and interpretable *occupational* differences are also evident.

Variation in the pattern of dimension usage

There is no reason why all the subjects should make use of each dimension, and the INDSCAL model is designed to accommodate such variation. In practice (Jones and Wadington 1975: 21) we know from simulation studies that a dimension which is used by only a few subjects is likely to be missed or distorted in subsequent analysis.

Virtually all subjects, (apart from a very few singularly ill-fit cases) use Dimension I to a considerable extent. A few do not use Dimension II, but about 6 per cent of subjects (almost all from Quadrant B) seem to ignore Dimension III. There are also a few 'one-dimensional men'; a clergyman, a teacher, an accountant (whose comments constantly returned to the theme of educational qualifications and training), and a chemical engineer.

But more interesting patterns exist than simple non-use of dimensions. The most intriguing differences occur in the *relative* predominance of one dimension over another. Those whose dimensional weights are in the same ratio can be thought of as attaching the same *relative importance* to the dimensions. Overall, the average degrees of relative emphasis were such that weights for the first dimension ('Educational Qualifications') were over two-and-a-half (2.66) times as large as weights for the second ('Service Orientation'), and over three-and-a-half (3.67) times as large as weights for the third ('Trades/Skill'). In turn, weights for the second dimension tended to be about one-and-a-half times (1.40) as big as weights for the third.

The weight ratios produce a very skew distribution, and when they are transformed to produce less skew distributions, then the differences in the predominance of Dimension I over Dimension II and Dimension III turn out to be a good deal more significant and substantial than any of the simple differences in (single) dimensional usage. The variations by occupational group are also quite interpretable (see T3.20, section II). The most sizeable differences in patterns of weights occur between the occupations found in Quadrant B and those in Quadrant D and the occupational groups which give greater predominance to 'Educational Qualifications' over 'Service-orientation' also tend to give predominance to Education over Skill:

Predominance of 'Education' over 'Service'
> *Strong:*   Accountants, Business Students, Professional Engineers, Actuaries
> *Weak:*   Engineers-Fitters, Police, Ambulance Drivers

Predominance of 'Education' over 'Skill/Trades'
> *Strong:*   Business Students, Professional Engineers, Accountants
> *Weak:*   Engineers-Fitters, Ambulance Drivers

3.7 EXAMPLES OF INDIVIDUAL VARIATION

Each subject who did the triadic similarities task made two implicit judgements on each of the 78 pairs of occupational titles. Such data are therefore well suited to individual analysis. The data of twelve of these subjects, separately scaled by the TRISOSCAL program (see T3.21) to yield individual maps, were selected to illustrate several of the important points which have been made so far. The summary statistics of the 12 individual solutions are given along with the most commonly used bases of similarity which were used. There seems little obvious relation between the dimensionality of the solution and the constructs used, but a common feature of the solutions is the large increase in stress in going from two dimensions to one.

The three cases which come closest to being one-dimensional are 6712, M207 and V851; a student teacher, an ambulance driver and a mature student respectively. 6712 uses a fairly typical repertoire of constructs — 'working with people' and 'having qualifications'. What produces a one-dimensional representation is the fact that, in satisfying his judgements, the scaling procedure splits the occupations into two clusters, one consisting of a combination of the 'qualified people' and 'helping people', and a second, strongly contrasted, manual group. It is the emphasis on qualifications, however, which is most salient.

M207 uses the antonyms of 'professionals *v.* just jobs' and 'trades *v.* labouring' to produce three clusters along the major dimension. Only the middle cluster, 'tasks', is split by the second dimension to any great extent.

Subject V851 is the only person among those making triadic judgements who uses status explicitly as a basis for similarity, and he does so in a clearly uni-dimensional way — each judgement is made in terms of higher or lower status. When his data are scaled in two dimensions, a group of occupations he describes as 'public service' (Policeman, Ambulance Driver, Male Psychiatric Nurse) form a tight cluster in the centre of the map, and half-way along the clearly evident status dimension, and it is clear that this construct adds little or nothing to his basic factor of status.

Two cases merit a more detailed description — 6718 (a student teacher) and M208 (an ambulance driver). In Figure 3.15 the bases which each cites for the most similar pair in each triad are mapped in to their respective similarity spaces, in a manner akin to Figure 3.6.

The bases which 6718 uses are virtually identical to those used to describe the aggregate map. In terms of the four main themes of 'working with people', 'professional', 'manual' and 'unskilled', the match is perfect.

The major differences are, first, that in his individual map, Commercial Traveller and Barman are located more towards the centre of the configuration (but apart from this, the familiar horseshoe-sequence is discernible); and, second, that the 'people-oriented' group occurs as a central cluster, rather than being arrayed as a sequence.

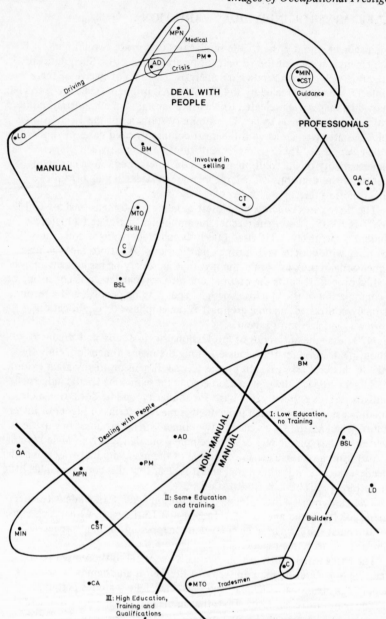

Fig. 3.15 Triads data, private spaces

Three major groupings of occupations are evident — what he calls:

'the professionals' (Qualified Actuary, Chartered Accountant, Comprehensive School Teacher, Church of Scotland Minister);
'people who deal with people' (Comprehensive School Teacher, Church of Scotland Minister, Policeman, Male Psychiatric Nurse, Commercial Traveller, Ambulance Driver, Barman); and
the manual group (Barman, Lorry Driver, Machine Tool Operator, Carpenter, Building Site Labourer).

The rest of the constructs which he uses refer to specific dyads:

'guidance' (Church of Scotland Minister, Comprehensive School Teacher); 'dealing with crisis' (Ambulance Driver, Policeman); 'medical connection' (Ambulance Driver, Male Psychiatric Nurse); 'selling' (Commercial Traveller, Barman); 'driving' (Ambulance Driver, Lorry Driver); and 'skilled' (Carpenter, Machine Tool Operator).

From this information an hierarchical (subset) structure can be inferred, indicating that his constructs exist at different levels of generality:

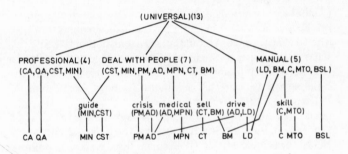

From this representation, it can readily be seen (Following the subset inclusion lines downward) that, for instance, a *Church of Scotland Minister* is a 'professional who guides' or a person who 'deals with people in a guidance role'; an *Ambulance Driver* is a person who 'deals with people in crisis, or in a medical capacity', and is also involved in 'driving', and a *Carpenter* is a 'skilled manual worker'.

From this representation it is also possible to infer a simple decision rule which, when applied to the 52 triads, correctly reproduces the 'most similar' judgements he makes in all but four triads and reproduces the verbal basis in all but nine instances. (It should perhaps be added that there is no direct

evidence that the subject used this particular rule.) This rule could be
expressed as follows:

For each triad,

(a)   separate out the three implied pairs of occupations. For each pair,
         identify the least upper bound (lub) of the two elements, and note
         the cardinality (or size) of the lub set. The pair having the smallest
         cardinality is chosen as the most similar pair, and the name of that
         set is cited as the basis of the construct. But

(b)   If the lub is the universal set, then two 'non-professional' occupations
         are chosen as most similar and on that basis.

For example (i) The triad (Ambulance Driver, Male Psychiatric Nurse,
         Commercial Traveller) consists of the pairs: (Ambulance Driver, Male
         Psychiatric Nurse), (Ambulance Driver, Commercial Traveller) and
         (Male Psychiatric Nurse, Commercial Traveller).
         Ambulance Driver-Male Psychiatric Nurse: have the lub of *medical*,
         size 2.
         Ambulance Driver-Commercial Traveller: have the lub of *deal with
         people*, size 7.
         Male Psychiatric Nurse-Commercial Traveller: have the lub of *deal
         with people*, size 7.

hence   (Ambulance Driver-Male Psychiatric Nurse) is chosen as most similar,
         on the grounds that they both 'have a medical connection'.

(ii)   The triad (Chartered Accountant, Policeman, Building Site
         Labourer) consists of the pairs: (Chartered Accountant, Policeman),
         (Chartered Accountant, Building Site Labourer) and (Policeman,
         Building Site Labourer). The lub of (Chartered Accountant,
         Policeman) is the universal set, size 13;
         (Chartered Accountant, Building Site Labourer) is the universal set;
         (Policeman, Building Site Labourer) is the universal set.
         Hence *(b)* is invoked, and (Policeman, Building Site Labourer) is
         chosen as most similar on the grounds of being non-professional.

This subject's data are the most obvious instance we have of the operation of
a simple set of rules (or algebra) upon a cognitive structure to produce
answers, and in this sense could be construed as evidence for the operation
of a primitive generative 'cognitive grammar' referred to in Section 3.4 above.

Indeed, even the exceptions — those judgements which were incorrectly
'predicted' — shed interesting light on the operation of such a grammar:

(1)   In the triad (Chartered Accountant, Machine Tool Operator and
         Male Psychiatric Nurse), since the lub for each pair is the universal
         set, rule *(b)* predicts that Machine Tool Operator and Male
         Psychiatric Nurse should be judged most similar, on the grounds
         that 'they don't deal with people' — i.e. the negation of the 'deal
         with people' construct. This information, and indeed rule *(b)*

itself, suggest that an important component of the 'cognitive algebra of occupations' is the operator of negation.

(2) In the triad (Machine Tool Operator, Male Psychiatric Nurse, Commercial Traveller), the rules predict that (Male Psychiatric Nurse, Commercial Traveller) will be judged most similar, on the grounds that they both 'deal with people'. In fact, Machine Tool Operator and Male Psychiatric Nurse were selected, on the grounds that they were 'non-professional' — i.e. Commercial Traveller became 'professional' in this set. This suggests that the occupations referenced by a given predicate or basis is not fixed, but may be affected by other occupations involved in the comparison.

(3) In the triad (Building Site Labourer, Commercial Traveller, Church of Scotland Minister) the rules predict that (Commercial Traveller, Church of Scotland Minister) will be chosen on the grounds that they work with people. In fact, the Building Site Labourer and the Commercial Traveller were judged most similar against the Church of Scotland Minister on the grounds of being 'non-professional'.

(4) In the triad (Church of Scotland Minister, Policeman, Barman), the rules do not predict an outcome (the 'depend on people' construct is the lub for all three). In fact (Church of Scotland Minister, Policeman) were selected on this basis.

These last two exceptions testify once again to the instability of the location of Barman and Commercial Traveller. It is also mirrored by the fact that eight of the 12 triads whose judged similarities are not monotonically related to the distances in the cognitive map involve these two occupations.

The second example of the Ambulance Driver (M208) provides a rather different picture. His judgements are based upon the conjunction of three main bases of similarity:

(1) an inclusive 'education' theme — qualifications, training, skill, apprenticeship used in specific circumstances with 'similar standard of education' as a fallback;

(2) 'dealing with the public';

(3) 'manual'.

The only other bases mentioned were 'drivers' (but not consistently), 'tradesmen' (applied to Carpenter and Machine Tool Operator), and 'job not at a standstill' — always a contrast to Machine Tool Operator.

The education-linked bases of judgement were not organised in a way that is sufficiently consistent to allow the mapping of clusters, but they seem to be unsystematic verbalisations of a genuine dimension. For example:

'Similar are Machine Tool Operator and Chartered Accountant, because both require a certain amount of education' [in the context of Building Site Labourer];

'Similar are Comprehensive School Teacher and Carpenter. They need

the same apprenticeship or training' [in the context of Commercial
Traveller] ;
'Similar are Commercial Traveller and Machine Tool Operator. Both have
to serve an apprenticeship, be educated' [in the context of Lorry Driver].

The term 'qualifications' was reserved for Qualified Actuary, Chartered
Accountant, Church of Scotland Minister and Comprehensive School Teacher.

Figure 3.15B is divided into three sections along the education
'dimension'. The titles Qualified Actuary, Chartered Accountant, Church of
Scotland Minister, Comprehensive School Teacher were never judged least
similar simply on the grounds of less education/training, whereas Barman,
Building Site Labourer and Lorry Driver were never cited as having more
education/training than anyone else. The other titles form an intermediate
group having more or less education/training, depending on context.

The occupations referred to as 'manual' include the three low-education
occupations, and also Carpenter, Machine Tool Operator, and more surprisingly, Commercial Traveller – as unpredictable as ever.

The occupations referred to as involving 'dealing with the public' form a
narrow band parallel to the education dimension and cross-cutting the
educational/manual categories. This would appear to be the natural configuration to be produced by a category ('dealing with the public') cross-cutting a
dimension ('level of education').

The exercise of interpreting individual sets of data can be self-defeating
if it simply becomes an attempt at verbal curve-fitting. In all the cases so far
cited it would be possible to go on to provide a more detailed, and individual-
ly more convincing 'explanation', but we have avoided this, since the main
purpose is to illuminate cultural communality, and not personal idiosyncracy.
We also recognise that many of the hypotheses advanced to explain particular
points can only be viewed as plausible until they are generalised and subject
to further testing. None the less, despite these necessary cautions, the main
burden of this chapter seems clearly established: there is undoubtedly a
considerable range of individual variation in occupational cognition. What is
important, however, is that this variation is socially structured.

3.8 SUMMARY

In this chapter, two main themes have been explored – the use of aggregate
occupational similarities data to describe cognitive maps of the occupational
structure, and the extent to which important and systematic social differences
exist in the ways in which the occupational structure is conceived. The main
results associated with the first theme are as follows:

(i)   Both the absolute (pairwise) and relative (triadic) similarities data
       give rise to highly similar findings when considered in aggregate,
       and the cognitive maps obtained from scaling both types of data are

also very similar. The INDSCAL Group Space is very much akin to the other maps, but it requires a larger number of dimensions and several distances have to be exaggerated in order to accommodate systematic individual differences. Due to the fixed orientation of the INDSCAL solution it is possible to identify the axes of the cognitive space. The first dimension, although multi-faceted, may be labelled 'Educational Qualifications' but subsumes properties such as work conditions, extent of training, income and status and contrasts such as professional/manual. The second dimension, labelled 'Service orientation', reflects the people *v.* data-and-things contrast, and the third dimension serves to differentiate the Carpenter and Machine Tool Operator from the other manual jobs, leading to its labelling as a 'Trades' or 'Skill' dimension.

(ii) When the highest average similarity judgements were embedded as a graph into the INDSCAL Group Space map, it gave rise to a C-shaped, 'horseshoe'-like structure, indicating a non-linear sequence (or subspace) of occupations. This characteristic shape can be interpreted as indicating that subjects make their judgement according to a kind of 'local Euclidean metric', judging all pairs beyond a certain threshold as maximally distant. Such an account also provides an interpretation of the high proportion of 'totally dissimilar' pairwise judgements noted in an earlier section.

(iii) An hierarchical procedure was used to examine the extent of clustering in the cognitive maps, showing that the 'horseshoe' sequence in fact consists of a connected set of linked clusters, centring upon the 'professional' and the 'manual' groups.

(iv) Subjects' verbalisations of the predicates they used in making the occupational judgements were mapped into both the INDSCAL cognitive map and the hierarchical clustering scheme. It was concluded that:

> the semantic predicates (or bases for judgement) are evidently at different levels of generality;
> the predicates repeatedly change as one moves along the occupational sequence (counter-indicating a purely dimensional interpretation);
> the predicates sometimes refer quite explicitly to a social or interactional context of judgement.

Whilst the *fact* of individual variation in conceptions of the occupational world has been frequently acknowledged, by sociologists, it has usually been argued that these differences do not have any coherent social basis, and may therefore be treated as idiosyncratic 'error'. The extent of individual differences evidenced in the INDSCAL analysis is certainly considerable. But it is more important to stress, first, that important and systematic differences exist in the ways in which different occupational groups view the occupational structure, and, second, that any particular viewpoint is restricted and partial.

The three basic types of systematic variation revealed by the analysis of the INDSCAL subject weights are:

(1) *Differences in the amount of variance in subjects' data accounted for by the model*
The data of the professional occupational groups are, on average, fitted better than those of skilled and unskilled groups.

(2) *Differences in the salience of the INDSCAL Dimensions*
The greatest salience tends to be ascribed to 'Educational Qualifications' (Dimension I) by higher-status, highly-qualified occupations. On the 'Service' and 'Trades' Dimensions, lower-status, unskilled occupations tend to attach greater importance in assessing similarity.

(3) *Differences in the pattern of relative importance ascribed to the Dimensions*
Patterns of relative predominance were assessed by taking the ratio of the dimensions. After suitable transformation, it turns out that it is the relative usage of Dimension I over Dimensions II and III that is the most substantial source of occupational difference.

It is, then, in patterns of *relative* dimensional predominance or usage that major and systematic sources of social variation in occupational cognition are to be found.

The analysis of individual cases has shown that the judgements which they make examplify the characteristics which were elicited at the aggregate level. Although occasional instances occur of subjects who have a quite distinct and coherent conception of occupational similarities, this does not appear as a frequent phenomenon in our data, and does not appear to be socially patterned. In a few cases there is sufficient auxiliary information to support the view that in generating judgments of similarity, individuals operate upon a cultural model, or 'internal representation' of the occupational structure in terms of a set of simple rules.

4 Occupational Evaluation

4.1 METHODS:

INTRODUCTION

The preceding chapter has demonstrated significant and patterned differences in the cognition of occupations. Different sub-groups of people cluster jobs together in different ways. We now turn to occupational evaluation. Are there similarly patterned differences in the invidious and odious comparisons that people make between occupations? In a sense, this question is unnecessary. Evaluation must depend upon cognition, since it is logically impossible to make orderings without some prior notion about the nature of what is being ordered. It follows that the existence of differences in cognition necessarily implies that there will be consequent differences in evaluation (though it is of course possible that the sociologist may choose techniques of data analysis that are insufficiently sensitive to detect these differences).

This chapter might very well have been called 'What are People Doing when they Evaluate Occupations?' Unfortunately a title very like this had already been used by Hope (1973) and so we have been forced to be more prosaic. The question can be partly answered by reference to a number of 'ideal typical' models of the logically possible things that people might be doing when they evaluate occupations. People might be:

(1) Assigning a real number to each occupational title in such a way that the magnitude of this number was some precise psychophysical function of the quality upon which the occupation was being evaluated.

(2) Making a complete rank order of occupations with no 'ties' allowed.

(3) Making a 'weak order' of occupations, all occupations being comparable with one another and 'ties' being allowed for equivalently evaluated occupations.

(4) Making a 'partial order' of occupations, certain occupations not being comparable with one another, and therefore being neither tied, nor ranked above or below certain others.

(5) Assigning occupations to subjectively defined categories or classes (such as 'the free professions', or 'trades', or 'essential jobs'). Such categories might or might not themselves be ordered.

(6) Analysing the skill-requirements, the type of personnel recruited and the duties and functions of the job, and combining the various

evaluations of these components into some overall summary of the
occupation's worth.

As happens with most social science research, we shall probably end up with
some combination of these six models in our explanation. Introspection and
informal observation suggest that people often reject the possibility of making
comparisons between some pairs of occupations (*vide* the 'chalk and cheese'
assertions quoted in the previous chapter). Generally speaking people also
dislike being required to make complete rank orders (without being allowed
to make 'ties'). As we shall see later, people tend to cluster occupations into
subjectively defined categories and to some extent they also make analyses
of the constituent attributes of occupations.

The sociological literature on occupational prestige favours the first two
of these six models. Sociologists have discovered that it is possible to score
occupations on equal interval scales (and therefore to make complete rank
orders of them) by using 'perceptual' data averaged over a very large number
of human judgements. The inference seems to be drawn that since a
statistically contrived 'collective representation' can be produced by
aggregating the judgements of many respondents, there must *therefore* be
some way in which an ideal form of that representation exists in the head of
each respondent. The somewhat Platonic arguments developed in the theory
of mental testing can be invoked to support such a view, but only at the cost
of drastically simplifying our notions of the cognitive structures on which
people operate in order to produce evaluative judgements. Nevertheless,
sociologists persist in talking of such abstract entities as *the* 'occupational
prestige hierarchy' of the USA, or of Brazil or wherever. This term
'occupational prestige hierarchy' means either a complete rank order of
occupations or a one-dimensional set of scores, one numerical score for each
occupation. It is surely implausible to suppose that each individual in a
society carries a clouded version of the 'true' rank order in his or her head.
But if this over-simple model is inadequate, then how can we account for the
aggregated prestige scores that sociologists have been able to produce?

COLLECTING DATA ON ORDERINGS OF OCCUPATIONS

Sociologists and psychologists have been investigating the subjective aspects
of occupations for at least fifty years now (see Crites 1968 and Treiman 1977,
for detailed bibliographies). During this period of time many legions of
schoolchildren, college students and members of the general public have been
requested (or sometimes required) to rank order occupational titles on
various criteria, or to make descriptive or numerical ratings of them on
similar criteria. Arguments are conducted about the comparative merits of
'allowing' subjects to make their own descriptive orderings with no ties
being permitted or forcing them to make a complete order. So far, at least,
the data-handling technologies of social scientists (or perhaps merely their

imaginations) have ruled out of account any rank structure among
occupations other than linear orders.

Most people who have taken an introductory course in psychology are
familiar with Bartlett's concept of a 'social schema', and the Gestalt
psychologists' notions about 'good' figure. Briefly, the notion is that some
types of shape or story are especially easy to recognise, remember or
reproduce, and such stimuli are called 'good' figures. It is a very well-
documented fact that shapes or stories tend to be distorted in perception,
memory or reproduction in such a way as to become more similar to 'good
figures'. These ideas become relevant to the study of occupational cognition
because of the frequently replicated finding that a complete linear ordering
is a conceptual 'good figure'.[1]

First, we should define some terms:

(a) Linear Ordering. This means a complete rank order with no ties.
DeSoto and Albrecht put it more formally as a relation among objects
that has the three properties of asymmetry, transitivity and completeness
(1968:507).

(b) Weak Ordering. This means a rank order where ties are allowed and are
to be interpreted as implying equality between the objects tied.

(c) Partial Ordering. This means a rank order that allows ties in the
different sense that some of the objects being ranked may not be
comparable with one another. The partial order relationship among
objects has the properties of asymmetry and transitivity, but it does not
have the property of completeness.

If we label eight occupations with the letters A to G, the difference between
a linear ordering and two partial orderings may easily be illustrated (the
arrow relation indicates 'domination' over the occupation towards which
the arrow points).

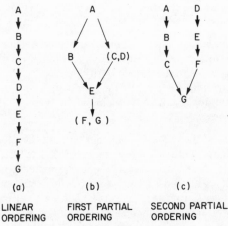

(a)	(b)	(c)
LINEAR ORDERING	FIRST PARTIAL ORDERING	SECOND PARTIAL ORDERING

Fig. 4.1 Three types of ordering

We can imagine for a moment that people think of occupations as partially ordered in a manner somewhat like the right-hand diagram of the figure ('second partial ordering'). The sociologist might have a linear ordering of occupations in mind (an arrangement like the left-hand diagram) and might arrange his interview schedule so that every subject was asked to make a complete or weak ordering of a set of occupations. Our experience suggests that a typical complaint on the part of the subject would be that it was difficult to say whether an eye surgeon, for example, was a higher-ranking person in the medical field than an airline pilot in the transportation field. However, most subjects would agree that both eye surgeons and airline pilots easily outrank such occupations as unskilled factory workers. When made into a diagram this looks like a tree structure (as in the 'second partial ordering'). Clearly, we are back to the concept of 'situs' as used by Morris and Murphy (1959), and by Nosanchuk (1972). Each 'branch' of the 'tree' is a 'situs' (perhaps each 'twig' is a 'sub-situs') and the 'trunk' represents those occupations which are so unskilled that they cannot claim to be specialised into any particular situs (a janitor may work in a hospital, but his claim to work in the health sector is obviously slight).

Our hypothetical sociologist might ignore any protests from his subjects and analyse his data so as to produce an averaged linear ordering of occupations. There would be nothing inherently wrong with this. However, it would be unwarranted for him to assume that his linear ordering at the aggregate level necessarily implied the existence of linear orderings in the heads of any of his subjects.

We are arguing that sociologists have been biased towards representing occupations as linear orderings. But why should this be so? Numerous experiments in the psychological literature show that people remember stories about linearly ordered social structures much better than stories about partially ordered structures. The linear ordering is a conceptual good figure while the partial ordering is not. Two further tendencies are apparent in such experiments: 'end anchoring' and 'upward tuning'.

(1)   *End anchoring* is the tendency for people to learn the top and bottom positions of a hierarchy more quickly and with fewer errors than they learn the middle positions.

(2)   *Upward tuning* is the tendency for people to learn more about the top and upper positions of a hierarchy than about middle and lower positions.

An examination of the various sociological scales of occupational prestige or occupational status strongly suggests that sociologists have been profoundly influenced by the 'good figure' quality of a complete linear ordering. But do people-in-streets really think in such a pattern? There is evidence that they do not. Some twenty years ago, Kahl (1957) tried to summarise the various empirical reports about what people do when they order occupations. His conclusions have been ignored by the mainstream literature on occupational prestige, but they are well-established and very pertinent to our concerns. They are as follows:

1. 'People perceive a rank order of occupations.'
2. 'People tend to enhance their own occupational position (egoism) *(a)* by raising their own position relative to others; *(b)* by varying the size of their own group. Here the evidence is not consistent: apparently there is a tendency to narrow the group when thinking of individual persons about whom invidious distinctions can be made (especially those lower on the scale) and to enlarge it when thinking of general categories of people who are closely similar to each other; *(c)* by perceiving separate but equal groups, thus accepting difference but denying hierarchy.'
3. 'People agree more about the extremes than about the middle of the prestige range. This may be a result both of clarity of stimulus and of aspects of perceptual organisation. There are more occupations in the middle, and they are less publicised.'
4. 'People agree more about the top of the range than the bottom and make more distinctions about the top than about the bottom. This may reflect social reality for those occupations at the top are more conspicuous and perhaps more differentiated.'[2]

In a sense, the distorting of partial orders into complete linear orders which takes place in the course of communication and remembering may all be part of the same 'social fact'. At one level of reality occupations may be partially ordered but due to the characteristics of our customary modes for communication they may most usually be spoken of as if a complete ordering existed. In the course of encoding, storage, decoding and transmission through various networks, there is likely to be a tendency for partially ordered conceptual structures to become assimilated to the 'good' linear ordering.

What seems likely to us is that sociologists have tried to talk about and even to quantify a whole linear continuum of occupational status, while people-in-streets have for most of their time been unconcerned with this 'big picture'. Harrison White remarks of occupational mobility that people devote great amounts of thought and emotion to changes in status which might seem miniscule in terms of overall social structure (1970:6). Indeed, there are many small-scale movements of this kind that would never be recorded under the standard procedures by which sociologists code occupations into analytical categories. If we take this assumption that men-in-streets are mostly concerned with the myriad complexities of day-to-day discussion about the relatively short rank orderings within small segments of a set of social roles, the task of the sociologist becomes one of integrating many such specialised world views into some kind of whole. One of the bases of the sociologists's claim to be a craftsman is that he can carry out such an integration without yielding to the temptations of good Gestalt that lie in wait for non-specialists.

All of the foregoing arguments imply two things for our methodology.

First, the methods chosen for gathering and storing data on orderings of occupations should not force the information into the pattern of a linear or even a weak ordering. We hope to follow Cicourel's (1974) approach in the sense that we are very much concerned with situating our evidence in the context of the interviews which produced it. As Cicourel puts the matter:

> Despite the continual attempts by researchers to extract simple quantitative findings from qualitative questioning, we cannot avoid the complex social processes that produce sociological information. Attempts to use statistical procedures to mask the qualitative judgements inherent in everyday social structures can create a misleading sense of quantitative inference (195).

Second, the methods chosen for analysing such data, and for representing the average of a number of orderings should preserve as much as possible of the integrity of the individual-level data.

We may not succeed in these endeavours (at least not in this report), but we hope that our attempts will stimulate others to work in the same general direction.

4.2 WHAT ARE PEOPLE DOING WHEN THEY COMPARE OCCUPATIONS?

WEAK ORDERINGS AND HOW THEY ARE CONSTRUCTED

It is a sure principle of interviewing that one should avoid forcing one's own definitions upon the interviewee. It seemed to us that our interest in occupational cognition required us to ask some very basic questions, such as:

(a)   Do people always think of occupations in rank orders?

(b)   If people do tend to arrange occupations into orders, are their bases for so doing idiosyncratic, or are there any general and compelling principles for ordering occupations?

(c)   To what extent do people agree about the strong, weak or partial orderedness of a set of occupations?

In order to investigate such questions as these, we used a fairly 'open-ended' task: we simply asked people to sort occupations into groups, and made careful notes of what they did and said during the task.

A standard set of 32 cards would be given to the interviewee, each card having the name of an occupation printed on it. The interviewee would then be asked to group the cards into piles in any way that seemed natural to him. He was encouraged to talk as he carried out the sorting. When the sorting was complete, he was asked to give an overall name to each of his groups (piles) of occupations. He was also asked if he felt that the groups could be put into any particular order. We carried out 82 interviews in which this technique was used but in only 32 of them were the groups of occupations ordered. In this chapter, we are concerned with invidious comparison, and therefore we only consider the data provided by the 32 subjects who were prepared to order their groups of occupational titles. It is important to bear in mind that the subjects were *not* required to order their groups on any particular specified dimension. Once they had sorted the occupational titles into groups (piles), they were asked if any ordering of those groups seemed appropriate.[3] The accompanying table shows the 32 subjects with the occupations they followed, the number of groups into which they sorted the occupational titles, and the criteria by which they said they had ordered their groupings. It is important to note that these 'criterion of ordering' labels are often rather inexact summary statements, and are furthermore produced with some help from the interviewer.

For these two reasons, the criteria the subjects 'said they had used' fail to do justice to the complexity of the reasonings they engaged in. Different individuals carried out this task in different ways. A small number of examples will give a flavour of the various approaches.

(a)   A Post Office Clerk (Y380) 'just identified "Professionals" and "Tradesmen" in the course of the task, and quickly made up two groups which he called "weekly-paid people" and "salaried people". In spite of my [the interviewer's] efforts to elicit subtler distinctions, he was adamant that he wanted to leave them in these two groups only.' (From interviewer report)

First, the 'Salaried Grades', 12 titles:

These are more the professional types you know. At the moment a Bank Clerk is a lower-paid grade, although he probably earns as much as a Primary School Teacher. A Secondary School Teacher would be paid a bit more. A Chartered Accountant would be better off again. A Minister of Religion is not very well paid, near the bottom. I am not sure what the Statistician and the Sales Manager get. A Sales Manager could be at the bottom or he could be at the top. But we are only left with two groups though. I don't want to make any subdivisions, but I would like to comment that there is no differentiation, money-wise, between the salaried people — what you called the professionals at one time — and the ordinary working people, because some of the people in the weekly-paid group earn probably more than some in the salaried group.

Second, the 'Weekly-paid Grades', 20 titles:

These people are all weekly-paid and in the more manual grades. You could order the weekly-paid people in the same way as you ordered the salaried people, like the Trawler Deckhands or Taxi Drivers. There is really no distinction between the two groups as far as money goes. But in my estimation, salaried people *should* be better off than these people.

TABLE 4.1 Summary of ordered groupings of occupations

Identifier	Occupation	Quadrant	Number of Groups	Criterion of Ordering
D365	General Medical Practitioner	A	7	Qualifications and social acceptability
S164	Sales Manager (Mechanical Engineer)	A	5	Importance to society
C304	Episcopalian Rector	A	5	Training
Y384	Comprehensive School Teacher	A	11	Training and specialisation
SW08	Social Worker	A	5	Status
C299	Episcopalian Rector	A	3	Training
A306	Church of Scotland Minister	A	2	Skill
C295	Episcopalian Rector	A	5	Skilled to unskilled progression
S161	Actuary (Qualified)	B	9	Intellectual content
S220	Insurance Manager (in a Bank)	B	4	Importance to the community
S017	Managing Director (of an Investment Firm)	B	6	Degree of responsibility
S028	Civil Servant: Principal (Revenue Department)	B	5	Skill
S029	Architect	B	11	Skill and responsibility
S061	Partner in a Firm of Quantity Surveyors	B	4	Training and ability
Y385	Civil Servant; Higher Executive Officer	B	8	Qualifications and ability
G292	Chartered Accountant	B	2	Education
F294	Actuary (Trainee)	B	7	Skill and training
G318	Chartered Accountant	B	5	Risk-takers versus non risk-takers
F315	Actuary (Qualified)	B	8	Definite order, but basis obscure
S039	Personal Assistant (to a Shipping Manager)	C	7	Qualifications and status
Y060	Salesman (in Industrial Protective Clothing)	C	5	Salary
Y035*	Retail Advisor (to Cooperative Wholesale Society)	C	2 or 7	Potential Salary
Y070	Newsagent and Sub-Postmaster	C	5	Skill
Y139	Sales Manager (in a Car Firm)	C	6	Skill
Y326	Master Jeweller	C	10	Contribution to society
Y007	Police Inspector	C	10	Social Standing
Y349	Motor Mechanic (recently promoted to Service Manager in his Garage)	D	8	Appeal and job satisfaction
Y380	Post Office clerk	D	2	Salaried versus weekly wage
Y381	Fitter's mate (though a Butcher by trade)	D	7	Qualifications
Y242	Heating Engineer	D	8	Importance to the Community
Y248	Chargehand (in firm of heating Engineers)	D	7	Pay
Y033	Contracts Manager (for Kitchen Engineering Firm)	D	7	Skill

*This interviewee felt that grouping the occupations into either 2 or 7 ordered groups was a satisfactory expression of his views.

(b)   A Higher Executive Officer in the Civil Service (Y385) took 33 minutes to sort and order the occupations. His comment on the ordering was, 'The only way I could do it is to put it in professionals coming down to unskilled, which I think you'd have to put at the bottom. Qualifications and ability.'

First, the 'Professionals, highly qualified,' 4 titles:

Professions. More or less of degree standard. University education or equivalent .. . . because of professional qualifications and as aspect of ability for the job. You know, some jobs require more ability than others.

Second, the 'Professionals, on-the-job training', 7 titles:

Professional, but not necessarily having to have the educational qualifications of the others, though some of the jobs are probably equally demanding. I know the Airline Pilot earns a hell of a lot more than the rest, but I'd classify them together. Less rigorous qualifications than [the first group] . On-the-job training.

Third, the 'Administrative, Executive, Clerical Jobs', 3 titles:

Once again, on-the-job training. A Computer Programmer could be defined as professional, but not necessarily. I didn't have any qualifications for becoming a Computer Programmer; we got 6 months' on-the-job training. I know we [i.e. the Civil Service] take lots of graduates for it, but I would say not a profession. I connect this lot with office work. . . .

Fourth, the 'Semi-Professional, Working Under a Professional', 1 title:

Difficult to define. I would near enough put him [Laboratory Technician] with Bank Clerk or Sales Manager [in Third Group] . You don't have to have professional qualifications or a degree or anything. He works under instruction of a scientist – he's obviously got to have some professional qualifications. I'll be quite honest, I'm not exactly sure of his function. Sort of semi-professional.

Fifth, the 'Tradesmen', 3 titles:

. . . next on ability and qualifications . . . skilled labour . . . skilled manual workers. They require an apprenticeship in each case. Having done an apprenticeship, your 5 years, you can go back to it. It's a sort of safe job to an extent. For example, professions are a safe job too to an extent, you can go back to them. You've got an expertise to them.

Sixth, the 'Vocational; – not educationally qualified, but at a higher level of training than [the seventh group]', 1 title:

Although it's in the medical profession, it's not a professional occupation. It [Male Psychiatric Nurse] requires training, probably quite intensive training. It probably requires a vocational aspect of it. I couldn't become one myself. A more demanding job, more vocational than the rest of them. But it's not a professional job. I don't think he has to have the qualifications or the ability of the class above, or should I say the category above, but he would have to have a vocation, a feeling for the job. Not necessarily ability at all, but able.

Seventh, the 'Semi-Skilled Labour, – average jobs', 7 titles:

These are guys who get a job with more or less minimum qualifications. They're no' daft, and it's a job that can be quite easily picked up; I think most people could do it. Sort of average jobs. . . . Very closely linked to [the bottom group]. These again require an amount of on-the-job training. Particularly Engine Driver. I'd put him near skilled labour, skilled manual worker [fifth group], but he's not a trade. Slightly more training involved [than for bottom group], for example you'd need qualifications as a driver. Barman is very near unskilled, but you've got to have certain qualifications; you can't be daft. You've got to count the change.

Eighth, the 'Unskilled Labour', 3 titles:

Unskilled manual workers. Require an amount of expertise which you learn on the job. You don't need an apprenticeship or suchlike for it. I wouldn't say that Building Site Labourers are necessarily thick, but you need very little qualifications at all for these three jobs.

(c)   A Church of Scotland Minister (A306) took 20 minutes over the task. 'He initially divided the titles according to "one general criterion", whether they were skilled or unskilled. He then dwelled for 10 minutes before sub-dividing the "skilled" group into those of "great technical ability", having much "involvement with technology" (10 titles) amongst whom only the Geologist was dubious; and into those of "people-orientated occupations", which he alternatively phrased as "helping-agencies in societies" (7 titles). The "unskilled" half of his initial dichotomy was, again, subdivided into two groups. This took less time than the first sub-division for, as he commented, "once you've got a criterion you keep to it". First were the people who "fulfil more mechanistic functions in society" [by "mechanistic" he seemed to intend "involved with machines", but he would not elaborate], who are "still people-orientated, but you're not completely dependent on them" (7 titles) and amongst whom the Actor and the Journalist were much the least "mechanistic" and the most "people-orientated". Second, and last, was a group he declined to label (8 titles). After a pause, he said "these would be mechanistic, too, I suppose." ' (Interview report) He produced four groupings in all – two large groups, one

ordered above the other, and each of which was subdivided into two sub-groups of equivalent rank.

(d)   A Chartered Accountant (G318) took 35 minutes over the sorting and ordering. First he listed the criteria by which he could make divisions. 'Given that I'm a chartered accountant, it's going to be the wage-earners and the salary-earners', to which he soon added the self-employed and lastly the 'miscellaneous' Actor. But, then, he could group by social class, or by whether he liked or was able to do the jobs, or by degree of education involved or by degree of technical skill involved, or by the political attitudes of the workers, or by age-groups. 'Come to think of it, however, most of these overlap with each other, and the exceptions aren't important.' Interviewer suggested he try to group by some combination of all these, and at that he declared that 'mental versus physical ability' was the summary version – only to revert, on being pressed to actually touch the sea of cards, to his initial division, which now, and finally, became that between 'Risk Takers' and 'Non-Risk Takers'. Each was divided, respectively, into 'Self-Employed' versus 'Salaried' versus 'Wage-Earning', and 'Salaried' versus 'Wage-Earning'.

First, the 'Risk-Takers, Self-Employed', 9 titles.

Second, 'Risk-Takers, Salaried', 4 titles.

Third, 'Risk-Takers, Wage-Earners', 7 titles, included some comment-worthy jobs. The building site labourer was 'out for nobody but himself', and lived in 'closed communities, like the miners'. The unskilled machine operator was 'just a layabout'. The trawler deckhand was in his job 'because he's brought up to do it'.

Fourth, 'Non-Risk-Takers, Salaried', 6 titles, included the teachers, who were 'frightened of the world' and the male psychiatric nurse, who – 'well, I don't know what the hell he's in it for; he probably likes the safety'. Again, the bank clerk was a 'safe chap'.

Fifth and last, 'Non-Risk-Takers, Wage-Earning', 6 titles, amongst which the Barman, Postman, and Policeman could be distinguished as 'public servants', but then so could others.

Handing over the piles he remarked that they reflected a 'difference in attitude of mind' which was, once again, a sign of 'physical or mental ability'.
Did it matter how Interviewer gathered up the piles? Yes, there was most definitely an order. [That in which I've described them.] Those at the top, especially the self-employed, tend to be both 'more individual' and 'more interesting' people. He would prefer to eat lunch with these than with the rest. He left the reasons for his ordering there. (Interviewer report)

(e)   A Chargehand Heating Engineer (Y248) took 50 minutes. Accord-

ing to the interviewer, he was very reticent, and it was obviously difficult for him to put his thoughts into words. His initial grouping of individual occupations remained rigid, but thereafter he spent a lot of time joining groups together and then separating them out again. Usually there was no well-articulated reason for doing this, and it took a fair amount of direct questioning to elicit the similarities and differences involved. When ordering the groups, he used three dimensions − pay, class and skill; when these became inconsistent, class was dropped first, and then skill. Several pairs of groups were given equal status in the ordering process; these groups have been identified by, e.g., 5(i) and 5(ii). His descriptions of the groups are worth quoting in full.

First, 'Top on skills, wages, and class structure. Highly qualified', 3 titles:

To be these professions you've got to work through a long apprentice-ship . . . to reach that standard you've got to be good. This group must be outstanding [on salary] , also the highest trained . . . upper class as well . . . minority jobs − very few people can achieve that standard.

Second, 'University-trained, higher-class jobs', 4 titles:

They all have about the same salary, higher than all the other groups except (1). They are also very qualified jobs, but slightly less than (1) . . . class again − very slightly lower [than (1)] . Obviously university-degree-type jobs. Higher-class jobs.

Third, 'Tradesmen'. 3 titles:

. . . working class, they're all grouped around the same wage bracket . . . skilled. [Ordered third] . . . because of skill. Definitely a drop in class. A definite drop in wages again, though they can earn a good standard of living, reasonable anyway.

Fourth, 'Moderately skilled, very specialised profession', one title:

Average sort of job; I don't think he's remotely connected with any of the others. As far as training is concerned he's on a level with Group 2 [i.e. university-educated] . You'd need a fair degree of intelligence. [I: Can you tell me the reason for keeping him on his own?] He just doesn't strike me as being a job you could say anything about, he's just a loner. He's obviously got to be good at figures. He's working for people further up the line like Group 5(ii) but I'd put him slightly above them. Middle to upper-class job, higher than average salary, a very individual job. In the order of class and pay I see him as equivalent to the primary school teacher [in Group 5(i)] . Moderately skilled sort of job; very small field that he works in.

Fifth Equal, 'Degree of training and responsibility' 3 titles:

Skilled people but not as skilled as tradesmen. In this respect of classing down, I'd group 5(i) and 5(ii) together. Slightly lower wage scale though possibly the class thing is higher [than tradesmen]. I see 5(i) and 5(ii) as different jobwise; as far as pay and class go they're about the same. [Interviewer: Why are they kept apart?] These jobs — 5(i) are a better-quality job — to be a school teacher, it's a better class than being a bank clerk. Also 5(i) have more opportunity for promotion and higher standards than 5(ii) . . . also responsibility comes into this group, more so than 5 (ii).

Fifth Equal, 'Higher-class labourers, employed by people one step up the latter', 4 titles:

They're higher-class labourers, i.e. the same as a labourer is to a tradesman, these people would be to their respective bosses. They're employed by people further up the scale.

Sixth Equal, 'Jobs that require dedication, a calling, natural ability', 4 titles:

They've chosen very individual professions, not run-of-the-mill; you've got to be dedicated to do these. These come next, very closely behind the previous group, as far as money — about the same for class. You've got to be dedicated — natural ability too.

Sixth Equal, 'Individual jobs, no great training, specialised', 2 titles:

. . . these two seem to run in parallel . . . one without the other wouldn't be very effective. Individual jobs that I think anyone could do, you don't need a great deal of training. [Interviewer: When you say they're individual jobs, do you mean that they're working on their own?) Not necessarily on their own; it's *chosen*, not like an ordinary trade, it's working in a very small field.

Seventh Equal, 'Unskilled, but requiring a little training and intelligence', 4 titles:

Unskilled but chosen professions, not labouring, requiring a slight element of training, and intelligence as well. [See also comments for group 7(ii).]

Seventh Equal, 'Unskilled jobs, poorly paid, lower class' 4 titles:

Unskilled. I'd lump 7(i) and 7(ii) together at the bottom, on all scales — wages, class. Dead-end jobs I suppose you'd call them. Little or no chance of promotion, or job satisfaction. Monotonous jobs, I should think.

(f) A Fitter's Mate (though a Butcher by trade, and a Docker by ambition) did the sorting and ordering task in 20 minutes. His criteria for sorting come out in his descriptions of his groups.

Unfortunately he did not give names to his groups.
First, 2 titles:

To be an Eye Surgeon you need to be good with your hands as well as
have brains. These are very intelligent men. You respect them for the good
work that they are doing. They are complicated jobs.

Second, 5 titles:

They are a cleverer sort of people. They have to have a bit of extra
brains to do that. You would have to have a bit higher qualifications. If I
picked the jobs I'd want to do, I'd pick these ones first. Obviously for
these jobs, you have to have a better education, it's a simple case of that!

Third, 7 titles:

It's the same sort of job really, dealing with people and that. Statistician
is a good job. It's not a job I would find interesting, I don't think I'll put
it besides the teacher; trying to learn things and, what you learn, you try
and teach to other people as well. These are better jobs [than those in
the following groups] although some of them don't appeal to me.
[Comparing Bank Clerk with Plumber] I would say one calls for brawn
and one calls for brain although in the long run a plumber on his own
account will earn more than the Bank Clerk nowadays. But just looking
at them on paper, a Bank Clerk looks a better job; security, smart dress,
all the loans, cheap rates etc.!!

Fourth, 4 titles:

'The Transport Workers.' As far as money goes, a Taxi Driver can make
fantastic money, they can make one hundred pounds in a week-end.
That's a very good job compared to the others.

Fifth, 2 titles:

I wouldn't consider that [Sales Manager] as a very good job. It is when
you get there but you couldn't start as a Sales Manager. You would have
to be a salesman for a number of years and work your way up. I wouldn't
fancy that. I am not sure where to put these, so I'll put them together.
They are both jobs that I don't know the qualifications, or certificates
needed. I wouldn't know whether to put them by the Chartered
Accountant [Group 2] or the Schoolteacher [Group 3]. They are better
jobs than [Group 6] ; it is easier to talk to people than to dig holes.

Sixth, (11 titles:

These are jobs that anybody can do. Anybody can put their hands to
these. Although Garage Mechanic is a trade, I would say they are easily
enough trained today. Photographer — some people say it's a hard job
but I don't think so, the camera does all the work. Male Psychiatric

Nurse — I've seen them, some of them are rather rough-and-ready, so I wouldn't put them with doctors. An unskilled machine operator — maybe when you put it as unskilled it makes it look a lesser job but he could probably get a job as a postman or barman. It's probably more complicated work than postman.

Seventh, one title:

I would put Actor last. It's not a very stable job. Very few make it. I wouldn't consider that a job at all. That's a gamble to me. If he [my son] was to grow up and say 'I want to be an actor', I would shudder, you know. It sounds a bit like a hippy.

SOURCES OF AGREEMENT AND DISAGREEMENT

Our main concern here is with the extent to which people disagree with one another in their orderings. (One subject produced two ordered sortings and both of these are included in the analysis below. The separate identifiers given to these two weak orderings from the same person are Y035 and Y935. So even though there are 32 subjects, there are 33 weak orderings.) It is interesting to look at the gross features of these 33 weak orderings of the 32 occupational titles. First, it is natural to look for areas of overwhelming agreement. Even though our interest is in lack of agreement, this must obviously take place within some context of agreement about something. Focusing upon the number of times each occupation is put into the group in first position, we find:

(1) No occupation is placed in the first position by all 33 subjects. The occupation which is nearest to this is Eye Surgeon, but two subjects, Y326 (a master jeweller) and Y033 (a contracts manager) each included Eye Surgeon in a group of occupations which were placed jointly second to Minister of Religion. The fact that 31 out of the 33 orderings placed Eye Surgeon in the first group is consistent with the previous literature which has shown that senior medical professionals are usually ranked high on almost all dimensions. However, we have here two instances of the belief that holds the cure of souls to be more important than the cure of disease, so that Minister of Religion should rank higher than Eye Surgeon.

(2) Six occupations are placed in a first-ranked group by no one. Thus there is unanimous agreement that whatever the qualities of Barman, Unskilled Machine Operator, Building Site Labourer, Restaurant Cook, Postman and Bus Conductor, they are not those that put an occupation in the first position on any of the usually employed criteria of evaluation. This is not surprising, but it is at least a base line.

(3)   Five occupations are placed in a first-ranked group in only one of
        the 33 orderings, and these are Garage Mechanic, Carpenter,
        Ambulance Driver, Trawler Deckhand, and Taxi Driver. What were
        the grounds of these idiosyncratic judgements? Were they random
        errors of judgement or are they understandable as parts of coherent
        cognitive structures?

Subject A306 (a Minister) accounts for two of these idiosyncratic placings
in a way which is easy to understand. He had insisted that there was no order
to the titles other than the very primitive ordering entailed by dividing them
into two groups, skilled and unskilled. Garage Mechanic and Carpenter fell
into his skilled category (which contained 17 of the 32 occupational
titles), so that it was in a sense easy for an occupation to get into his 'highest'
group.

Subject Y242 is more interesting. He places Ambulance Driver in his
first-ranked group, which is of size eight, and consists of three equally-ranked
sub-groups. The first of these is 'professions requiring great intelligence and
dedication' and contains Minister of Religion and Eye Surgeon. The
'professions' sub-group was described as 'men of great intelligence, but
they're also dedicated professions; they weren't in them just for financial
reward. I think that was what they wanted to be.'

The second sub-group contains Social Worker, Ambulance Driver, Male
Psychiatric Nurse and Policeman, and is described as 'I'd put them down as
giving service to the community, purposeful and necessary service. I could
link this group with [his 'professions'] as people who are interested in the
good and welfare of their fellow-men. I would keep them apart, because
[the first sub-group] have definitely had financial reward in mind before they
took these jobs, but [the professional pair] , I would say that they went for
that straight away. [The professional pair] are people who suddenly
realised they had a duty in life. They must have had a tendency in them to
want to serve the community. They weren't *just* looking for financial
rewards.' To summarise, it seems that Y242 (a Heating Engineer, whose
ordering was on the stated principle of 'importance to the community'),
places Ambulance Driver in a sub-group at the same level as Eye Surgeon,
even though he appreciates that there are important differences between
them. This is not to say that he (Y242) was unaware of the fact that an Eye
Surgeon earns more than an Ambulance Driver. It is of course, the essence of
a rank ordering that some information about differences is selected as being
important, and other information is ignored. At the time he made this weak
ordering of the occupational titles, Y242 was choosing to emphasise his
notion of 'importance to the community' above other possible bases for
comparison. (The third sub-group, by the way, contained Airline Pilot and
Railway Engine Driver.)

S164, a Sales Manager and Mechanical Engineer, is unusual in that he was
the only subject to place Trawler Deckhand in his first-ranked group (which
contained ten occupations). His stated criterion was the order of 'What I feel

is essential to society . . . in the economy we work in, rather than if these people were shipwrecked on an island'. Trawler Deckhand was placed in the first-ranked group along with Eye Surgeon, Geologist, Civil Engineer, Statistician, Railway Engine Driver, Airline Pilot, Male Psychiatric Nurse, Trawler Deckhand, and Computer Programmer. This group as a whole was dignified by the overall title, 'The foundations of society', (to distinguish it from other groups which were called the roof, bricks, mortar and plaster of society respectively). Trawler Deckhand and Male Psychiatric Nurse appear to have been included in the 'foundations' sub-group on the grounds that, 'They are both doing a very worthwhile job, both doing quite a dangerous job in their own ways. The rewards should be high.' He could also have carried out the grouping and ordering task on the different criterion of 'how important it is to be good at that particular job', but there was not time for this. On the point of defining what he meant by his phrase 'important to society', his view was: 'One can be considered more important to society than another person if an individual can prolong another individual's life and therefore his will to live, his self-respect, etc. [here referring to the Eye Surgeon] . My main reason for ranking people better than others is that these people have the drive, the honesty, the discipline to go for an academic qualification (for instance) and that qualification in itself being useful to society. By useful, I mean providing a continual employment for others, providing leadership qualities so that others, who don't have special discipline or drive, can earn a reasonable or good standard of living – and keeping the quality of life that we know today moving and perhaps improving.' Looking over his criteria, it seems that occupations that S164 sees as being in some sense 'demanding' of their incumbents are those that get into his first-ranked group.

G318, a Chartered Accountant, placed Taxi Driver into his first-ranked group, and was the only subject to do so. The basis of his ranking was to divide the occupations into five groups based on Risk-Taking and Type of Employment. The first-ranked group was called, 'Risk-takers, self-employed', and contained Eye Surgeon, Civil Engineer, Geologist, Plumber, Statistician, Chartered Accountant, Taxi Driver, Actor and Photographer. These people (that is, people in these 'self-employed' occupations) 'tend to be more individual and more interesting people'. G318 said that he would prefer to east lunch with these than with the rest. (See above for further discussion of G318.)

From examining these weak orders of occupational titles, we draw the following conclusion:

(1)   Invidious comparison is not such a pervasive characteristic of occupation names that all our subjects found it natural to sort occupations on the basis of a 'more' or 'less' criterion. Only 32 of the 82 subjects who made sortings of occupations made spontaneous orderings of their groupings.

(2)   Our subjects were free to choose their own criteria of invidious
       comparison, and they used a variety of bases of judgement. The
       amount of training required for the job, its skill and its qualification
       levels were given as criteria for ordering by about half of those who
       made any ordering. A significant minority of the subjects used some
       version of 'social usefulness' or 'importance to society' as a basis
       for an ordering.

(3)   There was considerable variation in the number of evaluative
       categories that subjects found it natural to use. The number varied
       between two groups through eleven groups (into which to sort 32
       occupational titles), with the most popular number to use being
       five. The range of variation casts a certain doubt upon the notion
       (put forward by Nosanchuk), that occupations are readily and
       naturally classified into a fairly standardised number of strata.

DETAILED COMPARISONS BETWEEN INDIVIDUALS

More detailed comparisons of the weak orderings made by the respondents
can be made by taking them two at a time and examining each pair
separately. As an example, we present a comparison between the ordered
sortings of two subjects (S039 and Y349), both employed in 'managerial'
jobs, but one of whom (Y349) had been a motor mechanic before becoming
a service manager; the other (S039) being described by the interviewer as a
'confident "public-school" type'. For ease of reference, we shall call S039
'Jim', and Y349 'Ian'.

Jim's interviewer was of the opinion that he used 'qualifications and
social status' as his main criterion for ordering. The summary statement for
Ian was that he differentiated between groups mainly on the basis of
'overall degree of appeal and job-satisfaction'.

Interviewer's report on Jim (S039)

Before starting the sorting task he mentioned such criteria as 'monetary
reward', 'job satisfaction', 'status'. But when he actually sorted the cards, he
used many other criteria rather unsystematically. I found it very difficult to
obtain descriptions that applied to *All* occupations found in any one group.
He used 'status' a lot as a final classification but was not aware of doing so.

First: 'Highly qualified persons in whom one trusts; people with
enormous skills and responsibilities.'
     Chartered Accountant
     Airline Pilot
     Eye Surgeon

Second: 'People who can carry a fair amount of responsibilities, sometimes rather underpaid' [implicitly of fairly high status] .
     Computer Programmer

Actor
Sales Manager

Third: 'People whose competence, status, usefulness, vary very widely.'
Civil Engineer
Photographer
Journalist

Fourth: 'People who made a direct contribution to society and have
responsibilities as individuals in their jobs.'
Secondary School Teacher
Primary School Teacher
Minister of Religion
Male Psychiatric Nurse
Ambulance Driver
Policeman
Postman

Fifth: 'People who serve a function, without much reward or prospects
for improvement in status.' [He thought of promoting Social Worker to the
fourth group because of its potential status in the future, but decided not
to.]
Statistician
Social Worker
Geologist
Taxi Driver
Bus Conductor

Sixth: 'People with some skill and responsibility.'
Garage Mechanic
Railway Engine Driver
Barman
Restaurant Cook
Laboratory Technician
Carpenter
Building Site Labourer
Plumber

Seventh: 'Low-paid, not very qualified people, who learn on the job but
have not taken the opportunity of increasing themselves.'
Bank Clerk
Unskilled Machine Operator
Trawler Deckhand

Interviewer's report on Ian (Y349)
Overall degree of job satisfaction emerged as the main criterion of
differentiation into 8 groups. The bottom three were all described as

unappealing and it was difficult to elicit the reasons for keeping them
apart — promotion, prospects, wages and training were finally
mentioned as the distinguishing features. Job satisfaction also formed the
basis for ordering the groups.

First: 'Specialised jobs, years of training, very high level of satisfaction.'

They're all specialised jobs, they've got to be specialised. I'd say a lot of
training, you'd have to be a few years at it. You'd probably take this
group first of all. There must be an awful lot of satisfaction at the end of
the day in doing that job [Eye Surgeon] operating on someone. Airline
Pilot — it must have its appeal, travelling to any part of the world, and
to handle a big machine like that. Laboratory Technician and Geologist
must do a lot of work and not get any credit for it. It's usually the man
at the top who gets his name on the paper.

> Airline Pilot
> Eye Surgeon
> Laboratory Technician
> Geologist

Second: 'Enjoyable jobs, scope for promotion.'
These must rate as the best jobs: there's quite a lot of scope there for
promotion. I would think these would be enjoyable jobs. Second, on
job satisfaction, they appeal to me. A certain amount of pleasure out of
those jobs as well.

> Chartered Accountant
> Civil Engineer

Third: 'Responsible jobs, acquired through experience rather than formal
training.'
You work up through stages, you build up to be these. It's not so much
training as experience more than anything. I think they're responsible
jobs, you've got a lot on your hands. I would take these 3 next because of the
responsibility. Responsible . . . a certain amount of trust in these jobs.

> Railway Engine Driver
> Postman
> Policeman

Fourth: 'Helping people, a lot of satisfaction.'
Obviously they deal with groups . . . they deal with people mainly.
Persons who help people . . . a lot of satisfaction . . . to see the end product
coming out.

> Minister of Religion
> Social Worker
> Primary School Teacher
> Secondary School Teacher

Fifth: 'Trades, time-served. High satisfaction because they are useful.'

These are the only ones (in the sample) where you have to serve time, what used to be five years, now you serve four years to qualify for these jobs. They're all what I think of as lowly paid. From the apprentice point of view, they're cheap labour. The basic rate is very low, it's all payment over the rate and bonuses that make up the wages.

I would take these next for the satisfaction of being able to do things. A Plumber can mend things, a Garage Mechanic again. A Carpenter, you can do it at your work and do it at home. Useful, all three of them.

Carpenter
Garage Mechanic
Plumber

Sixth: 'Unappealing jobs, but with some scope for promotion. Better wages than the following group.

There is a lot of promotion scope there but they don't appeal to me [different from Group 7] . . . because there's a lot more ability than Group 7. These two only come next because their wages come before the rest [i.e. the following groups] . There is room for promotion but I think it would be rather slow. The Bank Clerk does have some perks — mortgage, rates, etc.

Bank Clerk
Journalist

Seventh: 'Little training and little appeal.'

I wouldn't want to be any of these people, they just don't have any appeal [different from Group 6 because the latter have more training] . You don't need any training to be a Sales Manager. A small amount of training, you could be a Photographer. The rest are the same. None of them just don't appeal to me. [See also comments for Group 8.] Little training and little appeal.

Male Psychiatric Nurse
Photographer
Sales Manager
Restaurant Cook
Computer Programmer
Actor

Eighth and last: 'Dead-end jobs, no prospects.'

What's a Statistician? I suppose like in these national opinion polls: they go around the streets asking questions — somebody in like your own capacity? There doesn't seem to be anything in these jobs at the end of the day. You can't work up — dead-end jobs. They are different from Group 7 because there you can move up. You can advance in Group 7. Well, all these . . . I think just about *anyone* could do these: anybody that's not got a trade, these jobs are what they're landed with. If I had a choice of jobs these would be the last ones I'd take. These are dead-end jobs, no prospects at all.

Taxi Driver
Trawler Deckhand
Bus Conductor
Ambulance Driver
Statistician
Building Site Labourer
Barman
Unskilled Machine Operator

To what extent do these two men agree in their ordering of the 32 occupational titles? They both place Airline Pilot and Eye Surgeon in their highest-ranked group, and they agree in that they both place Trawler Deckhand and Unskilled Machine Operator in their lowest-ranked group. But there is also some disagreement: for example, Ian places Geologist in his highest-ranked group, while Jim places it in his fifth-ranking group. This can be verified from the interview summaries shown above, but it is more easily seen from the cross-tabulation of the two subjects' weak orderings of the 32 occupational titles which is shown as Table 4.2. The vertical axis of this table is divided into seven rows, each corresponding to one of Jim's grouping. The topmost row corresponds to Jim's highest group – and so on down to the seventh row, which corresponds to his bottom group of what he called, 'low-paid, not very qualified people' (Unskilled Machine Operator, Trawler Deckhand and Bank Clerk).

The horizontal axis of the table is used to represent the weak ordering of the occupational titles made by Ian. The eight groups he chose to use are ordered on the table so that his highest group is on the far right, and his lowest group (what he called 'dead-end jobs') is on the far left.

The tabulating of seven rows (for Jim) by eight columns (for Ian) yields Table 4.2, which has 56 cells. One can detect a clustering of occupations in the bottom left. These are occupations that are ranked low by both subjects. Similarly, there are three occupations which are ranked high by both subjects in the top left of the table. However, there are also occupations which occupy cells towards the top left or the bottom right of the table, and these are occupations about which there is disagreement. They are classified relatively high by one subject, but relatively low by the other.

Disagreement of this kind might be explained in a number of ways (and those to be mentioned are not mutually exclusive). It might be that one subject happens to order the occupations upon one criterion (say income), while the other happens to order them on a different criterion (say educational requirements). This might be so even though both subjects were capable of ordering the occupations in the same way on either criterion. An alternative possibility is that the subjects disagree about the meaning (reference) of one or more of the occupational titles. In the example under consideration, Jim and Ian seem to disagree about the meaning (reference) of the occupational title Statistician. Finally, there remains the possibility that the subjects have precisely the same criterion of ordering in mind (say social status), and

TABLE 4.2   Cross-sorting of weak orderings

Group:		8	7	6	5	4	3	2	1	
Group:	1							CA	AP ESG	1
	2		CP ACT SMG							2
	3		PHT	JN				CE		3
	4	AD	MPN			SST MOR PST	PM PO			4
	5	ST TDR BCR				SW			GEO	5
	6	BM BSL	RCK		GM		RED		LT	6
	7	UMO TDH		BCK						7
		8	7	6	5	4	3	2	1	

S 039 (left) · *S039* (right)

Y 349 (top) · *Y 349* (bottom)

GAMMA = 0.31
TAU-b = 0.28

32 Occupational Titles: Abbreviations
CA Chartered Accountant; GM Garage Mechanic; ST Statistician; C Carpenter;
CPR Computer Programmer; PL Plumber; BCK Bank Clerk; UMO Unskilled
Machine Operator; CE Civil Engineer; BSL Building Site Labourer;
AP Airline Pilot; RED Railway Engine Driver; GEO Geologist;
TDH Trawler Deckhand; ESG Eye Surgeon; LT Laboratory Technician;
SST Secondary School Teacher; BM Barman; SW Social Worker;
AD Ambulance Driver; MOR Minister of Religion; MPN Male Psychiatric
Nurse; PST Primary School Teacher; PM Policeman; PHT Photographer;
RCK Restaurant Cook; A Actor; PO Postman; SMG Sales Manager; TDR Taxi
Driver; JN Journalist; BC Bus Conductor.

agree about the nature of this criterion as well as about the meanings
(reference) of the occupational titles they were judging; but honestly
disagree about the meanings (connotation) of the occupational titles.

   It is interesting to find some quantitative measure of the degree to which
one ordered classification of occupations is similar to another. For example,
suppose that three people, whom we may call Brown, Jones and Smith, have

each sorted the same set of occupations into groups, and then have ordered
these groups. In this situation, it would be helpful to have some objective
method of evaluating the truth of a statement such as: 'Brown and Jones
have pretty similar weak orderings of the occupations, but neither of these
is very like Smith's weak ordering.'

In the case where we have two different rank orderings of the same set of
occupations, the rank correlation between them is an obvious index of their
similarity. Since each ordering contained many ties (because the subjects rank
ordered groups of occupations), the Goodman-Kruskal gamma coefficient
is an appropriate index of agreement between a pair of weak orderings. Like
many coefficients of association, gamma has an upper limit of 1.0 denoting
perfect agreement, with a value of 0.0 indicating the complete absence of any
relationship. Negative values indicate disagreement. Gamma is technically
described as an index of weakly monotonic agreement. When it is compared
with coefficients such as Kendall's tau-b, gamma is usually found to be
larger in absolute terms when computed over the same data. As an example,
we may take Table 4.2 where the ordering of Jim is tabulated across that of
Ian. The value of gamma between these two weak orderings is 0.31 while the
value of tau-b is 0.28. Clearly the orderings made by Jim and Ian are in some
agreement, though it is by no means complete agreement.

In the same way as for Jim and Ian it is possible to compute a gamma
coefficient for each of all pairs of the 33 orderings of the 32 occupational
titles. These gamma coefficients (multiplied by one hundred, rounded, and
with the decimal point omitted) are shown in Table 4.3, which conveniently
summarises the extent of agreement and disagreement between the 33 weak
orders. Even a cursory inspection of the lower triangular matrix of gamma
coefficients shows that one subject (Y326, a master jeweller) is unlike the
majority. Indeed only six out of the 32 comparisons with other subjects
yield positive gamma coefficients, and several of these are practically zero.

Excluding Y326 from consideration for a moment, there are only two
negative gamma coefficients out of the 496 which is the total number of pairs
that can be examined between the 32 remaining subjects. Only 9 of the 496
gamma coefficients reach the value of unity which denotes perfect (weak
monotonic) agreement. However, the overall picture that we gain from the
lower triangular matrix of gamma coefficients is one of fair agreement between
most pairs of subjects. Apart from Y326, the Master Jeweller, the subjects
who have little in common with the majority are Y242, a Heating Engineer,
and (to a lesser extent) G318, a Chartered Accountant.

The Master Jeweller appears to be the closest approximation we have to
Young and Willmott's famous 'upside-downers'. Clearly, this man's reasonings
ought to be worth a little close attention. He took 35 minutes over the task of
sorting the 32 occupational titles into ten groups and then ordering those
groups. His arrangement was idiosyncratic, but coherent and internally
consistent. The rationale he stated was 'the contribution of what I think is
important'. His ordered groups (from highest to lowest) were as follows:

TABLE 4.3 Goodman-Kruskal gamma coefficients between ordered sortings of 32 occupational titles
(times one hundred, rounded, no decimal point)

No.	Title	1	2	3	4	5	6	7	8	9	10	11	12	13	14	15	16	17	18	19	20	21	22	23	24	25	26	27	28	29	30	31	32
1	S039																																
2	Y349	31																															
3	D365	56	55																														
4	Y380	48	59	97																													
5	Y381	37	57	72	83																												
6	Y060	64	46	74	82	50																											
7	Y242	15	41	32	43	52	3																										
8	Y248	34	45	61	67	34	57	27																									
9	Y035	72	62	90	100	79	91	41	64																								
10	Y935	59	45	71	96	65	71	36	54	78																							
11	Y070	35	56	78	81	75	68	37	68	83	71																						
12	Y139	73	50	76	69	52	76	25	42	88	62	62																					
13	Y326	−24	16	−24	−24	1	−28	30	−17	−46	−18	−6	−22																				
14	S161	63	49	92	90	55	86	14	52	94	71	63	80	−31																			
15	S220	55	47	80	86	71	65	55	54	90	70	59	59	−10	69																		
16	S164	34	50	58	72	62	56	57	52	74	69	73	44	3	46	62																	
17	S017	69	46	83	76	55	80	17	56	84	68	69	74	−35	85	64	59																
18	S028	63	54	95	98	69	92	22	58	100	74	74	79	−30	97	80	64	59															
19	C304	41	49	84	91	60	69	36	55	92	64	68	87	−25	78	82	59	86	84														
20	Y007	64	50	88	90	64	89	23	61	100	72	72	58	−27	88	73	68	59	84	97													
21	S029	61	50	91	94	69	77	23	52	98	74	78	79	−31	89	66	84	80	87	94	78												
22	S061	54	54	91	100	68	90	24	60	100	78	78	76	−32	80	71	73	68	87	99	79	89											
23	Y384	27	48	55	58	40	55	7	45	60	53	54	50	3	95	57	44	33	38	54	63	47	96										
24	Y385	54	54	85	93	67	85	30	44	93	73	60	75	−30	84	76	50	45	91	84	89	76	57	60									
25	SW08	71	54	95	94	67	83	36	55	95	80	72	90	−22	77	74	76	61	82	99	86	94	53	94	88								
26	C299	42	62	90	97	60	83	5	75	100	74	83	67	−27	86	89	73	82	97	94	87	86	60	89	92	90							
27	G292	78	59	88	96	76	76	55	55	100	72	79	84	−35	96	88	53	63	94	86	91	85	94	76	94	93	94						
28	F294	66	38	70	65	40	65	−7	45	75	56	50	73	−23	87	53	30	73	100	87	70	51	48	48	48	75	70	86					
29	A306	23	77	62	42	54	39	65	62	57	38	57	46	−21	50	65	87	69	75	75	82	81	83	90	43	70	90	52	73				
30	Y033	47	61	86	88	72	72	40	63	97	66	81	59	−30	65	54	78	60	82	59	80	49	56	49	90	95	94	67	84	59			
31	C295	62	50	86	90	61	89	10	57	95	69	76	75	−9	69	65	84	81	94	71	85	52	51	54	88	94	89	90	95	84	86		
32	G318	26	11	43	43	15	59	−48	29	30	22	30	41	−48	48	27	41	40	52	57	27	41	45	15	47	40	41	36	59	67	54	47	
33	F315	68	51	83	88	65	73	37	57	96	82	73	79	−25	74	69	83	86	82	80	69	89	78	72	85	43	75	69	84	73	57	82	26

First, Geologist
He comes first: without him, you have really nothing to start on. He
would find the coal or the oil. He starts the chain.

Second, Trawler Deckhand
         Taxi Driver
         Airline Pilot
         Railway Engine Driver
         Postman
Without travel you'd be stuck in one place. [Postman added last because
'he walks a lot'.]

Third,   Unskilled Machine Operator
         Garage Mechanic
         Civil Engineer
All to do with engineering — metalwork . . . The engineers can make from
turbines to anything.

Fourth, Eye Surgeon
         Ambulance Driver
         Laboratory Technician
         Male Psychiatric Nurse
If you don't have the health, you're again confined to your place where
you're born.

Fifth,   Plumber
         Carpenter
         Building Site Labourer
         Bus Conductor
All tradesmen, to do with building. They're essential for keeping the
people housed.

Sixth,   Primary School Teacher
         Secondary School Teacher
         Teachers — we need education.

Seventh, Minister of Religion
         Police Policeman
         Social Social Worker
The police we need to keep law and order. The other two come into it as
well.

Eighth, Restaurant Cook
         Barman
They serve the public.

Ninth,   Photographer
         Actor
         Journalist

They are connected with each other in their employment . . . contribution to entertaining and social life.

Tenth,   Chartered Accountant
           Bank Clerk
           Computer Programmer
           Statistician
           Sales Manager

All to do with figures: they are concerned with money, with value. . . .
Last of all comes money.

With his ordered groups displayed, it is much easier to see why the Master Jeweller appears to be in disagreement with the majority. Clearly he has grouped the occupations in terms of a mixture of common function (like the industry classification of the British Census) and of on-the-job interaction. (For example, 'You've got to have the Photographer for photographing the Actor; the Journalist is describing what's happening through the medium of the paper.') His major idiosyncracy lies in his very low evaluation of occupations to do with figures and money and it is this which probably accounts for his negative gamma coefficients with other subjects.

The conclusions we draw from looking at between-person correlations (gamma coefficients) are that a moderate to high amount of agreement exists between interviewees who have sorted occupational titles on their own evaluative criteria — the disagreements which arise clearly do so because of different interpretations of the meaning (in the sense of reference) of unfamiliar occupations, or because of the use of varieties of 'usefulness to society' evaluative criteria, which assign low positions to occupations whose roles are not obviously in any kind of direct productive or service function. Agreement seems to arise from common usage of attributes such as educational qualifications and latent classifications such as 'professional' by different respondents.

4.3 GEOMETRIC MODELS FOR INVIDIOUS COMPARISON

In the previous section, we devoted considerable space to descriptions of the orderings that our subjects saw fit to make, and to their reasons for making them. There was abundant evidence of disagreement about orderings of occupations, but it was difficult to make any satisfactory description of the variety and extent of this disagreement. In order to discuss individual differences in judgements of this kind, it is necessary to have in mind some formal model of the cognitive and/or evaluative process. More than this, it is necessary to have a formal model which explicitly makes provision for certain kinds of disagreement, (or individual differences). If we are prepared to assume that our individual subjects' orderings of occupations are not too distorted by summarising them as linear or weak orderings (at the individual level), then some powerful and tractable geometric models are available.

One model well known to psychologists is Clyde Coombs' 'Unfolding' scheme, which explains variation in subjects' rank orderings of social stimuli as arising from the different locations of subjects in the social structure. A representation is therefore sought where both the judged (the occupational titles) and judges (the subjects) are represented in the same structure, or 'occupational space'. Coombs puts the basic notion rather well:

> A significant characteristic of joint spaces [i.e. a space in which there are points corresponding both to stimuli and individuals] is that they are constructed by putting together pieces from different individuals (and/or from different stimuli). The relations of an object in one set to the elements in the other set provide one view, one perspective, one image, one transformation, of the total space. A model specifies what this transformation is, and provides an algorithm by means of which a common space may be generated (Coombs 1964:549).

INTERNAL ANALYSIS BY VECTOR AND DISTANCE MODELS

The two basic models which meet Coombs' requirement are the *vector model* (where stimuli are represented by points, and individual orderings by a directed line) and the *distance model* (where both stimuli and individuals are represented by points and the relative distance between a subject's point and the stimulus points represents the individual ordering).

(i) *The vector model*
The vector model assumes that a subject's rank ordering (of preference, similarity etc.) is a decreasing (usually linear) function of separation between the vectors:

$$S_{ij} = F(\sum_a y_{ia} x_{ja})$$

where the x_{ja} define a *stimulus vector* (from the origin of the space to stimulus j, and the y_{ia} define the (unit length) *vector of individual i*. The individual i's scale value, or 'utility' for stimulus j (S_{ij}) is therefore equal to the (scalar) product of the appropriate stimulus vector with the individual's vector.

In its unidimensional form this is too restrictive a model to be of any interest, as all subjects must have either the same ordering or its mirror-image, since a one-dimensional space (line) cannot, by definition, accommodate any other line or vector at an angle to it. (However, a vector can be directed in either of the two opposite directions along the line, and one vector will give the reverse ordering to the other.) As a multidimensional model it is best known in its metric form as Tucker's (1963) 'Points of View Analysis', and as Carroll and Chang's (1964) Nonparametric Multidimensional Analysis of Pair Comparisons (MDPREF) model. The latter vector model is illustrated in Figure 4.2, where the 20 possible subject-orderings (I-scales) generated from a two-dimensional configuration of five points are illustrated. A vector model portrays an individual as a line directed to the *most preferred region* in the stimulus space. When the stimuli are projected on to this line, the order of the projections corresponds to the subject's ranking of the stimuli.[4]

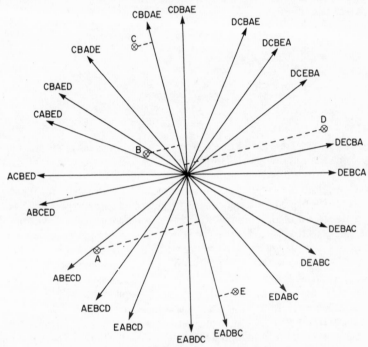

Fig. 4.2 Illustration of vector model

(5 stimulus points in 2 dimensions, generating 20 I-scale vectors)

The properties of the vector model are as follows:[5]

(1)   *Monotonicity.* For a given rank order (I-scale), an individual's preference 'increases monotonically with the object's loading on any attribute. The further out on the individual's line a stimulus projects, the more it is preferred.' (Coombs: 200)

(2)   *Mediocrity.* The model allows that some stimuli may never be *most* preferred, nor *least* preferred either (e.g. stimulus B in Fig. 4.2 is never most preferred, nor least preferred).

(3)   *Reversibility* (which is a consequence of Monotonicity). If a given
       rank-ordering occurs, then this *entails* the possibility of occurence of
       its mirror-image scale. A consequence of this is that all isotonic
       regions (each generating a unique ranking) are open and meet at the
       origin of the space.[6]

(ii) *The Distance model*

The distance model assumes that a subject's rank-ordering of stimuli (in
terms of preference, similarity etc.) is a decreasing (usually monotone)
function of the distance between the location of his ideal point i and the
location of stimulus j:

$$S_{ij} = F(d_{ij})$$

The generalised distance function is given by:

$$d_{ij} = (\underset{a}{\Sigma} |x_{ia} - y_{ja}|r)\, l/r$$

In the case of preference data, the matrix $\|x_{ia}\|$ represents the configuration of
stimulus points and the matrix $\|y_{ja}\|$ gives the location of the subject's (ideal)
points of greatest preference in the same space. In its unidimensional form,
Coombs' Unfolding Analysis is the most relevant distance model for the
analysis of rankings. In this model, an individual ordering is represented as
lying in a *segment* of the stimulus scale where the rank order of the distances
to the stimuli is the same. These notions generalise naturally to the multidimensional case, where an individual ordering is represented as an 'isotonic
region' of the space, where a particular rank-order of distance holds between
the stimuli and all individual 'ideal' points in that region. (See Good and
Tideman (1976) for a discussion of social science applications of the
distance model for representing preferences.)

When interpreted strictly as a substantive theory of human information-
processing, the distance function defining the model makes extremely strong
assumptions about how information is combined into a similarity judgement.
It implies that the subject has compared each pair of stimuli in terms of how
the stimuli differ on each dimension, and has then combined this information
into a final overall measure by a complex summative rule. In particular
(see Beals *et al.* 1968: 133-5) it asserts (by reference to the general distance
function above).

(i)   the absolute differences on each dimension (a)
(ii)   which are transformed by the same power function (r),
(iii)   combine in an additive manner
(iv)   to produce the overall distance measure between a pair of points.

In judgements of occupational prestige the task that the subject is supposed to perform is generally defined without reference to any specific attribute (indeed, it is viewed as the purpose of *analysis* to infer the dimensions), and these propositions can only be viewed as the coin paid to achieve a metric solution.

In effect, these four propositions form a theory of *how* subjects combine information into overall impressions or judgements, which is very akin to impression-formation theory in social psychology. However, the propositions advanced there have the advantage of being much weaker than those of the distance model, and tend to be restricted to straightforward summative, additive, and difference models (Anderson 1962, 1968). Almost no empirical evidence exists at present on how judgements about occupations are in fact made, and what theory there is almost entirely borrowed from impression-formation and cognitive consistency theories.[7]

IS PSYCHOLOGICAL SPACE EUCLIDEAN?

A further proposition assumed (at least by default) in the vast majority of analyses of occupational judgements is that the distance function is Euclidean. Apart from its greater familiarity (and possibly its greater robustness) there seems little compelling reason to accept it for occupational judgement data.[8]

The data-collection tasks usually specified for prestige-judgement require the subject to make quick decisions and simple judgements about a relatively large number of occupations. But there is reason to suppose that the Euclidean metric may well be the worst choice to make in this circumstance. The evidence for this is at present rather sketchy and analogical, but there is enough to make a good deal of sense of some of the more puzzling aspects of prestige data. Arnold (1971) has reported an experimental study of ratings of the semantic dissimilarity between words drawn from various word-classes, and he proceeds to test between the information-processing consequences which follow from the use of different Minkowski metrics.[9]

He concludes:

> The clearest finding was that semantic distance associated with judgments of similarity is not Euclidean. The evidence strongly suggests that, in forming a dissimilarity judgment, differences are suppressed on all dimensions *except the one that maximally* discriminates the members of a concept pair (ibid.: 349, emphasis added).

Whilst the Euclidean metric makes very strong assumptions about the information processing involved in making prestige judgements, the dominance metric (to which Arnold here refers) corresponds rather well to such a data-collection situation. As *r*-metrics approximate more closely to the dominance metric, the largest single component distance comes to dominate all others in determining the overall distance. Arnold interprets this as describing 'the output of a mechanism designed to make quick decisions about the similarities among objects that contain too much information to retain and process at once'. In information-processing terms, this is a perfectly understandable procedure:

> The rule for combining component dissimilarities into overall dissimilarities on pairs of concepts . . . appears to be 'consider the largest component distance and forget the others' (ibid.: 871).

Arnold goes on to point out that this may be considered a usefully adaptive procedure for two reasons — the largest component distance provides a least lower bound for the overall distance, and a single component distance may correspond to Miller's (1956) 'chunk' of information — remaining stable long enough to allow pairwise comparisons to be made. Sherman (1970: 12) and Hyman and Well (1967: 233) give an interpretation of the dominance metric which is similar to Arnold's but which is even more relevant to prestige judgement:

> The more component dimensions interact, the more the Minkowski exponent . . . will tend toward infinity . . . and [come to be] based on one *nondistinct* but dominant dimension of the stimulus (Sherman: 13).

In a similar vein, Shepard (1964) has documented the

> striking inability of subjects to take account of the independent way in which the objects vary along the different dimensions. Instead, there seems to be an overwhelming desire to collapse all dimensions into a single 'good versus bad' dimension with an attendant loss in detailed information about the configuration or pattern of attributes unique to any one object (264).

This is notably in contrast to the remarkable ability of humans to *extract* a manageable and relevant set of attributes from exceedingly complex phenomena.

The parallel with the 'unidimensionality' of occupational prestige (inferred from rating data) is notable. It is particularly relevant that the data-collection process itself should be pinpointed as the source of these characteristics, for it suggests that different methods which are more attuned to the analytic rather than the synthesising aspects of information-processing will differentiate and break up the apparently Procrustean nature of occupational prestige.[10]

This point should not be overemphasised, nor should it be thought that the argument is being made that occupational judgements are *always* complex. People may well use such a convenient and fast procedure in socially significant encounters. The point is rather that to *ask* subjects to make very general assessments of worth is to trade upon one of man's most notable deficiencies — to synthesise and combine multifaceted information into overall assessments. More directly, the nature of the data-collection process itself significantly affects inferences drawn from the data. In particular, *data obtained from simple ratings by no means provide unequivocal evidence of the essential simplicity of occupational judgments.*[11]

PROPERTIES OF THE DISTANCE MODEL

Three directly testable properties of the distance model have been singled out as particularly relevant to MDS models:

(1) *Single-Peakedness* (or 'boundedness'). Each individual has only one point of maximum preference, and the preference function is symmetric (see Luce and Raiffa (1957). It is because of this assumption that an individual's I-scale can be decomposed into pairwise distances, on the assumption that the subject will always prefer the most proximate of any two stimuli.

(2) *Excellence.* If the distance model holds, then each stimulus must necessarily be most preferred by at least one subject. (The vector model does not require this.)

(3) For the distance model, no property corresponds to the reversibility of all I-scales in the vector model. In the unidimensional case, *only one* pair of reverse orderings (Coombs' I-scale) is permissible, which, as in the unidimensional vector model, defines the order of the stimuli. In higher dimensional space, several (but always less than half) mirror-image pairs are permissible, and correspond to pairs of open isotonic regions.

IMPLICATIONS OF DISTANCE AND VECTOR MODELS FOR PRESTIGE DATA

How do these properties distinguish the two models? What other implications are there for the empirical and theoretical analysis of prestige orderings?

The most obvious difference is on the monotonicity *v.* single-peakedness characteristic. The vector models assume that subjects simplify the 'complexity' of the space by projecting the stimuli on to a single line, which points in the direction of highest evaluation. The distance model, by contrast, assumes that different linear orderings (I-scales) represent distinct 'local neighbourhoods of consensus' in a space which remains multidimensional in form.

The vector model assumptions seem to reflect most closely the 'high consensus' interpretation of occupational prestige, where occupational perception (whilst conceivably multidimensional) is believed to be entirely dominated by a single prestige factor.[12]

More specifically, if subjects are reporting on some consensual cultural *ordering,* then a two-dimensional configuration should be adequate, with subjects' I-vectors only slightly separated, and oriented towards the high-prestige end of the major axis. There should therefore only be slight individual variation on the prestige continuum, and the angle of separation between subject vectors (and between them and the prestige axis) should be small, denoting its high importance in the subject's judgements. It is worth noting, however, that the vector model could certainly not allow for the considerable dissensus over evaluation of occupations in the middle range of the prestige 'continuum' which is very characteristic of rating-scale prestige data (see Reiss 1961: 54-71; see also Hunter 1977).

The vector and distance models differ also in terms of the form which the individual's evaluation (or preference) function is assumed to take, and neither alternative is entirely satisfactory in analysing prestige data. The vector model assumes that evaluation increases (monotonically) with the dimension concerned – put idiomatically, 'the more the better'. By contrast, the distance model assumes that there exists a *unique* most preferred point for each individual or each dimension – 'I know what I like, and enough is enough'. In general, few properties seem to satisfy this assumption of the vector model although for occupational evaluation, it may be defensible over the usual range of judgement.

The distance model is a suitable model for the analysis of occupational rankings if it can be assumed that an individual's report of prestige is a monotonic function of the distances which separate an individual's 'own' point, and those representing the set of occupational titles. Some ambiguity resides in the notion of a subject's 'own' point. Put in the context of evaluating occupations, it could be construed as referring either to the location of the subject's *own* job, or to the location of some 'ideal' job, or it could refer to a consensual structure viewed from the location of the highest-esteemed occupation. If the first or second interpretations hold, then the conditional nature of the proximity judgement task must be made clear to the subject, or a mixture of absolute and relative distance estimates will be obtained preventing any consistent meaning being attached to ideal-point locations, and thereby destroying the purpose of the exercise.

In the case of absolute distances, all are taken from a common origin and are therefore directly comparable. If distances are measured from differently-located ideal points, then they will not be comparable.

If the third interpretation holds, then this effectively excludes the use of the distance model, for all ideal points will cluster at the highest point of the prestige dimension, and – as in the vector model – this lack of variability will prevent any metric information being obtained. A final consideration about the nature of ideal points is that it is quite conceivable that on some dimensions of occupational judgement the assumption that there is one *most preferred* point does not hold, and in this case it may be more realistic to postulate an 'anti-ideal' of single *least-preferred* point. An instance of this is where a person highly evaluates an occupation which has a very high degree of authority and also favours an occupation almost entirely free of authority, but most dislikes a 'middle-man' job, where authority is simply delegated, and where he would be restricted to implementing others' decisions. This complication need not detain us at present, although it has been incorporated in at least one distance model of preference judgement (Carroll 1972).

Finally, it may be thought that an important distinguishing feature of the two models is that the vector model implies the existence of *only* mirror-image I-scales (by virtue of the mediocrity and reversibility properties) whereas the distance model implies that I-scales *without* mirror-images may exist in the data. Roskam (1968:101) and others have pointed out that this is not a distinguishing characteristic as it stands — it simply implies the *necessary* absence in the vector model of closed isotonic regions.[13]

In this sense, the vector model can be viewed as a special, more restrictive, case of the distance model. There is a further sense in which the vector model is a special case of the distance model. Carroll (1972: 16) shows that the rank order of distances between a subject's ideal point located *at infinity* and the stimuli points is equal (in the limit) to the order of projections of the stimuli points on an ideal preference *vector* terminating at the same ideal point. Coombs (1964: 200) and Roskam (1968: 102) have argued a similar point — that the vector model 'constrains the data to I-scales that are compatible with infinite ideal points, where the distance model does not'.

EXTERNAL ANALYSIS OF DATA

We have seen that the unfolding models of preference (both distance and vector models) assume that subjects agree in their cognition of the objects being judged, and also assume that the source of individual variability is the different *evaluations* which subjects give to the dimensions of the cognitive structure. However, if subjects differ in their perceptions of the stimuli as well as in their evaluations of them, then an unfolding analysis will never be able to recover the cognitive space correctly, and it will never be possible to decide whether the reason for the badness of fit is due to differential perception, or to the fact that the distance model is not appropriate. To mirror this fact Carroll (1972) proposed a distinction between models for the *internal* analysis of preference data such as Coombsian unfolding (where both stimuli *and* subjects are parameterised from the same set of preference data) and *external* analysis (where the preference data are fitted in an *independently* derived space). In many cases of preference analysis, an independent set of judgements of similarity between the stimuli made by the same subjects can be scaled to obtain such an *a priori* cognitive space, and this is precisely what we shall do in section 4.6.[14]

Carroll (1972) developed a hierarchy of four external models for 'preference mapping' (collectively referred to as PREFMAP) which both generalises and particularises Coombs' Unfolding distance model for mapping preference data:

Phase (Level)	Name of Model	MODEL ALLOWS		
		Differential rotation of axes	Differential weighting of axes	Differential location of ideal points
I	General Unfolding	+	+	+
II	Weighted Unfolding	–	+	+
III	Simple Unfolding (Coombs)	–	–	+
IV	Vector	–	–	–

The preference scale values of individual i for stimulus j are assumed to be a linear function of the distances between his ideal point y_i and the stimuli locations x_j:

$$s_{ij} = F(d_{ij}^2) = a_i + bd_{ij}^2 + e_{ij} \ (b \geqslant 0)$$

The four models or levels of the PREFMAP hierarchy are distinguished in terms of how the distances d_{ij}^2 are defined. In Phase I subjects are permitted

(i)   to rotate the reference dimensions of the space, and
(ii)   *then* differentially weight them.

In Carroll's terms

> we allow distinct individuals additional freedom in choosing a set of 'reference axes' . . . and then to weight differentially the dimensions defined by this rotated reference frame, in addition to being permitted an idiosyncratic ideal point (Carroll 1972: 120).

A subject is assumed to apply his *own* orthogonal rotation T_i to both the stimulus and ideal point coordinates, and then weight the rotated dimensions. If $\|x_{ja}^*\|$ represents such transformed stimulus coordinates and $\|y_{ia}^*\|$ the transformed ideal points, then

$$s_{ij} = F_i\,(d_{ij}^2)$$

where

$$d_{ij}^2 = \Sigma_a w_{ia}\,(y_{ia}^* - x_{ja}^*)^2,$$

i.e. a Euclidean distance in an individually-rotated and weighted 'private space'.

In Phase II a subject is assumed to apply an *evaluative* weight w_{ia} to each dimension, so that

$$s_{ij} = F_i\,(d_{ij}^2)$$

where now,

$$d_{ij}^2 = \Sigma_a w_{ia}\,(y_{ia} - x_{ja})^2,$$

i.e. a Euclidean distance in a weighted 'private space'.

In Phase III — the simple Coombsian Unfolding case — subjects are each represented by an ideal (most preferred) point in the cognitive space. The greater the proximity of a stimulus to an individual's ideal point, the more he will prefer it. A given difference on a particular dimension is assumed in this model to have the same meaning and contribute identically to the overall distance for every subject.

$$s_{ij} = F_i\,(d_{ij}^2)$$

where now,

$$d_{ij}^2 = \Sigma_a\,(y_{ia} - x_{ja})^2,$$

i.e. the usual Euclidean distance metric.

In Phase IV, the preferences are assumed to be a simple linear function of the stimuli values:

$$s_{ij} = a_i + \Sigma_a b_{ia} x_{ja}$$

and this becomes the *external* analogue to the vector model encountered earlier.[15]

Since in the metric version of the PREFMAP models a subject's preferences are assumed to be linearly related to the (weighted, transformed or simple) distances between the stimuli locations and his ideal point, product-moment correlations between a subject's preference values and those estimated in terms of a particular model can be calculated to provide a useful measure of individual goodness of fit. Moreover, since each model is a special case of the higher one in the hierarchy, it is possible to use variance analysis to test whether the more general model explains a significantly greater amount of variation than the more particular one.[16]

4.4 THE EVALUATIVE MAP: ILLUSTRATIVE EXAMPLES OF INTERNAL ANALYSIS

Some readers may have found the algebra in the preceding pages to be somewhat tedious. If it is indeed useful to represent rank-order data with either vector or distance varieties of the general unfolding model, then it might be argued that the proof of the pudding should be in the eating. The vector or distance models ought to help the sociologist to make a sensible scaling of occupational titles and of the people who rank-order them.

We shall use analyses of a small set of occupational titles in order to illustrate the models. This set consists of eleven titles of the type found in official occupational classifications. In this case, they were selected from the (British) Registrar-General's *Classification of Occupations*. They were deliberately chosen from the very large number of occupational titles listed therein so that:

(i)   They would refer to 'identifiable work tasks'.
(ii)   They would be of approximately the same general social status.
(iii)   They would contain several specifications of detail within the same overall umbrella-title.

A set of 12 task-specific, socio-economically homogeneous occupational titles were chosen by means of a stratified random sample from four occupational Unit Groups within the Registrar-General's Socio-Economic Group V (Intermediate non-manual workers in Social Class II (non-manual)) (*Classification of Occupations* 1966: 140). Due to an error, the twelfth title was omitted from the computer-generated schedule. Hence our example deals with only eleven occupational titles.

These eleven titles were:

I   X-ray Operator
II   Newswriter
III   Scriptwriter
IV   Technical writer
V   Deputy Area Officer (Government)
VI   Higher Clerical Officer
VII   Customs and Excise Officer
VIII   Photographic Chemist
IX   Pharmacist
X   Industrial Radiologist
XI   Radiotherapist

As will be obvious, the titles are specifically defined and are concentrated in a relatively narrow range of social status and earning power. Various kinds of 'writer', civil servant and technician are represented.

Rankings of these eleven occupations were originally collected in the course of a check on the temporal stability of individual rank orders of occupations. Ten third-year students at Edinburgh University were contacted through the University's Placement Service. In the course of an interview they were asked to complete a computer-randomised schedule consisting of 55 pair comparisons (all possible pairs of the 11 occupational titles). Each student completed the pair comparisons task twice (on successive days). The students were asked to indicate which of each pair they thought had the better social standing. The resulting pair comparisons were converted into a weak order of 'social standing' scores (presented in Table 4.4) by summing across the rows of the individual pair-comparison matrices. Thus a score of n for occupational title k means that occupational title k was chosen as having better social standing than n other titles.

A glance over the data in Table 4.4 shows that there is a good deal of variation in the rank-scores assigned to these occupations. The title 'X-ray Operator' is something of an exception to this, since it is assigned to a low position with fairly high consensus. However the rank-scores for the majority of titles have a range of eight or more. Despite the close similarity of titles and the variability in ranks assigned, the individuals' implied rankings are generally quite stable. They correlate 0.83 (on average) over the one-day separation of test and retest. This indicates that the variability in rankings is systematic, and is not merely random fluctuation. Moreover, if this holds for occupational titles which have been deliberately sampled to reduce variation in prestige or status, it should hold *a fortiori* for sets of titles not so selected.

TABLE 4.4   Subjects' rank-scores (from pair comparisons data)

Subject No.	I	II	III	IV	V	VI	VII	VIII	IX	X	XI
T 1	9	3	1	6	7	10	3	11	8	3	5
R 2	10	2	1	6	9	3	4	11	8	7	5
T 3	9	10	7	11	1	3	2	8	4	6	5
R 4	10	9	6	11	1	2	3	8	4	7	5
T 5	6=	3	2	6=	1	10=	4	10=	8=	8=	4=
R 6	8	2	1	6	7	9	3	11	10	4	5
T 7	9=	2	1	9=	3	4=	6=	11	4=	8	6=
R 8	11	3=	1	9	2	3=	8	10	5	6=	6=
T 9	11	7	2=	2=	1	9	7	7	4	5	10
R 10	11	8=	4=	2	1	10	8=	6	3	4=	6=
T 11	11	10	9	4=	6=	4=	6=	8	2	3	1
R 12	11	9	5=	2	2	9	7	9	2	5=	4
T 13	10	4=	4=	4=	1	9	8	11	2	4=	7
R 14	10	1	4	7=	2	10	7=	10	4	6	4
T 15	11	6=	2	10	1	9	4=	4=	3	6=	8
R 16	11	6	3=	7=	1	10	7=	3=	2	5	9
T 17	11	5	9	5	1	3	2	10	7	5	8
R 18	10	5	8	4	1	3	2	11	7	6	9
T 19	9	10=	3=	8	1=	10=	6=	3=	1=	6=	5
R 20	10	9	7	4=	1=	11	3	4=	1=	7	7

OCCUPATIONAL TITLES:
    I X-ray Operator; II Newswriter; III Scriptwriter; IV Technical writer; V Deputy Area Officer (Government); VI Higher Clerical Officer; VII Customs and Excise Officer; VIII Photographic Chemist; IX Pharmacist; X Industrial Radiologist; XI Radiotherapist.

(i) *Vector model*
No subject's ranking is the exact reverse of another's, so *reversibility* does not hold for these data (the nearest approximation is for subjects E and A

whose rankings correlate − 0.36). Four of the eleven titles never feature as
the highest or lowest rank for any subject, hence the *mediocrity* property
holds.

The algorithm used to analyse the rank data by the vector model is
called MDPREF. The procedure was developed by Carroll (1964), and
performs a multidimensional analysis of sets of pair-comparison (or
conditional-proximity) data in terms of a linear model. It produces a joint-
space of stimulus points and unit-length vectors (representing subjects),
where the projections of the stimuli on a subject's vector match the rank-
order of stimuli on his preference scale as closely as possible. This is produced
by an Eckart-Young factorisation procedure. Goodness of fit of the model is
indicated by the proportion of variance accounted for in the rank data
(PVAF).[17]

When the test-retest data on eleven occupational titles are analysed by
the MDPREF model in two dimensions (Figure 4.3) 68 per cent of the total
variation in subjects' pair comparison is accounted for.

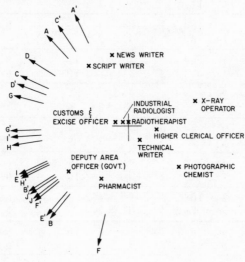

IO SUBJECTS BY 2 REPLICATIONS   TWO-DIMENSIONAL SOLUTION

REPRESENTED BY VECTORS   INDIVIDUAL

FIRST TEST DENOTED BY UNPRIMED LETTER (K)   PROPORTION OF VARIANCE
RETEST DENOTED BY PRIMED LETTER (K')   ACCOUNTED FOR (PVAF) : 0.4I TO 0.78

Fig. 4.3 Vector model analysis of eleven occupational titles

(Metric MDS analysis by Carroll   Chang's MDPREF alogorithm)

The configuration of occupational titles is not easy to interpret, nor does
the relatively even spread of subject-vectors make it easy to discern coherent
points of view. Most noteworthy is the way in which titles from the same

Unit Group usually *fail* to cluster — the only exceptions to this being News-writer and Scriptwriter and Industrial-radiologist and Radiotherapist.

If stimuli points are very close together, then the stimuli will occupy a similar location on the subject vectors, even though the precise position may change from vector to vector. In this sense, therefore, any rather tight clustering of titles can be interpreted as indicating that the occupational titles concerned are perceived as being similar to one another. But the difference between the Registrar-General's Classification (based largely on *task*-similarity) and the subjects' definitions of similarity seems rather large, and large enough to raise the question as to what characteristics and attributes form the basis of subjects' judgements.

The arrow-heads which represent the subject vectors are quite widely separated, though the reasonably high test-retest correlations are reflected by the small separations between 'first test' and 'retest' vectors (the former being indicated by unprimed and the latter by primed capital letters). The general *direction* of *lowest* evaluation is clear enough (X-Ray Operator is at the bottom), but in view of the wide separation of subject vectors, it would take an effort of faith to believe that a general prestige factor 'pops out' of the analysis.

(ii) *Distance model*
The *excellence* property of the distance model is fairly closely approximated for these data — five titles are given the highest prestige by at least one subject.

The algorithm used to analyse the rank data by the distance model is called MINI-RSA (Roskam, 1970). It is 'quasi-non-metric' in the same sense as other 'smallest space' procedures. It works iteratively in order to find a metric solution (in a certain number of dimensions, say two) where both stimuli and subjects are represented as points. The distances in the solution (when transformed to form the so-called 'disparities') are such as to reflect the rank-order information in the data. The badness of fit between data and solution is measured by a quantity called 'stress' which is a function of the squared differences between the distances in the solution space and the corresponding disparities.[18]

The test-retest data on our eleven occupational titles were analysed according to this distance (unfolding) model (using MINI-RSA), but while low values of stress were found (indicating good fit between data and solution) the representation of the data was close to trivial. Several points (occupations and subjects) occupy almost the same location in the solution space; and as a glance over Figure 4.4 will show, the occupations and subjects whose points are clumped together are not ones which would seem to go together naturally.[19] The vector model seems to provide a much more sensible evaluative map. There are technical reasons why the distance model seems to be so inappropriate and informative for this set of data, but we cannot go into them in the main text. Suffice it to say that a large number of analyses with rank orderings of occupations have left us with the strong impression that the vector model provides more interpretable results in the great majority of cases. If one is going to use geometric models and Euclidean spaces for describing occupational judgements, then the vector model is a useful work-horse.

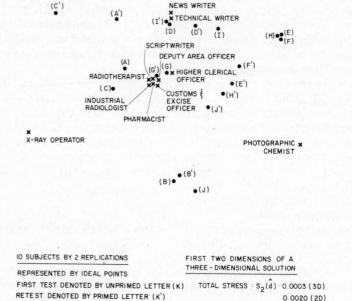

Fig. 4.4 Distance model analysis of eleven occupational titles
(Non metric MDS analysis by Roskam's MINI-RSA alogarithm)

IMPLICATIONS AND DEVELOPMENTS

The analysis in this section should not be construed as questioning the utility or the tenability of a unidimensional theory of prestige, at least for some purposes, and under certain circumstances. But however useful a unidimensional scale may be for some purposes it does *not* imply anything about how people conceive the occupational world, nor does it give any information about any cognitive processes involved in arriving at an overall judgement of occupational prestige. Nor, for that matter, do essentially *evaluative* judgements of prestige tell us much about the cognitions which underlie the evaluation. The desirability of separating cognitive and evaluative bases of judgement about occupations has, somewhat tardily, been recognised by social mobility theorists (see, for instance, Goldthorpe and Hope 1972: 38 *et seq.*), but a major difficulty arises here from the fact that it will not in general be possible to 'retrieve' representations of occupational cognitions from purely evaluative data. The reasons for this are in part substantive, and in part methodological, and are best illustrated in the context of data on preferences. Traditionally, preference has been construed as being the result of a subject evaluating a set of alternatives. The implicit — and important — assumption in comparing sets of individual preferences is that subjects perceive the alternatives in basically the same way. Preference is then viewed as some function of the prior cognitions and the source of individual variability in preferences is located in differences *in evaluation.* This conceptualisation translates well into Coombsian terminology, for if the cognitive relations between the objects are represented as a configuration of points in a multidimensional space (the 'cognitive space') and an individual is assumed to have a most preferred, or most highly evaluated, position on each of the dimensions of the space, then this fixes his 'ideal location'. The subject's set of preferences are then 'read off' as a monotonic function of the proximity of the stimuli points to his ideal point.

So long as subjects perceive the objects, or stimuli, in basically the same way, and so long as their preferences can justifiably be regarded as giving information about distances between the stimuli measured *relative* to the subject's own ideal point, then a distance model analysis of the preference I-scales will normally recover the joint space of locations of stimulus points and subjects' ideal points correctly. But if subjects do *not* perceive the stimuli in the same way, and/or if their data cannot be assumed to give conditional proximity information, then it will be impossible to recover accurately either the cognitive space or the individual 'ideal points'.

The increasing availability of computer programmes for carrying out 'internal' multidimensional scaling analyses of rank-order data gives rise to the possibility that sociologists may mistakenly interpret the 'evaluative map' configurations which are output from such procedures as if they were 'cognitive maps'. But in the absence of *independent* information about perceptions (or conceptions) of the occupational structure it is highly misleading to draw inferences about subjective occupational structure (cognitive maps) from evaluative rank orders of the kind found in occupational prestige data.

We can illustrate this point with a vector model analysis of rank orderings of the same 16 occupational titles for which individual differences-scaling of similarities and judgements produced the cognitive maps shown in Chapter 3. These occupational titles were rated in terms of 'Usefulness to Society' by the 34 individuals who are represented as vectors in Figure 4.5. A fair amount of consensus is evident in that the majority of the preferences are oriented in the direction of the horizontal axis of the figure. However, systematically different evaluations are also evident, and the range of preferences encompasses subjects with almost diametrically opposed rankings. Our main point here is made by comparing Figure 4.5 with the two-dimensional INDSCAL cognitive map from Chapter 3 (Figure 3.4). Although the overall patterns are not too different, the evaluative map differs from the cognitive map in a number of details, most notably in the position of Church of Scotland Minister, in the proximity between Comprehensive School Teacher and Policeman and in the proximity between Carpenter and Machine Tool Operator.

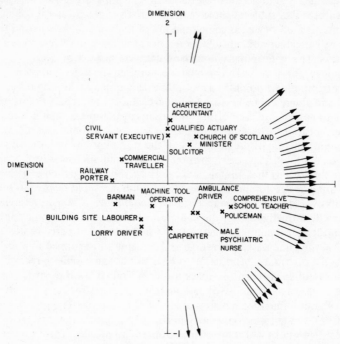

Fig. 4.5 Vector model analysis of rankings of social usefulness of 16 occupational titles (internal analysis)

It is our basic contention that prestige judgements *per se* give little direct information about the subjective occupational structure, or about concepts used to describe the occupational world, and that it is necessary to have prior information on the way in which subjects organise information and on their cognitions of the occupational world before a coherent account can be given of what prestige judgements mean. Indeed, prestige judgements are often stereotyped summaries of many more or less well-articulated pieces of information and evaluation (or even of pure ignorance) about occupations. This is why the analysis of occupational cognition is prior to the assessment of occupational prestige, and why we proceed to 'external' multidimensional scaling analysis of rank-orders of occupations in sections 4.6 and 4.7.[20]

4.5 CONVENTIONAL ANALYSES OF RATINGS AND RANKINGS ABOUT OCCUPATIONS

Simply asking people to rate or to rank-order a list of occupational titles can only yield the crudest information about how they perceive, evaluate and reason about occupations. Nevertheless, we decided that it was essential that our study should include a replication of the standard tasks of rating and ranking that so many papers in the learned journals have been based upon. The occupations to be judged were the standard set of sixteen, as discussed at length in the previous chapter. Interviewees were asked to judge these 16 occupations on one or more of five selected criteria; two 'normative' criteria, two 'descriptive' criteria, and one 'cognitive distance' criterion. The distinction between a normative judgement on the one hand and a descriptive judgement on the other occurs repeatedly in the sociological literature on invidious occupational comparisons; and, as we shall see, our interviewees were quite capable of making it themselves. Briefly, a 'normative' judgement refers to what 'ought' to be the case (i.e., it is deontic), while a 'descriptive' judgement refers to what 'is' the case. For example, in the context of occupational prestige, I may describe my experience that most people seem to be readier to accord status to physicians and surgeons than to mathematicians and physicists, while at the same time holding the view that the world would be a better place if this ordering was reversed. Another way of putting this distinction is that a descriptive judgement might in principle be checked against external evidence, while a normative judgement need not be affected by any evidence.

As our 'normative' criteria we took:

(a)   *Social Usefulness.* 'Their usefulness to society' (administered in a rating format, as 'percentage marks' out of 100).

(b)   *Rewards.* 'Your own personal opinion of the prestige and rewards they ought to receive' (administered in a ranking format with 'ties' permitted).

The first of these two criteria (social usefulness) clearly invites the interviewee to indicate his own private version of the functional theory of social stratification. Further, it is with this criterion that one would expect egoistic occupational ideology to be most easily detected. Goldthorpe and Hope (1972: 40) have reported the use of a similar criterion: 'value to society', and justify it as being essentially normative, on the grounds that:

> . . . regardless of how respondents themselves construed what they were doing, the judgments they made must be determined primarily by values which they held rather than directly by their perception of some aspects of social fact.

Our second normative criterion (rewards) was devised so as to be even more sensitive to personal values held by interviewees. In the administration of this ranking task, interviewers were instructed to supplement the criterion of 'your own personal opinion of the prestige and rewards they ought to receive', with the suggestion that it might be helpful for the interviewee to think of himself as a benevolent dictator, having absolute powers over the allocation of prestige and rewards to occupations. As with the first normative criterion, our reasoning was that a respondent's ordering of occupations according to their position in his Utopia would reveal his notions about social stratification. The two normative criteria were therefore meant to be similar and indeed several respondents pointed this out. For example, an actuary we interviewed (F312) pointed out that 'In the end, "prestige and reward they ought to get" could only mean "value to the community" could it not?'

One can draw no simple conclusion from studying the comments made by interviewees while they were making invidious comparisons between occupational titles on these normative criteria. Some people appear to accept one version or another of the functional theory of social stratification as the basis for their Utopia. The notion that 'our priorities are all wrong' is common, though people do not agree about the direction in which these priorities should be altered.

> Example (F311). A qualified Actuary placed Policemen and Comprehensive School Teachers in the highest positions on both social usefulness and rewards. 'The Actuary doesn't benefit society − rather, the country − as much as the Comprehensive School Teacher does . . . If we don't teach the kids anything, then we can't carry on as we are at the moment . . . Our priorities are all wrong: the policeman will be better paid in Canada for example . . . If we didn't have a decent police force, this society would just collapse in a heap.'

(c) Cognitive distance

Interviewees were asked to rate each occupational title according to the criterion of 'How much you know about what is involved in the job'. This criterion was chosen as an index of 'cognitive distance'. We argue that some occupations are highly visible in that a large majority of the population feel that they know about the tasks involved − for example, almost all adults have attended elementary schools and think that they know what is involved in being a teacher in such an institution. By contrast, our results show that most people feel that they have very little idea about the duties of an actuary (little at least beyond the assumption that he is some sort of 'desk-wallah'). This criterion is clearly descriptive rather than evaluative in nature, though since it describes the interviewee's personal feelings about how much knowledge he has about occupations it would be difficult to check it against external criteria. We can note in passing that since most interviewees rate their own occupations highest on this criterion, it serves to some extent as a (highly exaggerated) model for the pattern of judgements which might emerge from a fully fledged egoistical 'occupational ideology'.

(d) Social standing

As the first purely descriptive criterion of judgement, we took the classical operational definition of occupational status as first used in an American survey carried out by NORC in 1947 (see Reiss *et al.*). Our interviewees were asked to rank-order the 16 occupational titles in terms of 'your own personal opinion of their general standing in the community'. This criterion is curious because of the stress upon 'your own personal opinion' — implying a possible danger lurking in the opinions of others — this stress being followed by a request to make the personal opinion an opinion about what the average opinion is. While few problems arose with regard to its meaning we commonly found that people denied the assumption which they found implicit in the wording of the NORC criterion, that a man's social standing arises from his job only.

(e) Earnings

The second descriptive criterion was simply 'as accurate a guess as you can about the average earnings of a man in the job (aged about thirty)'. We adopted this criterion because it seemed to be the most obvious index of an occupation's perceived material desirability.

THE SAMPLE

The individuals who judged the sixteen occupations were sampled from enumeration districts in the city of Edinburgh, using a quota sampling plan, whose aim was to maximise the heterogeneity of different types of

TABLE 4.5   Assignment of individuals to the four quadrants

Quadrant A		Quadrant B	
Clergymen	19	Qualified Actuaries	14
Schoolteachers	23	Chartered Accountants	9
(Education Students)	30	(Chemical Engineering Students)	17
(Social Work Students)	4	(Electrical Engineering Students)	18
(Theological Students)	9		
(Journalists)	6		

Quadrant C		Quadrant D	
Ambulance Drivers	13	Joiners, Fitters and Engineers	60
Policemen	11	Printers	4
(Nurses)	3		
(Nursing Students)	16		

Subjects from the following groups were not assigned to any quadrant;
Law Students
Business Administration Students

occupation. This was supplemented with data from students following vocational courses. Precisely as in the previous chapter, our aim was to obtain a sample of individuals with theoretically relevant variation on factors likely to bring about differences in occupational thinking. We were not attempting to draw any kind of 'representative sample'.

(See Arnold 1970, for discussion of 'dimensional sampling'.)

Conventional analysis

The conventional way to find an average rank order from a large number of individual rank orders is to average the rank numbers assigned to the first object, average the ranks assigned to the second object, and so on until one gets to the last object. The average rank order is then the rank order of these separately-arrived-at average ranks for each object. It should be obvious that the integrity of each individual rank ordering is entirely lost in this process of aggregation. (See Guilbaud 1952.)

We have drawn up Tables 4.6 to 4.10 in order to show how a conventional averaging of occupational orderings is carried out. Each of these tables examines one criterion of rating or ranking, and is laid out so as to show up differences between the four quadrants of the typology (which is discussed in the previous chapter).

TABLE 4.6 'Social Usefulness' rating criterion: percentages of subjects giving more than half marks (50%) to each occupational title, by quadrants

Occupa- tional Titles	*Overall*	*Quadrants*			
		A	B	C	D
MIN	69.6	73.0	70.5	89.7	50.9
CST	96.6	95.5	97.7	100.0	95.0
QA	66.2	67.0	63.6	71.8	63.3
CA	72.6	74.7	77.3	74.4	65.0
MPN	83.6	85.4	77.3	89.7	81.7
AD	87.5	91.0	79.5	89.7	86.7
BSL	46.7	57.3	36.4	41.0	42.4
MTO	61.9	68.5	60.5	61.5	53.3
SOL	74.5	79.5	72.7	79.5	65.0
CSE	66.1	77.5	63.6	70.3	48.3
CT	26.4	28.1	18.2	28.2	28.8
PM	94.0	93.3	95.5	94.9	93.3
C	67.5	69.7	65.1	74.4	61.7
LD	50.2	50.0	45.5	61.5	46.7
RP	19.9	23.6	2.3	20.5	27.1
BM	23.2	19.3	11.6	12.8	44.1
N	232	89	44	39	60

(a) Social Usefulness (Table 4.6). Each occupation is scored with the percentage of subjects who gave it more than 'half marks' (50 out of a

possible 100). Over the whole sample (left-hand column of the table), Comprehensive School Teacher has the highest score (96.6), closely followed by Policeman (whose score is 94.0). Railway Porter has the lowest overall score, since only 19.9 per cent of subjects give Railway Porter more than half marks. A fair amount of disagreement between the four quadrants is evident.

As a very rough rule of thumb, we can decide that a subgroup is 'out of line' in its average opinion of any occupation if the percentage of 'high social usefulness' judgements is ten percentage points or more distant from the overall figure. Applying the rule to this table, we find that quadrant A subjects are out of line in their excessively generous ratings of Building Site Labourer and Civil Servant. Quadrant B subjects are out of line in having extra low opinions about the social usefulness of Building Site Labourer, Railway Porter and Barman. Quadrant C subjects are excessively generous in their view of the social usefulness of Minister and Lorry Driver, but like quadrant B, they have an extra low opinion of Barman. Quadrant D subjects seem to have rather different biases: they alone discern social usefulness in the work of a Barman, but they have extra low opinions of Minister and Civil Servant.

TABLE 4.7 'Rewards' ranking criterion; percentages of subjects placing occupational titles in the top half of their ranking, (in top eight); by quadrants

Occupa- tional Titles	Overall	*Quadrants*			
		A	B	C	D
MIN	75.9	83.3	86.0	95.7	46.0
CST	95.3	98.8	97.7	91.3	89.6
QA	78.1	73.8	90.7	95.7	66.0
CA	78.9	75.0	93.0	82.6	71.4
MPN	81.6	85.0	83.7	69.6	80.0
AD	61.6	57.5	46.5	60.9	81.6
BSL	15.3	16.3	14.0	4.3	20.0
MTO	32.4	28.8	32.6	17.4	44.9
SOL	83.7	81.3	97.7	87.0	74.0
CSE	79.5	75.9	81.4	91.3	78.0
CT	28.0	21.3	32.6	17.4	39.6
PM	88.8	87.5	97.7	87.0	84.0
C	40.8	41.3	39.5	26.1	48.0
LD	19.4	13.8	18.6	21.7	28.0
RP	11.4	10.3	4.7	4.3	22.4
BM	12.8	8.8	4.7	13.0	26.0
N	196	80	43	23	50

(b) Rewards They Ought to Receive (Table 4.7). Here each occupation is scored with the percentage of people who rank-ordered it in their top eight

(out of 16). Looking down the left-hand column of Table 4.7, we see that
the order of the overall percentages used as scores places Comprehensive
School Teacher first and Policeman second, just as occurred in the social
usefulness criterion. Using the same ten per cent difference rule as before,
it turns out that quadrant A subjects are not too different from the averages
of all the cases. However quadrant B subjects show several differences from
par. This group (which includes Actuaries and Accountants) ranks each of
Minister, Actuary, Accountant and Solicitor at least ten percentage points
higher than the overall figure, and also gives Ambulance Driver a markedly
low position. Quadrant C subjects place Minister, Actuary, Psychiatric
Nurse, and Civil Servant especially high and they put Machine Tool
Operator, Commercial Traveller and Carpenter lower than others do.
Quadrant D subjects show a little *proletarierstolz,* since they mark up
Ambulance Driver, Machine Tool Operator, Commercial Traveller, Railway
Porter and Barman, and they mark down Minister and Civil Servant.

(c) 'Cognitive Distance' ratings (Table 4.8). As was the case for 'social
usefulness', each occupation is scored with the percentage of subjects who
gave it more than half marks. Over the whole sample, Comprehensive School
Teacher has the highest score. This is the occupation (of these 16) that our
subjects felt they knew most about. Second to Comprehensive School Teacher

TABLE 4.8 'Cognitive Distance' rating criterion; percentages of subjects
giving more than half marks (50%) to each occupational title; by quadrants

Occupa-tional Titles		Quadrants			
	Overall	A	B	C	D
MIN	53.6	72.5	60.3	51.4	22.0
CST	67.6	79.7	83.1	51.4	45.1
QA	25.2	11.6	57.6	8.1	18.4
CA	33.4	29.0	66.1	13.9	15.7
MPN	36.7	40.6	33.9	54.1·	22.0
AD	52.3	36.2	50.8	83.8	52.9
BSL	52.3	37.7	52.5	62.2	64.7
MTO	28.2	14.5	27.1	16.2	56.9
SOL	30.6	21.7	52.5	32.4	15.7
CSE	29.8	33.3	40.7	16.7	22.0
CT	32.9	26.1	37.3	40.5	31.4
PM	60.2	56.5	69.5	64.9	51.0
C	46.4	30.4	44.8	45.9	70.0
LD	57.8	49.3	54.2	75.0	60.8
RP	43.1	33.3	45.8	56.8	43.1
BM	59.6	53.6	55.9	66.7	66.7
N	216	69	59	37	51

was Policeman, and third was Barman. Shifting to the least understood occupational titles, qualified Actuary was bottom, closely followed by Machine Tool Operator and Civil Servant (executive). As is only to be expected, most of the 16 occupational titles show large differences between the four quadrants.

(d) 'Social Standing' – the NORC wording (Table 4.9). As with 'rewards', each occupation is scored with the percentage of people who rank ordered it in their top 8 (out of 16). The overall figures show that Comprehensive School Teacher is in first position yet again (Schoolteachers have traditionally enjoyed high prestige in Scotland), followed by Solicitor, Chartered Accountant and Civil Servant. Bringing up the rear are Railway Porter, Building Site Labourer and Lorry Driver. Applying our rough 10 per cent rule again, quadrant A appears to be much the same as the overall average. Subjects from quadrant B mark down Male Psychiatric Nurse and Ambulance Driver for some reason. Quadrant C subjects mark no occupation down very much, but they overestimate the social standing of Minister and Male Psychiatric Nurse. Finally quadrant D shows *proletarierstolz* yet again (this time on a descriptive criterion), marking down Minister, Accountant, and Solicitor, and overestimating the social standing of Psychiatric Nurse, Ambulance Driver, Machine Tool Operator and Barman.

TABLE 4.9 'Social Standing' ranking criterion; percentages of subjects placing occupational titles in the top half of their ranking (in top eight) by quadrants

| Occupa-tional Titles | *Overall* | *Quadrants* | | | |
		A	B	C	D
MIN	87.6	90.8	95.2	100.0	71.0
CST	93.8	97.4	91.9	100.0	88.7
QA	84.7	85.5	93.5	82.1	76.2
CA	89.1	94.7	93.5	92.9	76.2
MPN	68.1	65.8	46.8	85.2	84.1
AD	41.7	36.8	30.6	42.9	58.1
BSL	10.2	5.3	9.7	11.1	16.1
MTO	23.1	14.5	19.4	17.9	39.7
SOL	91.3	93.4	96.8	96.4	81.0
CSE	88.6	90.8	91.9	96.4	79.0
CT	43.6	44.6	43.5	42.9	42.9
PM	82.5	73.7	90.3	85.7	84.1
C	35.8	34.2	37.1	32.1	38.1
LD	13.5	9.2	9.7	14.3	22.2
RP	7.4	2.6	6.5	10.7	12.7
BM	15.4	10.5	11.3	14.3	25.8
N	229	76	62	28	63

(e) 'Earnings' (Table 4.10). Each occupation was scored with the percentage of subjects who guessed its average earnings to be more than 140 pounds per months. From the overall figures, Solicitor, Chartered Accountant and qualified Actuary emerged as the top trio. Railway Porter, Barman and Ambulance Driver were at the Bottom. Again, quadrant A showed no differences from the overall pattern. However, quadrant B subjects over-estimated the incomes for Building Site Labourer, Commercial Traveller, Carpenter and Lorry Driver. Subjects from quadrant C overestimated the earnings of Minister and Policeman, but tended to make lower guesses than did other subjects about the income of Lorry Driver. Finally for this eminently descriptive 'earnings' criterion, quadrant D subjects made abnormally low income estimates for Comprehensive School Teacher, Accountant, Building Site Labourer, Machine Tool Operator, Commercial Traveller, Production Manager, Carpenter and Lorry Driver, and they tended to make an extra high estimate for Psychiatric Nurse.

TABLE 4.10   'Earnings' rating criterion; percentages of subjects guessing the monthly income to be more than 140 pounds for each occupational title by quadrants

Occupa-tional Titles	Overall	Quadrants			
		A	B	C	D
MIN	37.3	37.1	34.9	52.6	30.2
CST	58.9	64.0	68.3	57.9	41.4
QA	91.5	93.3	96.8	92.1	82.8
CA	91.1	96.6	98.4	89.5	75.9
MPN	23.8	14.6	20.6	26.3	39.7
AD	9.7	5.6	14.3	13.2	8.8
BSL	45.6	52.8	57.1	47.4	20.7
MTO	48.8	56.2	57.1	39.5	34.5
SOL	93.5	94.4	98.4	97.4	84.5
CSE	87.5	85.4	95.2	92.1	79.3
CT	66.7	67.4	83.9	68.4	45.6
PM	35.1	39.3	30.2	50.0	24.1
C	32.3	28.1	42.9	39.5	22.4
LD	54.0	60.7	65.1	47.4	36.2
RP	2.4	3.4	4.8	0.0	0.0
BM	8.5	11.2	9.5	7.9	3.4
N	248	89	63	38	58

DISCUSSION OF CONVENTIONAL ANALYSIS

Crude as it is, our conventional analysis shows intriguing differences between our four quadrants of subjects. Many though not all of these differences are

consistent with an occupational egoism account. A few of them may be due
to chance. The analysis might be pursued with a finer subdivision of the
quadrants (into occupational groups for example) — or with the use of means
and standard deviations to characterise the scores of occupational titles on
the various evaluative and descriptive criteria. A considerable proliferation
of tables results from such a strategy and this provides one argument against
it. The second argument against conventional analysis has already been
mentioned. It seems quite wrong to take an individual subject's set of
interlinked occupational judgements (sixteen of them with our data) and
to average each one separately. What we should be doing is to maintain the
interlinked quality of an ordering all through the averaging procedure. This
can be done through an appropriate scaling procedure, and it is this strategy
we adopt in the following sections.[21]

4.6 PUTTING COGNITION AND EVALUATION TOGETHER — EXTERNAL ANALYSIS OF INDIVIDUAL DATA

We have argued that the rank orderings which are made by individuals should
only be aggregated in a way which preserves their integrity. This can be
carried out if each evaluative rank order is fitted into the cognitive map that
the subject had in mind when he was making invidious comparisons. As a
proxy for this cognitive map, we shall use the 'group space' configurations
(in two and three dimensions) from the scaling of similarities data carried
out in the previous chapter. It then turns out that proper aggregation of rank
orders can be carried out if we 'put cognition and evaluation together' first.

In the analyses which follow, we are concerned to relate rank orderings
of the standard set of 16 occupations on the five criteria already discussed
in the previous section. For the three criteria where the original data were
collected in the form of 'marks out of 100', we translated the information
into the implied rank order (with tied ranks allowed). This translation
completed, the data were in the form of rank orderings of the 16 occupational
titles upon five different criteria by people from a variety of social backgrounds. These rank orderings were then examined one by one for the
extent to which they could be understood as arising from simple transformations of distances in the cognitive map.

The reader may feel puzzled here. How can some transformation of
distances between occupational titles in a cognitive map be turned into a
rank order of the occupations in terms of social standing, earnings or
whatever? There are in fact two basic ways of doing this, and a geographical
example may clarify the point. For the first approach (known technically as
the 'simple unweighted distance model') we may imagine a man's preferences
for towns to live and work in, and we may assume that his cognitive map of
towns is based solely on distances between them in ordinary physical units
such as miles or kilometres; in short his cognitive map happens to be the

same as a geographical map with the two axes (dimensions) of north-south and east-west. We may then make up a simple model or conjecture that there is some town which is the man's first preference, or 'ideal point', and that his rank order of other towns is determined solely by the relative distance of those towns from the 'ideal point'. Given an accurate map, it is easy to rank order towns in terms of their distance from some most preferred town.

This example is meant to indicate the logic of the 'simple unweighted distance model' as it is called in technical jargon. We may think of it as the model of 'man with a pair of compasses' in that, given a cognitive map of some stimulus domain (say occupations), a rank ordering of those stimuli can be understood in terms of their relative distances from some 'ideal point' on the cognitive map. If the point of a pair of geometrical compasses were set down upon that 'ideal point' then one would be able to draw concentric circles about it, and the unfolding model asserts that for all of those circles whose origin is the ideal point, stimuli inside the circle are ranked higher (closer to the ideal point) than stimuli outside the circle. We would emphasise that the distance model as we have described it is merely a conjecture which may not be supported by data we collect.

A rather more restrictive model of the relationship between rank orders and a cognitive map is based, not on the idea of an ideal point, but rather on the notion of an ideal *direction* (since the technical geometrical name for a direction is a vector, this is called a 'vector model'). This implies that there is a direction (or, if you like, a compass-bearing) over the cognitive map. Supposing that in one case this direction over the cognitive map was north-easterly. If this were so, it could be related to a rank order of the points on the cognitive map by the rule that one point is ranked higher than another point only if it is further towards the north-east. In this model then, a rank order is summarised as a direction in a cognitive map. Given a 'cultural' cognitive map of 16 occupational titles, the vector model can be used to summarise a rank order of those 16 occupational titles by a single direction (or compass-bearing) which can be described by two numbers.

We can now report the results of relating the rank orderings of 16 occupational titles on five different criteria to the two-dimensional cognitive map which was produced as a result of individual differences scaling, as described in the previous chapter. So far as the analysis of individual rank orders is concerned, only the direction of a vector is of interest: its length is arbitrary. For ease of representation then, all vectors are scaled so as to be the same length (unity) when measured from the origin to the arrowhead. A vector can be described by the coordinates (upon the dimensions of the cognitive map) of the arrowhead at its end.

It may seem perverse to take so great an amount of trouble merely to replace a rank order of 16 occupational titles by the coordinates upon two dimensions of the arrowhead at the end of the unit vector whose direction in a cognitive map provides a summary of that rank order. However, the advantage of this mode of representation rapidly becomes apparent when we need to compare large numbers of rank orderings, and ask whether or not the variation in judgement between occupational groups is greater than the variation within occupational groups. In their raw form, orderings are difficult to handle in any quantitative way. This is partly because many sociologists rightly feel unhappy about applying powerful statistical techniques to data which so clearly fail to satisfy the 'equal interval' level of measurement properties prerequisite to the use of such techniques. More important perhaps, the conventional survey analytic methods of presenting and analysing rank orders given by interviewees fail to maintain the integrity of the individual rank order: instead they simply count the number of times each stimulus is ranked first, the number of times it is ranked second, and so forth. We have already argued this point at length. The mode of analysis undertaken here is superior to this in that *ordinal* rank orders are fitted *as a whole* (maintaining their integrity) into a *metric* space (the cognitive map), in which they are represented by *metric* quantities – the coordinates of the ends of the unit length vectors whose directions in the cognitive map provide a representation of those rank orders. This accomplished, it is a simple matter to use statistical methods for the analysis of directional data in order to manipulate these coordinate values. For example, one can easily compute between group and within group sums of squares in analysis of variance (see Mardia, 1972). In this way, we achieve what we might call 'appropriate aggregation' of rank orders. However before describing groups and group differences, we should illustrate the model with individual-level data.

INDIVIDUAL LEVEL ANALYSES

As usual, diagrams are worth many words. The simplest way in which to picture the relationship between rank orders of occupations and their positions in a cognitive map is as follows. The occupations that were judged are pictured as points and each of the rank orders is pictured as a directed line passing through the origin of the space. We may illustrate by looking at a single case, G264, a chartered accountant.

Figure 4.6 shows a two-dimensional map of the five rank orderings made by this man. The cognitive map of the 16 occupations is the two-dimensional group space from the individual differences scaling. There are five directed lines drawn through the origin of the cognitive map, and each of these lines (the arrowheads indicate the direction) represents one of the rank orderings made by G264. If we refer to the diagram by a 'clock-face' convention, we have the social usefulness rank ordering depicted as an arrow pointing to 'one o'clock' while earnings points approximately to 'four o'clock'. Male Psychiatric Nurse, Church of Scotland, Minister and Policeman were the first three in terms of social usefulness, while Chartered Accountant, Qualified Actuary, Civil Servant (Executive Grade) and Country Solicitor were judged highest in earnings. Clearly, G264 sees no necessary inter-relationship between the social usefulness of an occupation and its emoluments. Indeed, the angle between the directed line (or vector) for social usefulness and that for earnings is 95 degrees, which corresponds to a slight negative correlation.

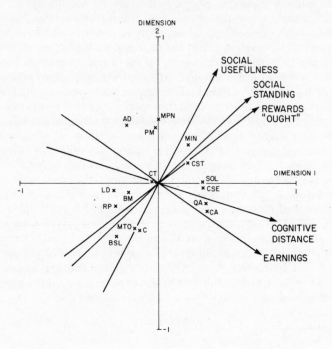

Fig. 4.6 Case G264 (Chartered Accountant): two-dimensional solution

His general comments on the ranking and rating tasks are of considerable interest, especially when he touches on the interrelationship between general standing and usefulness to society:

The questions are probably inevitably very vague. For instance, the income of solicitors, just to take an example. A solicitor's income varies tremendously. Some legal firms make a lot of money and the partners get a very high income accordingly. Some solicitors make very little. It's quite a difference — it's really amazing. To put down a certain figure for country solicitors, say, is very, very misleading. Same for chartered accountant. A chartered accountant who is in industry or, say, an organization like the health service, is on a scale that's fixed. In a smaller firm, a chartered accountant firm, he may have to negotiate his own and naturally they will try to keep it as low as possible. So it's very, very difficult to answer this— very difficult for you to interpret them, I should think, because of the gradations. And then too, grading them as to standing, this, that and the other. You may say that a chartered accountant or that a civil servant (executive) has a greater standing in the community in terms of class and prestige and social scale, etc., etc. If we were all shipwrecked on a desert island it would be the carpenter and the bricklayer, etc., etc., who would be the valuable members of the community (chartered accountant — G264).

The cognitive distance vector points in a similar direction to that of the earnings vector indicating that G264's rank ordering of occupations in terms of his knowledge of them is much the same as his rank ordering in terms of earnings.

A second point to notice about Figure 4.6 is that the vector for social standing points in almost the same direction as the vector for the prestige and rewards criterion. This indicates that the two rank orders are nearly the same, so it seems that G264 was interpreting social standing (which is supposed to be a descriptive criterion in a similar way to 'prestige and rewards' (which is supposed to be a normative criterion). In both cases, Church of Scotland Minister is ranked first, followed by Country Solicitor, Civil Servant (Executive Grade), Comprehensive School Teacher, etc. This is confirmed by the interviewer's report, where it was noted that the respondent (G264) chose to interpret general standing as 'usefulness to the community'.

He queried whether general standing was social standing. I said general standing. 'So standing can mean anything — all things to all men.' General standing was interpreted as 'usefulness to the community'.

Figures 4.7 to 4.10 show vector representations of rank orderings for a Church of Scotland Minister, an Apprentice Bricklayer, an Actuary and a Journalist. The vector corresponding to the social usefulness rank ordering points to approximately one o'clock on the first four of these five figures, indicating that the first four subjects have much the same social usefulness rank ordering. However, the journalist whose rankings are represented in Figure 4.10 appears to be a case of what Lockwood has called *Proletarierstolz*. The vector corresponding to his social usefulness rank ordering of the 16 occupations is directed towards seven o'clock in Figure 4.10 and this indicates that his social usefulness rank ordering is almost exactly the inverse of those made by the other four subjects under consideration here.

The Church of Scotland Minister (Figure 4.7, case A268) had the curious characteristic that his cognitive distance vector pointed to the northwest, indicating that he judged himself to be more knowledgeable about working-class occupations than about middle-class ones. It turns out that this can be explained by his occupational history, since before becoming a minister he had worked as a sanitary inspector for seventeen years. This involved not only being a 'drain brain', but also overseeing the work done on building sites, and acting as a meat and food inspector. His judgements of similarities and differences between occupations were permeated with contrasts made upon the 'people versus machines or data' dimension (this is the style of thinking one would expect of workers in 'people-oriented' jobs, of which the ministry is a paradigm case).

Figure 4.10 shows our 'upside-downer' (a news sub-editor and father of the NUJ Chapel). A glance at the positions of the vectors for descriptive and evaluative criteria shows that while he is aware of the existence of rank orderings among occupations in terms of the objective criteria, 'earnings' and 'general standing', his own evaluations are quite opposite.

He said several times that he was 'prejudiced' against policemen and ministers and a very salient construct was whether you are 'authorised' in a job, by which he meant 'under others' control'.

General Standing

He insisted it is how he *interprets* public opinion, *not* his personal view — 'cliches'. Strategy: started at the first rank (Church of Scotland Minister), then worked up from the bottom (ranks 16 to 10) and finished by working from 2 to 9.

Social Usefulness

He strongly stressed value of zero for minister (compare with his descriptive judgement).

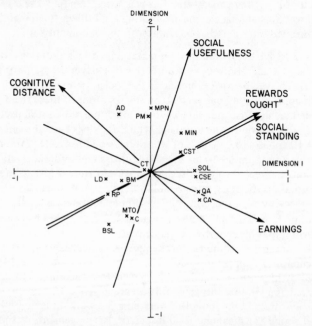

Fig. 4.7 Case A268 (Church of Scotland Minister): two-dimensional solution

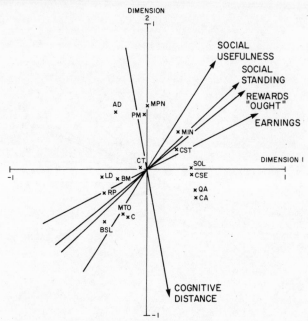

Fig. 4.8 Case A248 (Apprentice Craftsman): two-dimensional solution

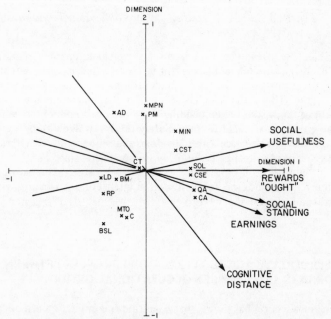

Fig. 4.9 Case F312 (Actuary): two-dimensional solution

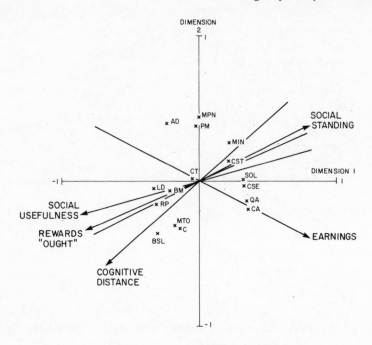

Fig. 4.10 Case J271 (Journalist): two-dimensional solution

This subject has already been discussed in the previous chapter (section 3.6) as an 'ill-fitting but coherent case'. It is interesting that independent analyses by the two authors were successful in identifying the same man as being a 'deviant case'. The reader who has followed our argument so far will be doubtful of the wisdom of embedding this journalist's rank orders in the general 'group space' cognitive map. Surely this is not likely to be a good proxy for his 'private space' (his individual, and probably idiosyncratic, cognitive map). As it happens, intuition is wrong here, since J271's rank orders fit into the group space very well. Even so, statistical measures of goodness of fit are not the only criterion of intellectual satisfactoriness, and we devote a technical appendix to an exhaustive analysis of this man's data (T4.6).

4.7 APPROPRIATE AGGREGATION – DIFFERENCES BETWEEN QUADRANTS AND BETWEEN OCCUPATIONAL GROUPS

The previous section has shown that cognition and evaluation can be 'put together' in a way which represents each individual's rank orders by a set of vectors (directions) in the overall cognitive map. Diagrams of this kind are helpful aids to communication, but it would clutter a figure impossibly if any very large number of rank orders were to be represented as vectors in the same cognitive map. (The present study analyses more than one thousand rank orders of our standard set of 16 occupational titles.) Clearly some method of averaging rank orders is needed. Fortunately for our aggregation problem, the treatment of rank orders as vectors (directions or compass-bearings) over a cognitive map means that an average rank order can be thought of as an average direction. Fortunately again, there exists a considerable body of technical literature concerning the statistical analysis of directional data.[22]

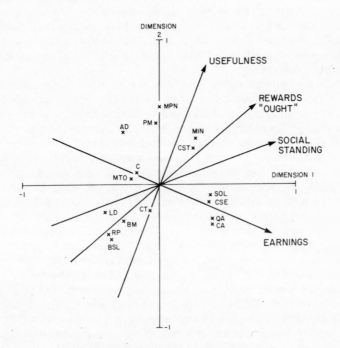

Fig. 4.11 Average over all groups for each criterion of judgement

We begin by looking at the average vectors for the four invidious rank orderings ('social usefulness', 'prestige and rewards', 'social standing' and 'earnings'). These are shown in Figure 4.11, which is a picture of the first two dimensions of the three-dimensional cognitive map (the three-dimensional 'group space' from the individual differences scaling of similarities judgements). It should be borne in mind that each of the four vectors shown in the figure is an average direction formed from some two hundred vectors, each of which represents an individual's rank-ordering of the 16 occupational titles. If we use a clock-face representation for the directions of the vectors, the average 'social usefulness' vector points approximately to four minutes past the hour, 'prestige and rewards' points to nine minutes past, 'social standing' points to twelve minutes past, and 'earnings' points to twenty minutes past. Given the positions of the occupational titles which are represented as points in the cognitive map, the projections of the occupational titles on to the four vectors are such that Chartered Accountant and Qualified Actuary tie for first position on the earnings criterion, Church of Scotland Minister is in first position in terms of 'prestige and rewards' and also in terms of 'social standing', and Male Psychiatric Nurse is in first position in terms of 'social usefulness'. It should be noted that the 'social usefulness' vector is approximately at right angles to the 'earnings vector'. This indicates that 'social usefulness' and 'earnings' are independent of one another (at least so far as the limited nature of the sample of subjects and the selection of occupations permit one to generalise).

We can now proceed to the formalities of statistical hypothesis testing. Our research hypothesis is a simple one — that when individuals make comparative rank orderings of occupations, these orderings tend to be systematically related to the occupational backgrounds of the rankers. The kind of effect that we should expect is some version of the 'occupational egoism' phenomenon. This may seem to be a simple enough hypothesis to test. However (and here we are labouring a point already touched on previously), we can hardly overemphasise the extent to which *all* previous investigations in the area have been hamstrung by the technical difficulties involved in comparing the central tendency of one group of rank orders with the central tendency of another group of rank orders. The usual approach has been to analyse the data in piecemeal fashion — comparing the average rank of one occupational title as assigned by different groups of subjects; then doing the same for another occupational title; and so on. The approach adopted here is much superior in that the integrity of each individual rank order is maintained. This is accomplished in two stages. First, each rank order is represented as a vector in a two-dimensional or three-dimensional space. Then the direction of that vector is used to represent the rank order and statistical techniques developed for the analysis of directional data are used to test the hypothesis that the average direction in one group of subjects is different from the average direction in another. In the vector representation, averaging the direction of the vectors corresponds to averaging rank-orders.

The careful reader will easily see that the averaging procedure we propose is only valid so long as the rank order data are a good vector model fit to the cognitive map that the investigator uses. We claim this as a virtue, on the grounds that our method for representing rank orders as vectors is a testable measurement hypothesis. Carroll (1972) has proposed a set of nested models forming what he calls a 'linear quadratic hierarchy', and the vector model is the simplest of these. We carried out F-tests of the kind proposed by Carroll, and these showed that the overwhelming majority of our rank orders could be best represented by the vector model (rather than by the distance model, or the weighted distance model, or by the rotated-then-weighted distance model).

Suppose, for example, that two different rank orders are fitted through a vector model into a cognitive map of two dimensions. Each rank order will be represented by a unit length vector in the space, each vector being described by the coordinates of the arrowhead at its end. One intuitively supposes that an average of these two vectors would be one which cut in half the angle between them, and in fact the coordinates of such a vector are given by the arithmetic of averaging the coordinates on each dimension. If the vectors being averaged are of unit length, then their average vector (if calculated in this way) is of less than unit length and the greater the angular separation (up to 180 degrees) between the vectors being averaged, the shorter is this average vector. This provides a useful diagrammatic representation of average rank orders for different sub-groups, since the shorter the average vector for a sub-group, the less the consensus between the individual rank orders in that sub-group. This does not influence the conclusions drawn about the direction of the resultant vector, for the direction of a vector does not depend upon its length. Indeed, the figures in this chapter which show average vectors show them all standardised to the same length. However, the information about the length of the resultant vector arises in the course of computation anyway, and is quite interesting, since the shorter it is, the less consensus.

When we examine the lengths of the average resultant vectors for the five rank-ordering criteria, it is perhaps not surprising that the shortest resultant vector is for the 'Cognitive Distance' criterion, with a length of 0.32, and this summarises the fact that there were great differences between the 215 rank orders of this kind. The normative criteria for rank-ordering the 16 occupations were associated with rather longer resultant vectors, 'Social Usefulness' having one of length 0.77, and 'Prestige and Rewards' having one of length 0.74, these values denoting a moderate amount of consensus. The descriptive criteria for ranking the occupations were associated with a little more consensus, 'Social Standing' having a resultant vector of length 0.80, and 'Earnings' having one of 0.90. To summarise, there was most consensus about the 'Earnings' criterion and this was followed in terms of degree of consensus by the 'Social Standing' criterion, then the 'Social Usefulness' criterion, then 'Prestige and Rewards' and finally by 'Cognitive Distance'. These results square with the conventional sociological opinion that there is less agreement about evaluative judgements than there is about descriptive judgements concerning occupations.

A form of one-way analysis of variance for directional data was used in order to test the hypothesis that there are differences in average direction between different sub-groups of subjects. Five analyses of variance were carried out, one for each of the ranking criteria. In each of these analyses, the rank orders made by the subjects were fitted as directions in a three-dimensional space[23] and these directions were classified into the familiar quadrants produced by the two-way tabulation of educational requirements versus contact with people as against data or machines. Analysis of variance tables are shown as Tables 4.11 to 4.15.

We also carried out analyses of variance (for directional data) with our subjects classified on a rather finer basis. For this, we used their occupational backgrounds, classified into nine groups. These were:

1. Clergy
2. Teachers
3. Actuaries
4. Accountants
5. Ambulance Drivers
6. Police
7. Joiners, Fitters and Apprentices
8. Electrical Engineers
9. Student Teachers

TABLE 4.11 One-way analysis of variance* for average directions of 'Social Usefulness' vectors in the three-dimensional INDSCAL space.
Null hypothesis: no difference between average directions of the four quadrants

Quadrant	N	Sums of cosines I	II	III	Length of resultant R	Cosines in the unit sphere I	II	III
A	87	22.72	64.09	−12.60	69.155	0.329	0.927	−0.182
B	41	14.53	26.87	−6.61	31.254	0.465	0.860	−0.211
C	40	14.28	30.30	0.63	33.502	0.426	0.904	0.019
D	58	15.08	39.04	6.25	42.315	0.356	0.923	0.148
Total	226	66.61	160.30	−12.33	174.026	0.383	0.921	−0.071

Length of average resultant vector = 0.77

Analysis of variance table

DF	SS	MS	F
6	2.201	0.367	3.3
444	49.773	0.112	
450	51.974		

F is significant at the 1% level

*See Mardia (1972: 268)

TABLE 4.12   One-way analysis of variance* for average directions of 'Rewards' vectors in the three-dimensional INDSCAL space.
Null hypothesis: no difference between average directions of the four quadrants.

Quadrant	N	Sums of cosines			Length of resultant	Cosines in the unit sphere		
		I	II	III	R	I	II	III
A	79	47.40	38.99	−3.05	61.451	0.771	0.634	−0.050
B	43	32.92	18.15	−0.85	37.601	0.875	0.483	−0.023
C	26	18.84	11.20	0.98	21.940	0.859	0.510	0.045
D	48	15.46	21.77	1.34	26.735	0.578	0.814	0.050
Total	196	114.62	90.11	−1.58	145.808	0.786	0.618	−0.011

Length of average resultant vector = 0.74

Analysis of variance table

DF	SS	MS	F
6	1.919	0.320	2.5
384	48.273	0.126	
390	50.192		

F is significant at the 5% level

*See Mardia (1972: 268)

TABLE 4.13   One-way analysis of variance* for average directions of 'Knowledge' vectors in the three-dimensional INDSCAL space.
Null hypothesis: no difference between average directions of the four quadrants.

Quadrant	N	Sums of cosines			Length of resultant	Cosines in the unit sphere		
		I	II	III	R	I	II	III
A	73	−7.52	23.64	21.79	33.018	−0.228	0.716	0.660
B	57	8.77	−1.45	7.43	11.585	0.757	−0.125	0.641
C	36	−18.83	12.92	11.59	25.609	−0.735	0.505	0.453
D	49	−26.93	8.37	−11.24	30.358	−0.887	0.276	−0.370
Total	215	−44.51	43.48	29.57	68.891	−0.646	0.631	0.429

Length of average resultant vector = 0.32

Analysis of variance table

DF	SS	MS	F
6	31.679	5.280	19.5
422	114.429	0.271	
428	146.109		

F is obviously significant

*See Mardia (1972: 268)

TABLE 4.14   One-way analysis of variance* for average directions of 'Social Standing' vectors in the three-dimensional INDSCAL Space. Null hypothesis: no difference between average directions of the four quadrants.

Quadrant	N	Sums of cosines			Length of resultant	Cosines in the unit sphere		
		I	II	III	R	I	II	III
A	78	60.53	17.63	−0.04	63.045	0.960	0.280	−0.001
B	62	53.49	9.67	2.31	54.406	0.983	0.178	0.042
C	30	26.67	9.67	2.09	28.446	0.938	0.340	0.073
D	61	34.37	23.31	6.30	42.004	0.818	0.555	0.150
Total	231	175.06	60.28	10.66	185.454	0.944	0.325	0.057

Length of average resultant vector = 0.80

Analysis of variance table

DF	SS	MS	F
6	2.447	0.408	4.3
454	43.099	0.095	
460	45.546		

F is significant at the 1% level

*See Mardia (1972: 268)

TABLE 4.15   One-way analysis of variance* for average directions of 'Earnings' vectors in the three-dimensional INDSCAL space. Null hypothesis: no difference between average directions of the four quadrants.

Quadrant	N	Sums of cosines			Length of resultant	Cosines in the unit sphere		
		I	II	III	R	I	II	III
A	92	76.67	−39.53	−5.05	86.408	0.887	−0.457	−0.058
B	61	51.90	−26.36	−3.44	58.312	0.890	−0.452	−0.059
C	41	34.91	−12.54	−1.04	37.109	0.941	−0.338	−0.028
D	54	41.87	−9.09	−2.78	42.935	0.975	−0.212	−0.065
Total	248	205.35	−87.52	−12.31	223.562	0.919	−0.391	−0.055

Length of average resultant vector = 0.90

Analysis of variance table

DF	SS	MS	F
6	1.203	0.200	4.2
488	23.236	0.048	
494	24.438		

F is significant at the 1% level

*See Mardia (1968: 268)

Analysis of variance tables are shown as Tables 4.16 to 4.20. Statistically significant differences between occupationally based groups of subjects (and between quadrants) were found for all five criteria of ranking. The F-ratios were significant beyond the 1 per cent level for the Social Usefulness, Social Standing and (not surprisingly) for the Cognitive Distance criteria, and at the 5 per cent level for the Prestige and Rewards criterion. The orthodox view in Sociology has been that while different social groups *may* have different *evaluations* of the various parts of the occupational structure, (see Della Fave 1974), it must still be true that the different social groups make the same *descriptive* rank orders, for example in terms of guessed earnings or social standing. However, we find statistically significant differences between occupationally defined sub-groups in terms of *both* descriptive *and* evaluative criteria of ranking.

Figures 4.12 through 4.15 show the average vectors for the nine occupational sub-groups. (The figures show the cognitive map in dimensions I and II of a three-dimensional configuration.) Each figure is concerned with one of the criteria for invidious comparison. (There is no figure for the 'cognitive distance' criterion, but curious readers can construct one with the information in the three right-hand columns of Table 4.18.) Figure 4.12 shows the positions of the nine average vectors for the Social Usefulness criterion. The vectors look like a loose sheaf of arrows pointing in a more or less north-easterly direction. The average vector for the sub-group of Actuaries (coded number 3 on the figure) is the 'Social Usefulness' vector whose direction lies furthest clockwise. This indicates that Actuaries tended to interpret 'Social Usefulness' in such a way that occupations like Solicitor, Civil Servant, Actuary and Accountant were ranked higher than by other sub-groups, a finding which is consistent with an 'occupational egoism' hypothesis.

Figure 4.13 shows the positions of nine averaged vectors for the second of the normative criteria, 'Prestige and Rewards'. Again the vector for the sub-group of Actuaries has the furthest clockwise direction. Two of the nine vectors form a pair whose common direction is some thirty degrees anti-clockwise of the average direction of the remaining seven vectors. These two sub-groups are Clergy (coded 1) and Apprentice Joiners and Fitters (coded 7). When compared with the other seven sub-groups, the directions of their average vectors are such as to place the 'helping occupations' a little higher, and the 'legal-financial' occupations a little lower.

The nine average vectors for the 'Social Standing' criterion are shown in Figure 4.14 and again we find that the vector for the sub-group of Actuaries (coded 3), has the furthest clockwise direction. Eight of the nine average vectors form a loose sheaf pointing to approximately twelve minutes past the hour, but the large sub-group of Joiners and Fitters (coded 7) lies more or less by itself pointing to approximately eight minutes past the hour. As in the previous figures, this indicates that these Joiners and Fitters ranked the 'helping occupations' relatively higher than did other sub-groups.

TABLE 4.16   One-way analysis of variance* for average directions of 'Social Usefulness' vectors in the three-dimensional INDSCAL space

Null hypothesis: no difference between average directions of the nine occupational sub-groups

	N	Sums of Cosines			Length of resultant	Cosines in the unit sphere		
		I	II	III	R	I	II	III
Clergy	19	4.35	14.89	−3.57	15.918	0.273	0.935	−0.224
Teachers	23	10.37	13.43	−2.29	17.121	0.606	0.784	−0.134
Actuaries	14	8.76	7.57	−1.07	11.627	0.753	0.651	−0.092
Accountants	9	3.19	6.45	−2.64	7.665	0.416	0.842	−0.344
Ambulance Drivers	13	4.91	9.96	0.91	11.142	0.441	0.894	0.082
Policemen	10	3.24	7.85	−0.21	8.495	0.381	0.924	−0.025
Fitters, etc.	55	12.89	38.50	7.47	41.282	0.312	0.933	0.181
Electrical Engineers	17	3.26	12.13	−3.00	12.914	0.252	0.939	−0.232
Student Teachers	28	6.44	22.26	−3.67	23.462	0.274	0.949	−0.156
TOTAL	188	57.41	133.04	−8.07	145.123	0.396	0.916	−0.056

Length of average resultant vector = 0.77

Analysis of variance table

DF	SS	MS	F
16	4.502	0.281	2.625
358	38.375	0.107	
374	42.877		

F is significant at the 1% level

TABLE 4.17   One-way analysis of variance* for average directions of 'Rewards'.'vectors in the three-dimensional INDSCAL space

Null hypothesis; no difference between average directions of the occupational sub-groups

	N	Sums of cosines			Length of resultant R	Cosines in the unit sphere		
		I	II	III	R	I	II	III
Clergy	10	5.03	7.70	-1.19	9.274	0.542	0.830	-0.128
Teachers	20	14.82	9.91	-2.07	17.948	0.826	0.552	-0.115
Actuaries	17	14.89	5.70	-0.06	15.944	0.934	0.358	-0.004
Accountants	9	7.13	3.30	-1.03	7.924	0.900	0.416	-0.130
Ambulance Drivers	10	5.53	3.92	0.92	6.841	0.808	0.573	0.134
Policemen	13	11.10	5.59	-0.18	12.429	0.893	0.450	-0.014
Fitters, etc.	45	13.13	21.10	2.01	24.933	0.527	0.846	0.081
Electrical Engineers	17	10.90	9.15	0.24	14.233	0.766	0.643	0.017
Student Teachers	30	20.03	12.07	0.99	23.407	0.856	0.516	0.042
TOTAL	171	102.56	78.44	-0.37	129.118	0.794	0.608	-0.003

Length of average resultant vector = 0.76

Analysis of variance table

DF	SS	MS	F
16	3.814	0.238	2.029
324	38.068	0.117	
340	41.882		

F is significant at the 5% level

TABLE 4.18 One-way analysis of variance for average directions of the 'Knowledge' vectors in the three-dimensional INDSCAL space

Null hypothesis: no difference between average directions of the occupational sub-groups

	N	Sums of cosines			Length of resultant R	Cosines in the unit sphere		
		I	II	III	R	I	II	III
Clergy	15	0.69	9.05	2.25	9.351	0.074	0.968	0.241
Teachers	7	0.58	2.18	2.52	3.382	0.171	0.645	0.745
Actuaries	15	4.70	−7.79	5.58	10.673	0.440	−0.730	0.523
Accountants	9	3.49	−4.80	3.29	6.786	0.514	−0.707	0.485
Ambulance Drivers	9	−7.26	2.66	2.13	8.020	−0.905	0.332	0.266
Policemen	11	−8.31	1.33	3.53	9.126	−0.911	0.146	0.387
Fitters, etc.	46	−28.97	9.23	−9.86	31.964	−0.906	0.289	−0.308
Electrical Engineers	16	−5.13	0.24	−2.59	5.752	−0.892	0.042	−0.450
Student Teachers	31	−4.38	8.24	11.07	14.478	−0.303	0.569	0.765
TOTAL	159	−44.59	20.34	17.92	52.183	−0.854	0.390	0.343

Length of average resultant vector = 0.33

Analysis of variance table

DF	SS	MS	F
16	47.348	2.959	14.929
300	59.468	0.198	
316	106.817		

F is obviously significant

TABLE 4.19 One-way analysis of variance for average directions of 'Social Standing' vectors in the three-dimensional INDSCAL space

Null hypothesis: no difference between average directions of the occupational sub-groups

	N	Sums of cosines			Length of resultant R	Cosines in the unit sphere		
		I	II	III	R	I	II	III
Clergy	20	16.27	5.23	−0.47	17.096	0.952	0.306	−0.027
Teachers	7	6.34	1.52	0.17	6.522	0.972	0.233	0.026
Actuaries	18	17.22	1.82	0.00	17.316	0.994	0.105	0.000
Accountants	9	8.28	1.95	−0.57	8.526	0.971	0.229	−0.067
Ambulance Drivers	15	12.94	5.37	0.82	14.034	0.922	0.383	0.058
Policemen	12	10.83	3.68	1.13	11.494	0.942	0.320	0.098
Fitters, etc.	57	31.04	22.45	6.86	38.917	0.798	0.577	0.176
Electrical Engineers	18	16.62	3.89	1.29	17.118	0.971	0.227	0.075
Student Teachers	30	26.24	4.93	0.03	26.699	0.983	0.185	0.001
TOTAL	186	145.78	50.84	9.26	154.668	0.943	0.329	0.060

Length of average resultant vector = 0.83

Analysis of variance table

DF	SS	MS	F
16	3.053	0.191	2.389
354	28.278	0.080	
370	31.332		

F is significant at the 1% level

TABLE 4.20   One-way analysis of variance* for average directions of 'Earnings' vectors in the three-dimensionsl INDSCAL space

Null hypothesis; no difference between average directions of the occupational sub-groups

	N	Sums of Cosines			Length of resultant	Cosines in the unit sphere		
		I	II	III	R	I	II	III
Clergy	19	15.47	−7.74	−2.93	17.545	0.882	−0.441	−0.167
Teachers	22	18.40	−10.47	−1.29	21.210	0.868	−0.494	−0.061
Actuaries	19	15.85	−8.04	−1.26	17.817	0.890	−0.451	−0.071
Accountants	7	5.86	−3.06	−0.49	6.629	0.884	−0.462	−0.074
Ambulance Drivers	13	11.50	−3.40	−0.70	12.012	0.957	−0.283	−0.058
Policemen	9	7.97	−1.42	−0.74	8.129	0.980	−0.175	−0.091
Fitters, etc.	51	39.27	−8.07	−2.34	40.159	0.978	−0.201	−0.058
Electrical Engineers	18	15.31	−8.22	−0.92	17.401	0.880	−0.472	−0.053
Student Teachers	32	26.25	−14.57	−1.10	30.043	0.874	−0.485	−0.037
TOTAL	190	155.88	−64.99	−11.77	169.295	0.921	−0.384	−0.070

Length of average resultant vector = 0.89

Analysis of variance table

DF	SS	MS	F
16	1.650	0.103	1.959
362	19.055	0.053	
378	20.705		

F is significant at the 1% level

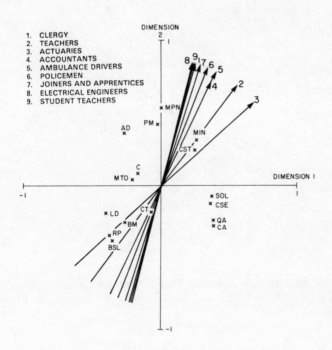

Fig. 4.12 Average 'Social Usefulness' vectors for nine sub-groups

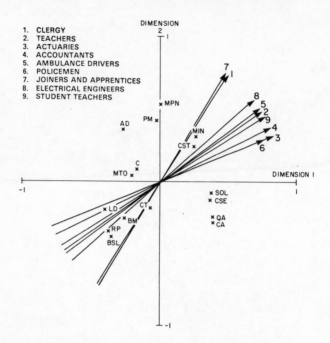

Fig. 4.13 Average 'Rewards' 'Ought' vectors for nine sub-groups

The last criterion for ranking the 16 occupational titles was 'Earnings'. Subjects were simply asked to make as accurate a guess as they were able to, about the average earnings in each occupation. Since this criterion is purely 'descriptive' as opposed to 'normative', it would surprise many sociologists to see the clear separation in Figure 4.15 between a cluster of three vectors (for Ambulance Drivers, Policeman and Joiners and Fitters) and another cluster of six vectors (for the remaining occupational sub-groups). The three-vector cluster (with codes 5, 6 and 7 in the figure) is for those occupational sub-groups classified as C or D in our quadrant system; i.e., they are occupational sub-groups whose educational requirements are relatively low. This contrasts with the occupational sub-groups for the other cluster of vectors, which are all of type A or B; i.e., they have relatively high educational requirements. From the relative directions of these two clusters, it appears that the subjects in occupations with lower educational requirements tend to rank the 'helping occupations' slightly higher in terms of judged earnings than do subjects in occupations with higher educational requirements.

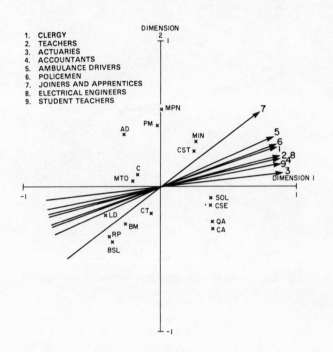

1. CLERGY
2. TEACHERS
3. ACTUARIES
4. ACCOUNTANTS
5. AMBULANCE DRIVERS
6. POLICEMEN
7. JOINERS AND APPRENTICES
8. ELECTRICAL ENGINEERS
9. STUDENT TEACHERS

Fig. 4.14 Average 'Social Standing' vectors for nine sub-groups

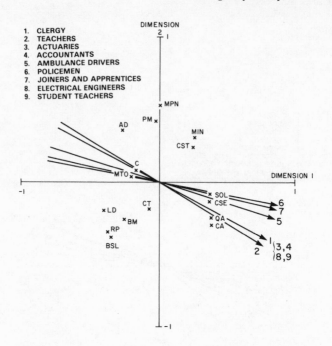

1. CLERGY
2. TEACHERS
3. ACTUARIES
4. ACCOUNTANTS
5. AMBULANCE DRIVERS
6. POLICEMEN
7. JOINERS AND APPRENTICES
8. ELECTRICAL ENGINEERS
9. STUDENT TEACHERS

Fig. 4.15 Average 'Earnings' vectors for nine sub-groups

4.8 CONCLUSIONS AND SUMMARY

In this chapter we have examined the invidious comparisons that people make between occupations, that is, comparisons in which one occupation is evaluated as being better or worse than another. From the point of view of studying semantics and cognition in the domain of occupation names, we have been interested in the extent to which there are salient evaluative gradients over this domain. Invidious comparison may be a natural operation to carry out with occupations, or it may not. Furthermore, there may be one or many bases of evaluation. Finally, individuals and sub-cultures may differ in the importance they give to evaluations of occupations, or the bases upon which these evaluations are made.

Examining the weak orders of occupations that were implied when subjects ranked the groups into which they had sorted occupation names upon the basis of overall similarity gave the following results.

(i)   Invidious comparison was not such a pervasive characteristic of occupation names that all our subjects found it natural to sort occupations on the basis of a 'more' or 'less' criterion. Indeed, less than half of the subjects who made sortings of occupations made spontaneous orderings of their groupings.

(ii)   When subjects were free to choose their own criteria of invidious comparison, they used a variety of bases for judgement. The amount of training required for the job, its skill, and its qualification levels were given as criteria by about half of the subjects. A significant minority of them used some version of 'importance to society' as a basis for ordering.

(iii)   This method of asking subjects to sort occupations upon the basis of general similarity, and then asking them about any order in their groupings also gave information on the numbers of evaluative categories that subjects found it natural to use. There was considerable variation between subjects in the number of categories used (for 32 occupation names) varying from two to eleven, with five being the most popular number to use.

(iv)   A coefficient of rank correlation (the gamma coefficient) was computed between the weak orderings of occupations for each pair of the subjects. Inspection of these coefficients showed moderate to high amounts of agreement between persons. More detailed examination suggested that such agreements as there are arise from common usage of attributes such as educational qualifications and of latent classifications such as 'professional' by the different subjects. Disagreements arose because of the use of different criteria of evaluation, and also because of different interpretations of the meaning (in the sense of reference) of unfamiliar occupations.

In a second, and more structured investigation, subjects were asked to rate or rank occupation names on criteria (dimensions) that had been predetermined by the investigators. We used two 'normative' criteria, two 'descriptive' criteria, and one 'social distance' criterion. Subjects either ranked or rated a standard set of sixteen occupation names upon these five criteria. These rank orders of occupations were scaled in two and also in three dimensions in the course of a detailed examination of the bases for differences between individuals and between sub-groups (as defined by occupational membership). The scaling was carried out by a 'preference mapping' method in which rank orders are fitted into a given, and sometimes *a priori* configuration. In this chapter, the given configuration used had been obtained empirically, as the 'cognitive map' derived by an individual differences scaling of similarity judgements of pairs of occupations (see Chapter 3). The procedure we adopted is entirely new in the history of studies upon evaluations of occupations, and has a number of advantages.

(i)   The scaling of the rank orders of occupations provided an explicit link between 'evaluative' data (rank orders) and 'cognitive' data (similarity judgements). Each rank order might be best scaled by any one of four models which differ in complexity, and it is of some interest that it was the simplest of these four, the 'vector' model which provided the closest fit to the data for the overwhelming majority of rank orders.

(ii) Having been scaled by the 'vector' model, each rank order of occupations could be represented as a direction (or vector) in the cognitive map (i.e. in the given configuration). This led to considerable advantages in terms of data reduction. Since the rank orders of occupations had been scaled into a vector representation, it was possible to carry out formal statistical analyses using methods developed by physicists and biologists for the analysis of directional data.

(iii) Detailed examination of individual subjects showed that interview data could be used to fill out the picture given quantitatively by a 'cognitive map' with associated evaluative vectors traversing it. This mode of presentation considerably facilitated comparisons between the occupational ideologies of different individuals.

(iv) Statistical analysis (using methods for directional data) showed that there were significant differences between the sub-groups that had been defined upon the basis of occupational membership. Significant differences of this kind were found for each of the five predetermined ranking criteria (two 'normative', two 'descriptive' and one 'social distance'). The differences were by no means of large size. We did not find any sub-groups of individuals who consistently inverted the status order of occupations that is reported in textbooks of sociology. However, since the whole investigation was carried out using subjects from the city of Edinburgh, an *a fortiori* argument seems justified in suggesting the conclusion that differences between occupationally defined sub-groups of people do indeed exist, and may be found to be larger than we have been able to show, when sub-groups from more widely separated cultures are compared.

(v) The sub-group differences just described are concerned only with differences between *rank orders* of occupations. (This remains true even though the rank orders were 'metricised' in the course of being scaled into a vector representation.)

5 Review

The first two chapters of this book were concerned with the ways that professional sociologists and psychologists have tried to represent occupational images. In Chapters 3 and 4 we presented our own attempts to model such images with a general metaphor of a continuous space. We identified two major issues in the sociological and psychological literature. The first of these is concerned with the extent to which occupational structure is in some sense 'real' and 'objective', in such a way that occupational images are derivative of it. We favour the counter-argument to this view, which holds that occupational images are most usefully studied *sui generis* and that information about these images cannot in general be used to make inferences about any 'objective' structure that may exist.

The second major theme of this book relates to debates among sociologists about the degree to which occupational images held by different segments of the population are essentially the same or, on the other hand, reflect the different perspectives (or points of view) of these sub-groups. Both our literature-review and our own empirical investigations lead us to support the view that occupational images do in fact differ, not only from individual to individual but also from group to group. Put into sociological jargon, this means that images of the occupational structure differ from one another not accidentally, but because of socially structured causal processes.

A related issue is the degree to which occupations can all be ranked on a single dimension of general desirability. Empirical sociologists have found it a useful simplification to assume this. We argue that it is an oversimplification, and a dangerous one at that. The rank-ordering of occupations in terms of income is not the same as the rank-ordering of occupations in terms of such factors as the degree of autonomy they offer, the amount of contact with other people they involve, the level of prestige they confer and so on. It is precisely the trade-offs between these different forms of desirability that is of most interest when people move from one occupation to another, and therefore it is curious that sociologists have been so attracted to the use of a single dimension of overall occupational status.

The technical uses to which sociologists and policy-makers put occupational information are almost all based upon crude and often incorrect theories about occupational cognition and evaluation. It is assumed, first, that knowledge of the replies a person makes to questions concerning his or her occupation tells us a great deal about his or her status in society. It is also assumed that all people in a society draw the same status-relevant conclusions from any given piece of occupational information. It is further assumed that of occupational information into the same status category (of a set of status categories).

Our reasons for regarding these assumptions as being highly dubious are indicated throughout this book. We affirm that not only 'subjects' of sociological research, but also the interviewers and coders employed by sociological researchers are subject to the processes that generate individual differences in occupational cognition and evaluation.

All this may seem rather negative. We have criticised sociologists' notions about occupational cognition, but we have not yet made any constructive suggestions about the valid uses that can and should be made of occupational information. These themes will be developed in a second volume.

Notes

Chapter 1

1. The considerable difficulties attendant on the aggregation of individual cognitive structures to the level of the group, and the subsequent interpretation of group averages as 'idealised individuals' (or 'collective representations', Arrow 1951, Guilbaud 1952, Alker 1969, Hirschi and Selvin 1967, Ross 1970; and Horan 1969, Smyth 1971, Cliff 1968), have been steadfastly ignored in the literature on occupational perception.

2. Quillian (1968) presents a different model, designed to represent the objective part of meaning, as against the affective (feeling) component tapped by the semantic differential. The use of the Semantic Differential further commits the researcher to a set of rather strong psycholinguistic assumptions, (see Carroll 1959, Green and Goldfried 1965, Deese 1965). For example, the assumption that all semantic scales are bipolar is called into question almost every time one carries out a Kelly Repertory Grid interview (from the writers' experience, it seems that people use contructs which have *no* opposite pole). Scott (1969) has tried to develop a dimensional theory of meaning which will accommodate such objections.

3. Such perceptual processes are very similar to those discussed by Bartlett (1932), Allport and Postman (1947), and Lloyd (1966). There are even similarities to the Jacobs and Campbell (1961) demonstration of the 'perpetuation of an arbitary tradition' (concerning the Sherif autokinetic effect), through several generations of a laboratory micro-culture (it is comforting to note that Jacobs and Campbell claimed to show the gradual effect of reality on their respondents' judgements).

4. This viewpoint on the way in which people use occupational terms frames the question of how global stereotype judgements of occupational titles get incorporated into analytic judgements of particular occupations.

5. This 'popular' account in fact conflates Engels' more positivistic elements with Lenin's version of materialism, but it characterises the orthodox Comintern position in 1922 in its struggle against European 'deviationism'. As such, it proved the sounding board for 'sociological Marxists' such as Lukács and Korsch. See Watnick (in Labedz 1962) and Lichtheim (1970).

6. Most of the evidence for this statement is provided in Warner's account of 'Rating by Matched Agreements of Social Class Configurations', 47-70. That is not to say, of course, that subjects do *not* perceive the status structure as a single ordered scale, only that Warner presents little evidence, apart from assertion, of the basis for the claim. Certainly in the informative 'social class configuration' (verbal reports) which Warner presents, there is plenty of evidence that some respondent 'stubbornly speak of society as composed of different kinds of people rather than different ranks' (De Soto 1968: 538).

7. A number of occupational prestige studies were performed in the 1920s, beginning with Counts' 1925 study. These are cited in Smith (1943).

8. Shils adds three further conditions which do not have the same salience and cognitive importance as those stated here.

9. These are discussed in Coxon and Jones 1974b.

10. Averaged ratings are usually fairly stable over time, and these form the basis of the multinational comparisons of occupational prestige (Inkeles and Rossi 1956; Hodge, Treiman and Rossi 1966). It will also be noted that the number of occupational titles common to a number of national studies are small and fairly stereotyped, which will tend to inflate the size of the correlations, as is indeed the case.

11. The cognitive approach in sociology has been heavily dependent upon previous psychological, linguistic and social psychological work associated with Allport, Bartlett, Chomsky and Piaget, and latterly has been based upon artificial intelligence (Simon 1969) and psycho-linguistics (Miller 1967). Parsons and Shils (1959) made some use of the notion of Tolman's concept of 'cognitive map', but most cognitive analysis entered sociology by way of occuaptional choice (Musgrave 1967) and ethnomethodology (Cicourel 1973). A good deal of Weberian and action-theory can be construed as being concerned with basic cognitive problems at a social level.

Chapter 2

1. By 'instrumental' social interaction is meant interaction which is only a means to some (usually economic) goal: for example, the squire may chat with the bank clerk as he cashes a cheque, but this does not imply any kind of social equality between them.

2. Further remarks on the sociolinguistics of forms of address may be found in Ervin-Tripp (1971) and in Grimshaw (1973).

3. Some researchers in the field correct their profile correlations for attenuation. This makes them bigger. The enterprise of correction for attenuation is based on the idea that a subset of occupational titles (say the subset of blue collar titles) might have a smaller spread in prestige than exists in the total set. Because of issues concerning the representative sampling of occupational titles, (see the main text), it seems arguable that the corrections for attenuation ought to be applied so as to make profile correlations *smaller* than empirically estimated with the regular formulae, not larger (as seems to be routinely done). This practice of correction for attenuation is related to an unspoken tendency for cross-national profile correlation between occupational prestige scorings to be interpreted as if they were reliability coefficients (like test-retest coefficients). This is tenuous to say the least. The first objection is that the profile correlation weights all occupations equally, no matter how infrequently one comes across them in everyday mobility studies. If Supreme Court Justice is in the list, it is weighed equally with more frequently encountered occupations. The second objection is that it takes no account of the unreliability that occurs when occupational information is coded into prestige-scored categories. Clearly we cannot make any reasonable analogy between the reliability coefficient

for (say) an intelligence test, and the profile correlation between the occupational prestige scorings of the same set of occupations in two different societies.

4. The classic case of professional organisation in an occupation is of course medical and surgical practice in Britain and the USA. So far as Britain is concerned, Parry and Parry (1976), Elliott (1972) and Eckstein (1960) have described how the British Medical Association looks after the interests of its members.

5. It is well known that Blacks are a numerical minority in the USA, (Siegel gives the mean of the 'proportions non-White' for the occupations in his study as being 8.5 per cent). It follows then that the averages for the educational attainments and for the incomes of Whites in the occupations he studied are likely to be much the same as the average educational levels and incomes for all the personnel (White together with non-White) in at least the vast majority of the occupations he studied.

6. Not many students have used 'unemployed' as a category of occupation. One exception is Pineo and Porter (1967), who asked their respondents to judge the social standing of 'someone who lives on relief'.

7. Thinking more positively, it is of course natural to attempt a combination of the work of Siegel and of Nosanchuk. Nosanchuk, it may be recalled, proposed the model that perceivers (or cultures) agree about the presence of strata, and the assignments of occupations to them, but disagree about the ordering of situses within strata. The psychological interpretation of the strata that people agree about might be the classification of occupations into categories such as 'professions', 'white-collar workers other then professionals', 'skilled workers' and 'unskilled workers'. Within-stratum correlations between the characteristics of occupations should then be computed, and these within-group correlations used as data with which to estimate the coefficients of the structural equation models.

8. Nevertheless, the tools are available (Cadzow 1973; Sprague 1976) and progress in this area is to be expected.

9. Elaborations and special cases of the occupational egoism hypothesis have been made. The phenomenon is supposed to be particularly marked among people who work in morally marginal occupations. Strippers and topless waitresses are said to be at pains to distinguish their profession from an older and less prestigious one, though moralists who are unfamiliar with the finer gradations in the world of burlesque entertainment may lump them together as 'no better than prostitutes'. Another special case of the hypothesis is that some occupations are supposed to be evaluated *lower* by people in them than by the general public. In Britain it is often said that the teaching profession as a whole has been undergoing downward social mobility in terms of pay, conditions of work and general prestige in the community. However we might conjecture that news of this percolates only slowly through the social structure, the teachers themselves finding out first, and manual workers finding out last. Such a hypothesis has been used to account for puzzles such as Kelsall's (1957) report that the frequency of sons and daughters following in their father's occupational footsteps is smaller in teaching than in any other professional group (the suggestion being that the children of teachers have direct experience of the level of rewards in teaching). We have already mentioned other studies which show the existence of negative occupational egoism (Sarapata and Wesolowski 1961).

10.   A study of the labour aristocracy in the late nineteenth-century Edinburgh (Gray 1973) shows that this familiar picture of status rivalry is broadly valid, but oversimplified. Economically speaking, the members of the labour aristocracy were upwardly mobile, and according to a simple status-rivalry hypothesis we might expect them to have retained proletarian values in their new economic position. As Gray shows, this did not happen. The highly skilled working man pursued 'respectability', but defined this in his own idiosyncratic terms, which were neither those of white-collar workers nor traditionally proletarian.

11.   This sort of situation is often regarded as an instance of the politically destabilising consequence of disagreements about the status of occupations or social strata. However, Brittan (1975) has argued that processes of occupational egoism ought, at least under some circumstances, to have a politically stabilising influence upon a society. It has commonly been maintained that agreement about the relative status of occupations is a prerequisite of social stability. However, this is only the case for status as meaning 'entitlement to material reward'. Where status is taken to mean prestige in the sense of honour or deference, a high degree of 'egoism' on the part of each occupational group (which would of course indicate dissensus between these groups) might be quite compatible with social stability, and even conducive to it. Brittan argues on these lines that a society in which manual workers, professional and white-collar workers all regarded themselves as the true aristocrats would be good for people's self-respect. See also Hirsch (1976)

12.   It can hardly be an accident that the use of 'Prestige-scores', (or the closely-related 'Socio-Economic Index' scores), from the individual's occupation (assuming it is correctly coded), in order to assign to that individual a score on a finely divided social class continuum has become popular at the same time that the use of regression models have become routine tools for data analysis (guaranteed to produce a readily interpretable 'path analysis diagram' from any set of data).

13.   It is interesting to note that Bogardus' use of social space is roundly dismissed as subjective and psychological by Sorokin (10).

14.   But this is not a question which can be settled *a priori*. There is a lot to be said for the idea (of Coombs 1964: 331) that to the extent that cognitive relations are strongly, uniformly and unequivocally formed by social, cultural and educational forces, to this extent we may expect that they will yield to highly structured quantitative representation. However, relations which correspond to less common experiences, or are simply less intensely thought about are likely to require weaker (or even strong but over-simple) representation. The principle of multiple representation is not simply a cautious strategy in the area of cognition, but a necessary one.

15.   In a lucid treatment of indexical statements Barnes and Law (1976) go so far as to argue that (all) human discourse is constitutively indexical. Acceptance of this viewpoint considerably simplifies our ensuing argument.

16.   We ourselves explicitly examine the problems of the indexicality of class terminology in the second volume.

Chapter 3

1. The pairwise rating schedules in this, and other, tasks were generated by a computer program so that systematic positioning effects could be avoided by randomising the order in which pairs of occupational titles appeared on each schedule and also by randomising the left-right position of pairs. Full detail of the task and the instructions given to interviewers is given in *Methods of Data Collection Used in the Project on Occupational Cognition* (Edinburgh, mimeo, 1973 and 1975, section 5.1), and our third volume.

2. A similar but somewhat more restrictive method is used by Personal Construct theorists (Kelly 1955; Bannister and Mair 1968) to elicit from the subject an antonymous construct which differentiates two of the objects from the third. We obtain two judgements, and do not require that the construct must be an antonymn.

3. From this point on, technical information and discussion, together with most tables, are relegated to the technical appendixes collected together in the third volume. Appendix sections are signalled in the main text by bracketed references starting with the letter T - e.g. (T3.2).

4. The pairwise and triadic similarities data are available as Project files DPB106AD (pairwise similarities) and DTB110AD (triadic similarities) from the SSRC Survey Archive at the University of Essex.

5. The terms 'normal attribute space', 'Group Map' and 'Group Space' will be used interchangeably in the rest of this chapter to refer to a configuration of stimulus points in r-dimensions to which individual cognitive maps may be referred.

6. The assistance of Mr Stephen Kendrick in the analysis of the data in this section is gratefully acknowledged.

Chapter 4

1. Some relevant papers are DeSoto 1961; DeSoto *et al.* 1965; DeSoto and Albrecht 1968; Trabasso *et al.* 1975; Walker 1976.

2. This implies that a funnel-shaped evaluative map of stimulus points (or a hyper-funnel) with high status occupations at the broad end of the funnel, ought to emerge from analysis of ratings and rankings.

3. Eight of the 32 subjects who ordered their ranked occupational titles were in occupations involving high educational qualifications and high contact with people, eleven were in occupations involving high educational qualifications and contact with data or machines, seven were in occupations not requiring high educational qualifications but involving contact with people, and six were in occupations not requiring high educational qualifications and involving work with data or machines.

4. See Roskam (1968: 27-8 and 99 *et seq.*); Coombs (1964: 200 *et seq.*); and Carroll (1972: 16).

5. It is easier to explain the model by reference to *preference* rankings, but this should not be taken to imply either that these models refer only to preferences, or that prestige need be viewed as a type of preference.

6. To these properties Roskam (1968: 28) adds a particular type of

additivity which complements the excellence and boundedness properties of the distance model.

7. Triandis *et al.* (1959, 1972) examined cross-culturally the role which *occupation* plays in social judgements, and Himmelfarb and Sen (1969) present an approach to the similar problem of impression-formation of social class.

8. Discussed in Shepard (1969: 34), and in Rapoport and Fillenbaum (1971: 23-5). See also Hyman and Well (1967: 245 *et seq.*).

9. Every value of *r* of 1 or above substituted in the general distance function above yields a different Minkowski metric. Our interest is restricted to cases where *r* = 1, 2 and infinity; *r* = 1 defines Landahl's 'City-Block' metric (where distance is simply the sum of the differences on each dimension), *r* = 2 defines the Euclidean metric, and r = ∞ defines the so-called dominance metric, where the largest dimensional difference makes the greatest contribution to the distance.

10. This is very similar to what has happened in the case of the Osgoodian Evaluative factor in semantic differential research, and the similarity to occupational prestige is interesting. The most relevant instance is provided in Miller's (1967: 68-71) use of the classification method to obtain data on the relations between Osgood's antonymous adjective pairs. His analysis shows a clear differentiation of three distinct varieties of 'unidimensional' evaluation.

11. Shepard (1964) and Yntema and Torgerson (1961) go as far as to argue that in many decision-making situations, humans should be used to extract relevant information, but machines should be relied upon to combine it in a decision-rule.

12. High consensus is shown in the vector model representation by the fact that subject vectors have small angles of separation.

13. When stimuli are arrayed on a circle, sphere, or hypersphere the distance (unfolding) model *also* produces only sets of mirror-image scales, and in this case there are no closed isotonic regions in a distance model either.

14. If considerable differences in perception do exist, then the results from an Unfolding Analysis may lead, quite incorrectly, to abandoning a distance model. It might be that all subjects' preferences are in fact a monotone function of the separation of their ideal points and the stimuli points, but that the distances refer to different cognitive spaces.

15. Carroll (1972) has proved that the vector model is a special case of the simple distance (unfolding) model. As an ideal-point of the distance model is moved further and further out from the origin of the space, the circular isopreference contours (joining points of equal preference for this subject) more and more closely approximate straight lines in the vicinity of the stimuli points; and isopreference 'contours' in the vector model consist of precisely such straight lines, perpendicular to the subject's vector.

16. In the program implementing the PREFMAP models an option also exists for the non-metric (i.e. monotonic) regression of preference values on the model distances (or projections on the subject vector in the case of model IV).

17. The score value of stimulus *j* for subject *i* (S_{ij}) is assumed to be the scalar product of the stimulus vector from the origin of the space to the location of stimulus *j*, and the subject-vector for subject *i*. If $\|x_{ia}\|$ give the

stimulus coordinates and $\|y_{ja}\|$ the termini of the subject vectors, then $S = XY$. Eckart-Young factorisation yields the matrix S_r which is the best least-squares fit to S in r dimensions. Carroll (1964: 4-9) proves that this procedure maximizes C_1, an index of linear agreement between the data and reproduced values.

18. 'Raw stress' (the residual sum of squares from monotonic regression) forms the basis for all commonly used measures of badness-of-fit between the empirical data and the configuration produced by non-metric MDS procedures. Since any uniform contraction (or expansion) of a given configuration will automatically decrease (increase) the raw stress value, a scale factor is necessary to prevent this. For conditional data (such as I-scales) normalisation of raw stress must be by $\Sigma (d_{ij} - \bar{d})^2$ if the risk of degenerate solutions is to be avoided. (see Roskam 1969: 25) and Kruskal and Carroll (1969: 661 *et seq.*).

19. Whilst the two (and higher) dimensional solutions have very low values of stress, several points occupy almost the same location. This can be interpreted in at least two ways. One alternative is to say that this representation capitalises on the fact that non-metric algorithms require only *weak-order monotonicity* between data and solution distances, and this allows low-stress solutions by producing equivalences among the distances of the solution which do not occur in the data. However, the use of stress formula 2 in the stress-minimisation algorithm (see Roskam 1968: 43 *et seq.*, 59-60) usually guards against this eventuality. The alternative explanation is simply that the subject-rankings are so diverse that the only configuration of occupational titles that can satisfy the data is a totally 'compromise' or averaged one where the subject points are all approximately equally distant from the subject points. In fact, these are two sides of the same coin; inspection of the disparities fitted to the data (I-scales) confirms the suspicion that the solution capitalises on weak monotonicity, and we have already commented on the diversity of subjects' rankings, which would lead to an 'averaged' solution when analysed by a non-metric distance model.

20. As Moore *et al.* (1949: 793) express it in a slightly different context: 'It is only where the specific attributes of individuals and specific context are unknown, ignored, or irrelevant that the more general category of class is likely to have any significance.' This point is also well expressed and documented by Bott (1971: 163 *et seq.*).

21. Some readers may feel that more conclusions could be drawn from conventional analyses of these data. We shall be presenting such conclusions, together with the data on which they are based, in a technical appendix (T4.1).

22. We have been unable to find any reference to the statistical analysis of directional data in the sociological literature, and so our application of these techniques here seems to be something of an innovation in sociological data analysis. Most of the developments and applications so far have been in such disciplines as Geology and Biology. See Mardia (1972) for a thorough review.

23. In the vector model, each rank order of the 16 occupational titles is summarised by three direction cosines, (one for each of the dimensions of the INDSCAL space). The parameter setting used for the PREFMAP analyses were as follows:

Dimensions: 3 Phase (i.e. model): vector model only. Fitting criterion: code 2 (squared distances in the solution to be related to the scale values monotonically (block monotone with ordering within blocks) as is recommended for use with tied data). This is the so-called 'primary approach to ties'. The criterion for stopping the iterative procedure on the monotone fit was set to 0.0005; this is a finer tolerance than customarily used and requires correspondingly more computer time.

The number of rank orders available for analysis was 1262; however since some of these rank orders were not complete (there were 'ranks' of zero), the number actually analysed was 1204; these broke down into;
245 for the 'first normative criterion', (social usefulness)
202 for the 'second normative criterion', (rewards ought to have)
236 for the 'cognitive distance criterion', (knowledge)
252 for the 'first descriptive criterion', (NORC Social standing)
269 for the 'second descriptive criterion', (earnings).

In a tidily designed investigation, equal numbers of rank orders for the different criteria would have been obtained. This was not attained here because of the fact that some interviewees were being asked to complete a number of tasks as well as the rank orderings, and in some of those cases, it was considered advisable to have only two or three of the ranking/rating criteria used, rather than the complete set of five.

List of Abbreviations

Acronyms of multidimensional scaling models used in this volume and computer programmes implementing them (Edinburgh-Cardiff MDS(X) programmes)

INDSCAL   *Individual Differences Scaling,* by a weighted Euclidean distance model (Carroll and Chang 1969)
           Originator: J. D. Carroll, Bell Laboratories (Section 3.5 *et seq.*)

MDPREF   *Multidimensional Preference Analysis,* by a non-parametric analysis of a rectangular data matrix using a vector model (Carroll and Chang 1964)
           Originator: J. D. Carroll, Bell Laboratories (Section 4.4 *et seq.*)

MINIRSA   *Rectangular Similarity Analysis,* of a rectangular data matrix using a non-metric distance model (Multidimensional Unfolding) (Roskam 1975a)
           Originator: E. E. Roskam, Nijmegen University (Section 4.4 *et seq.*)

MINISSA   *Smallest Space Analysis*, of a square symmetric data matrix using a non-metric distance model (Roskam 1975b)
           Originator: E. E. Roskam, Nijmegen University (Section 3.4 *et seq.*)

MRSCAL   *Metric Scaling,* of a square symmetric data matrix using a metric (linear) distance model (Roskam 1972)
           Originator: E. E. Roskam, Nijmegen University (Section 3.4)

PREFMAP   *Preference Mapping* (External), scaling of rectangular data matrix in a user-supplied *a priori* space, using a hierarchy of distance and vector models, with metric and quasi-non-metric options (Carroll 1972)
           Originator: J. D. Carroll, Bell Laboratories

TRISOSCAL *Triadic Scaling,* Edinburgh version of integral scaling of triadic similarities, using a non-metric distance model. (Roskam 1970 and Prentice 1973)
           Originators: E. E. Roskam, Nijmegen University, and M. J. Prentice, Edinburgh University.

Technical Appendixes (in Third Book)

References

Aberle, D.F., A. Cohen, A. Davies, M. Levy and F. Sutton (1950). 'The functional prerequisites of a society'. *Ethics, 60,* 100-11.

Agar, M. (1973). *Ripping and running: a formal ethnography of urban heroin addicts.* New York: Seminar Press.

Alexander, C.N. (1972). 'Status perceptions', *Am.Sociol.Rev., 37,* 767-73.

Alker, H.R., Jr. (1969). 'A typology of ecological fallacies', Dogan, M., and Rokkan, S. (eds), *Quantitative ecological analysis in the social sciences.* Cambridge Mass.: MIT Press.

Allport, G.W., and L. Postman (1947). *The psychology of rumour.* New York: Holt.

Anderson, N.H. (1962). 'Application of an additive model to impression formation', *Science, 138,* 817-18.

———(1968). 'A simple model for information integration', R.P. Abelson *et al,* (eds), *Theories of cognitive consistency.* Chicago: Rand McNally.

Anglin, J.A. (1970). *The growth of word meaning.* London: MIT Press.

Arnold, D.O. (1970). 'Dimensional sampling: an approach for studying a small number of cases', *The American Sociologist, 5,* 147-50.

Arnold, J.B. (1971). 'A multidimensional scaling study of semantic distance', *Journ.Exp.Psychol., 90,* 349-72.

Arrow, K.J. (1951). *Social choice and individual values.* New York: Wiley.

Asch, S.E. (1946). 'Forming impressions of personality', *J.Abnorm.Soc. Psychol, 41,* 258-90.

Axelrod, R. (1973). 'Schema theory: an information processing model of perception and cognition', *American Political Science Review, 67,* 1248-66.

Bailey, K.E. (1974). 'Interpreting smallest space analysis', *Sociological methods and research, 3,* 3-29.

Bannister, D., and J. Mair (1969). *The evaluation of personal constructs.* London: Academic Press.

Bar Hillel, Y. (1954). 'Indexical expressions', *Mind, 63,* 359-79.

Barkow, J.H. (1975). 'Prestige and Culture', *Current Anthropology, 16,* 553-65.

Barnes, B., and J. Law (1976). 'Whatever should be done with indexical expressions?', *Theory and Society, 3,* 223-37.

Bartlett, F.C. (1932). *Remembering: A study in experimental and social psychology.* Cambridge: Cambridge Univ. Press.

Beals, R., D.H. Krantz and A. Tversky (1968). 'Foundations of multidimensional scaling', *Psychol.Rev., 75,* 127-42.

Beardslee, D.C., and D.D. O'Dowd (1961).'The college student image of the scientist', *Science, 133*, 997-1001.

———(1962). 'Students and the occupational world', N. Sanford (ed.). *The American College,* New York: Wiley.

Becker, H. (1970). *Sociological Work.* London: Allen Lane.

Bendix, R., and S. Lipset (eds) (1966). *Class, status and power* (2nd edition). New York: Free Press.

Berliner, J.S. (1961). 'The situation of plant managers', in A. Inkeles and K. Geiger (eds), *Soviet Society.* Boston: Houghton Mifflin.

Beshers, J.M., and S. Reiter (1963). 'Social status and social change', *Behav.Sci., 8,* 1-13.

Biddle, B.J. *et al,* (1966). 'Shared inaccuracies in the role of the teacher', in B.J. Biddle and E.J. Thomas (eds.), *Role Theory: concepts and research.* New York: Wiley.

Blau, P.M., and O.D. Duncan (1967). *The American occupational structure.* New York: Wiley.

Blishen, B. (1967). 'A socio-economic index for occupations in Canada', *Canadian Rev. of Sociology and Anthropology, 4,* 41-53.

Bohm, D. (1972). 'Indication of a new order in physics, in Shanin (q.v.).

Bolte, M. (1959). *Sozialer Aufstreg and Abstieg: eine Untersuchung über Berufsprestige und Berufsmobilität.* Stuttgart: Enke.

Bott, E. (1971). *Family and social network* (2nd edition). London: Tavistock Publications.

Brigham, J.C. (1971). 'Ethnic stereotypes', *Psychol.Bull., 76,* 15-38.

Brittan, S. (1975). 'The economic contradictions of democracy', *Brit. J. Polit.Sci., 5,* 129-59.

Brown, R., and P. Brannen (1970). 'Social relations and social perspectives amongst shipbuilding workers', *Sociology, 4,* 71-84, 197-211.

Brown, R., and M. Ford (1961). 'Address in American English', *J.Abnorm. Soc.Psychol., 62,* 375-85.

Bulmer, M.I.A. (ed.) (1975). *Working Class Images of Society.* London: Routledge and Kegan Paul.

Burton, M.L. (1972). 'Semantic dimensions of occupation names', in A.K. Romney, R.N. Shepard and Sara Beth Nerlove (eds), *Multidimensional scaling: Vol. II Applications.* New York: Seminar Press.

Burton, M.L., and Sara Beth Nerlove (1971). 'Brevity with balance: an exploration of a judged similarity task', Working Paper No. 2, School of Social Sciences, University of California at Irvine, mimeo. Published (1976) as 'Balanced designs for triads testing: two examples from English', *Soc.Sci.Res., 5,* 247-67.

Cadzow, J.A., (1973). *Discrete-time systems.* New Jersey: Englewood Cliffs.

Cauthen, N., *et al.* (1971). 'Stereotypes: a review of the literature, 1926-1968', *J.Soc. Psychol., 84,* 103-25.

Cain, G.G. (1974). 'Review Essay on Socio-economic background and achievement by O.D. Duncan *et al., Amer.J.Sociol., 79,* 1497-509.

Campbell, J.D. (1952). 'Subjective aspects of occupational status', unpublished Ph.D. thesis, Harvard University.

Carroll, J.B. (1959). 'Review of Osgood, Suci and Tannenbaum. The Measurement of meaning', *Language, 35,* 58-77.

Carroll, J.D. (1972). 'Individual differences and multidimensional scaling', in R.N. Shepard, A.K. Romney and Sara B. Nerlove (eds), *Multidimensional scaling: Vol. I Theory.* New York: Seminar Press.

Carroll, J.D., and J.J. Chang (1964). 'Nonmetric multidimensional analysis of paired comparisons data', Murray Hill, New Jersey: Bell Laboratories, mimeo.

——(1969). 'Analysis of individual differences in multidimensional scaling via an N-way generalization of "Eckart-Young" decomposition', *Psychometrika, 33,* 283-319.

Chun, K.T., *et al,* (1975). Perceived trustworthiness of occupations: personality effects and cross-cultural generalizability', *J. of cross-cultural psychology, 6,* 430-43.

Cicourel, A.V. (1974). *Theory and Method in a Study of Argentine Fertility,* New York: Wiley.

Cliff, N. (1968). 'The "Idealized Individual" Interpretation of.Individual Differences in Multidimensional Scaling', *Psychometrika, 23,* 225-32.

Coleman, J.S. (1964). *Introduction to Mathematical Sociology.* London: Macmillan.

Cook, M. (1971). *Interpersonal perception.* Harmondsworth: Penguin.

Coombs, C.H. (1964). *A theory of data.* New York: Wiley.

Cormack, R.M. (1971). A review of classification. *J.Roy.Stat.Soc.A. 134,* (3) 321-67.

Coxon, A.P.M. (1967). 'Patterns of occupational recruitment: the anglican ministry', *Sociology, I,* 53-67.

——(1971). 'Occupational attributes: constructs and structure', *Sociology, 5,* 335-54.

——(1975). 'Multidimensional scaling'. Colchester: ECPR Monographs on Social Science Data Analysis.

Coxon, A.P.M., and C.L. Jones (1974a). 'Occupational similarities: subjective aspects of social stratification', *Quality and Quantity, 8,* 139-54.

——(1974b). Problems in the selection of occupational titles. *Sociological Review, 22,* 369-384.

Cramer, P. (1968). *Word Association.* New York: Academic Press.

Crites, J. (1968). *Vocational Psychology.* McGraw Hill.

D'Andrade, R.G. (1971). 'A propositional analysis of U.S. American beliefs about illness', paper presented at Mathematical Social Science Board Workshop on natural decision making processes. Palo Alto, California.

Davis, A., B.B. and M.R. Gardner (1941). *Deep South: a social anthropological study of caste and class.* Chicago: University Press.

De Fleur, M.L., and Lois B. De Fleur (1967). 'The relative contribution of

television as a learning source for children's occupational knowledge',
Amer.Sociol.Rev., 52, 777-89.

Della Fave, L.R. (1974). 'Success Values: are they universal or class
differentiated?', *Am.Journ.Sociol., 80,* 153-169.

De Soto, C.B. (1961). 'The predilection for single orderings',
J.Abnorm.Soc.Psychol., 62, 16-23.

De Soto, C., and F. Albrecht (1968). 'Cognition and social orderings. In
R.P. Abelson *et al.* (eds), *Theories of Cognitive Consistency,* Chicago:
Rand McNally.

De Soto, C.B., and J.J. Bosley (1962). 'The Cognitive structure of a social
structure', *J.Abnorm.Soc.Psychol., 64,* 303-307.

Deese, J. (1965). *The structure of associations in language and thought.*
Baltimore: Johns Hopkins Press.

DiCesare, Constance B. (1975). 'Changes in the occupational structure of
U.S. jobs', *Monthly Labour Review,* March, 24-34.

Duncan, O.D., D.L. Featherman and B. Duncan (1972). *Socio-economic
background and achievement.* New York: Academic Press.

Durkheim, E. (1938). *The rules of sociological method.* Chicago: University
Press.

Eckstein, H. (1960). *Pressure group politics.* Stanford: University Press.

Eisler, H., and E.E. Roskam (1973). 'Multidimensional similarity: an
experimental and theoretical comparison of vector, distance, and set
theoretical models', Nijmegen: Psychological Laboratory Report
73-MA-12.

Ekman, G., and L. Sjöberg (1965). 'Scaling', *Ann.Rev.Psychol., 16,* 451-74.

Erdos, P.L. (1970). *Professional mail surveys.* New York: McGraw Hill.

Ervin-Tripp, Susan M. (1971). 'Sociolinguistics', in J.A. Fishman (ed.),
Advances in the sociology of language. The Hague: Mouton. 15-91.

Ervin-Tripp, Susan M. (1972). On sociolinguistic rules: alternation and
co-occurrence. In Gumperz and Hymes, 1972, 213-50.

Elliott, P. (1972). *The sociology of the professions.* London: Macmillan.

Fararo, T.J. (1970). 'Theoretical studies in status and stratification',
Gen.Systems, 15, 71-101.

Field, M.G. (1960). 'Medical organization and the medical profession', in
C.E. Black (ed.), *The transformation of Russian society.* Harvard:
University Press.

Fillenbaum, S., and A. Rapoport (1971). *Structures in the subjective
lexicon.* London: Academic Press.

Form, W.H. (1946). Toward an occupational social psychology. *J.Soc.
Psychol., 24,* 85-99.

Garfinkel, H. (1967). *Studies in ethnomethodology.* Englewood Cliffs:
Prentice-Hall.

Ginzberg, E., S.W. Ginsburg, S. Axelrad and J.L. Herma (1951).
Occupational choice: an approach to a general theory. New York:
Columbia University Press.

Glenn, N.D. (1963). 'Negro prestige criteria', *Am.Journ.Sociol.*, *68*, 645-57.

Goblot, E. (1961). 'Class and occupation', in T. Parsons *et al.* (eds), *Theories of society.* New York: Free Press.

Goldmeier, E. (1972). 'Similarity in visually perceived forms', *Psychological Issues, 8* (Monograph 29).

Goldthorpe, J.H., and K. Hope (1972). 'Occupational grading and occupational prestige', in K. Hope (ed.), *The analysis of social mobility,* Oxford: Clarendon Press.

Good, I.J., and T.N. Tideman (1976). 'From individual to collective ordering through multidimensional attribute space', *Proc.Royal Society of London,* Series A, *347,* 371-85.

Granovetter, M.S. (1974). *Getting a job: a study of contacts and careers.* Cambridge, Mass.: Harvard University Press.

Gray, R.Q. (1973). 'Styles of life, the "labour aristocracy" and class relations in later 19th century Edinburgh', *Int.Rev.Soc.Hist., 18,* 428-52.

Green, R.F., and M.R. Goldfried (1965). 'On the bipolarity of semantic space', *Psychol.monographs, 79,* 1-31.

Gregson, R.A.M. (1975). *The psychometrics of similarity.* New York: Academic Press.

Grimshaw, A.D. (1973). 'Sociolinguistics', in I. de S.Pool *et al.* (eds.), *Handbook of Communication.* Chicago: Rand McNally.

Gross, N., W.S. Mason and A.W. McEachern (1958). *Explorations in role analysis: studies of the school superintendency role.* New York: Wiley.

Guilbaud, G.T. (1952). 'Theories of the general interest and the logical problem of aggregation', translated from the French, in P.F. Lazarsfeld and N.W. Henry (eds.), *Readings in Mathematical Social Science.* Cambridge, Mass.: MIT Press.

Gumperz, J.J. and D. Hymes (eds.) (1972). *Directions in socio-linguistics: the ethnography of communication.* New York: Holt, Rinehart and Winston.

Gusfield, J.R., and M. Schwartz (1963).'The meanings of occupational prestige: reconsideration of the NORC scale', *Am.Sociol.Rev., 28,* 265-77.

Guttman, L., and E.A. Suchman (1947). Intensity and a zero point for attitude analysis. *Amer.Sociol.Rev. 12,* 56-67.

Haller, A.O., D.B. Holsinger and H.U. Saraiva (1972), 'Variations in occupational prestige hierarchies: Brazilian data', *Amer.J.Sociol., 77,* 941-56.

Hammel, E.A. (1970). 'The ethnographer's dilemma: alternative models of occupational prestige in Belgrade', *Man* (Journal of the Royal Anthropological Institute) *5,* 652-70.

Harder, T. (1969). *Introduction to mathematical models in market and opinion research.* Dordrecht: Reidel.

Hartigan, J.A. (1967). 'Representation of similarity matrices by trees', *J.Am.Stat.Ass., 62,* 1140-58.

Hartman, Moshe. (1975). 'Prestige grading of occupations using sociologists as judges', paper presented at the 70th annual meeting of the American Sociological Association, San Francisco.

Heise, D.R., and Essie M. Roberts (1970). 'The development of role knowledge', *Genetic psychol.monographs, 82,* 83-115.

Hirsch, F. (1976). *Social limits to growth.* Harvard: University Press.

Hirsch, W. (1958). 'The image of the scientist in science fiction: a content analysis', *Amer.J.Sociol., 63,* 506-12.

Hirschi, T., and H.C. Selvin (1967). *Delinquency research: an appraisal of analytic methods.* New York: Free Press.

Hodge, R.W., P.M. Siegel and P.H. Rossi (1964). 'Occupational prestige in the United States 1925-1963', *Amer.J.of Sociol., 70,* 286-302.

Hodge, R.W., D.J. Treiman and P.H. Rossi (1966), 'A comparative study of occupational prestige', in R. Bendix and S.M. Lipset (eds.), *Class, Status and Power* (2nd edition). New York: Free Press.

Hodson, F.R. (ed.) (1971), *Anglo-Romanian conference on mathematics in the archaeological and historical sciences.* Edinburgh: Edinburgh University Press.

Hoijer, B. (1970a). On the consistency of similarity judgments', Uppsala: Report 77, Department of Psychology.

——(1970b). 'Isosimilarity contours of two-dimensional cognitive judgements', Uppsala: Psychology Research Report 79.

——(1971). 'Cognitive processes in similarity judgments', Uppsala: Psychology Research Report 84.

Holland, J.L. (1963). 'A theory of vocational choice: vocational images', *Voc.Guid.Quart., 11,* 232-9.

Hollander, P. (1973). *Soviet and American society.* New York: Oxford University Press.

Holman, E.W. (1972). 'The relation between hierarchical and Euclidean models for psychological distances', *Psychometrika, 37,* 417-23.

Hope, K. (1973). 'What are people doing when they grade occupations?', paper presented at the British Sociological Association Annual conference.

Horan, C.B. (1969). 'Multidimensional scaling: combining observation when individuals have different perceptual structures', *Psychometrika, 34,* 139-65.

Hudson, L. (1966). *Contrary imaginations.* London: Methuen.

——(1967a). 'The stereotypical scientist', *Nature, 213.*

——(1967b). 'Arts and sciences: the influence of stereotypes on language', *Nature, 214,* 968.

——(1968). *Frames of Mind.* London: Methuen.

Hunter, A.A. (1977). 'A comparative analysis of Anglophone-Francophone occupational prestige structures in Canada', *Canad.J.Sociol., 2,* in press.

Hyman, R., and A. Well (1967). 'Judgments of similarity and spatial models', *Percept. and Psychophysics, 2,* 233-48.

Inkeles, A., and P.H. Rossi (1956). 'National comparisons of occupational prestige', *Amer. J.Sociol.*, *61*, 329-39.

Jackson, E.F., and R.F. Curtis (1968). 'Conceptualization and measurement in the study of social stratification', in H.M. Blalock and A.B. Blalock (eds.), *Methodology in social research.* New York: McGraw Hill.

Jackson, J.A. (ed.) (1968). *Sociological Studies 1: Social Stratification.* Cambridge: University Press.

Jacobs, R.C., and D.T. Campbell (1961). 'The perpetuation of an arbitrary tradition through several generations of a laboratory microculture', *J.Abnorm.social psychology*, *62*, 649-58.

Jencks, C.S., and D. Reisman (1962). 'Patterns of residential education: a case study at Harvard', in N. Sanford (ed.), *The American College*, New York: Wiley.

Johnson, S.C. (1967). 'Hierarchical clustering schemes', *Psychometrika*, *32*, 241-54.

Johnson, T.J. (1972). *Professions and Power.* London: Macmillan.

Jones, L.E., and J. Wadington (1975). 'Sensitivity of INDSCAL to simulated individual differences in dimension, usage patterns and judgmental error', Urbana: University of Illinois, mimeo.

Kahl, J.A. (1957). *The American class structure.* New York: Holt Rinehart & Winston.

Katz, M.B. (1972). 'Occupational classification in history', *J.of interdisciplinary history*, *3*, 63-88.

——(1973). *The people of Hamilton, Canada West.* Harvard: University Press.

Katz, D., and K.W. Braly (1933). 'Racial stereotypes of 100 college students', *J.abnorm.and soc.psychol.*, *28*, 280-90.

Kelly, G.A. (1955). *The psychology of personal constructs.* New York: Norton.

Kendall, D.G. (1971). 'Seriation from abundance matrices', in Hodson 1972, 215-52.

Komorita, S.S., and A.R. Bass (1967). 'Attitude differentiation and evaluative scales of the semantic differential', *J.Pers.Soc.Psychol.*, *6*, 241-4.

Kruskal, J.B. (1964a). 'Multidimensional scaling by optimizing goodness of fit to a nonmetric hypothesis', *Psychometrika*, *29*, 1-27.

——(1964b). 'Nonmetric multidimensional scaling: a numerical method', *Psychometrika*, *29*, 115-29.

Kuhn, T.S. (1970). *The structure of scientific revolutions* (2nd edition). Chicago: University of Chicago Press.

Labedz, L. (ed.) (1962). *Revisionism: Essays on the history of Marxist ideas.* London: Allen & Unwin.

Laumann, E.O. (1973). *Bonds of pluralism: the form and substance of urban social networks.* New York: Wiley-Interscience.

——(1966). 'Prestige and association in an urban community', Indianapolis: Bobbs-Merrill.

Laumann, E.O., and L. Guttman (1966). 'The relative associational contiguity of occupations in an urban setting', *Am.Sociol.Rev., 31,* 169-78.

Lazarsfeld, P.F., and N.W. Henry (eds.) 1968). *Readings in mathematical social science.* Cambridge, Mass.: MIT Press.

Lewis, L.S. (1964). 'Class and perceptions of class', *Social Forces, 42,* 336-40.

Lichtheim, G. (1970). *Lukács.* London: Collins-Fontana.

Lindzey, G., and E. Aronson (eds.) (1969). *The handbook of social psychology,* (2nd edition). Reading, Mass.: Addison Wesley.

Lloyd, G.E.R. (1966). *Polarity and analogy: two types of argumentation in early Greek thought.* Cambridge: University Press.

Lockwood, D. (1958). *The blackcoated worker.* London: Allen & Unwin.

——(1966). 'Sources of variation in working class images of society', *Sociol.Rev., 14,* 249-67.

Luce, R.W., and H. Raiffa (1957). *Games and decisions.* New York: Wiley.

Lukács, G. (1971) (tr. R. Livingstone). *History and class consciousness.* London: Merlin Press.

Macdonald, K.I. (1972). 'MDSCAL and distances between socio-economic groups', in K. Hope (ed.), *The analysis of social mobility.* Oxford: Clarendon Press.

——(1974). 'The Hall-Jones scale: a note on the interpretation of the main British prestige coding', in J.M. Ridge (ed.), *Mobility in Britain reconsidered.* Oxford: Clarendon Press.

McFarland, D.D., and D.J. Brown (1973). 'Social distance as a metric: a systematic introduction to smallest space analysis', in Laumann (1973), 213-53.

Manning, P.K. (1971). Talking and becoming. In Douglas 1971.

Mardia, K.V. (1972). *Statistics of directional data.* London: Academic Press.

——(1975). Statistics of directional data. *J.Royal statistical society, series B (Methodological), 37,* 349-93.

Martin, F.M. (1954). 'Some subjective aspects of social stratification', in D.V. Glass (ed.), *Social mobility in Britain.* London: Routledge & Kegan Paul.

Mayer, K.U. (1972). 'Dimensions of mobility space: some subjective aspects of career mobility', *Social Science Information, 11,* 87-115.

Mead, Margaret, and R. Metraux (1957). 'The image of the scientist among high school students', *Science, 126,* 384-90.

Merton, R.K., G. Reader and P.L. Kendall (eds.) (1957). *The Student-Physician.* Harvard: University Press.

Miller, G.A. (1967). 'Psycholinguistic approaches to the study of communication', in D.L. Arm (ed.), *Journeys in science.* Albuquerque: University of New Mexico Press.

——(1969). 'A psychological method to investigate verbal concepts', *J.Math.Psychol., 6,* 196.

Mills, C.W. (1951). *White collar: the American middle classes.* Oxford: University Press.

Morris, R.G., and R.J. Murphy (1959). 'The situs dimension in occupational structure', *Amer. Sociol.Rev., 24,* 231-9.

Moser, C.A., and J.R. Hall (1954). 'The social grading of occupations', in D.V. Glass (ed.), *Social mobility in Britain.* London: Routledge & Kegan Paul.

Moss, W.W. (1967). 'Some new analytic and graphic approaches to numerical taxonomy, with an example from the dermanyssidae (Acari)', *Syst.Zool., 16,* 177-207.

Musgrave, P.W. (1967). 'Towards a sociological theory of occupational choice', *Social.Rev., 15,* 33-46.

Neisser, U. (1967). *Cognitive psychology.* New York: Appleton-Century-Crofts.

Newby, H. (1975). 'The deferential dialectic', *Comp.studies in society and history, 17,* 139-64.

North, C.C., and P.K. Hatt (1947). 'Jobs and occupations: a popular evaluation', *Opinion News, 9,* 3-13. Reprinted in R. Bendix and S.M. Lipset (eds.), *Class Status and Power* (1st edition), Free Press, 411-26.

Nosanchuk, T.A. (1972). 'A note on the use of the correlation coefficient for assessing the similarity of occupation rankings', *Canad.Rev.Soc. and Anth. 9,* 357-65.

Oldman, D., and R. Illsley (1966). 'Measuring the status of occupations', *Sociol.Rev., 14,* 53-72.

Oliver, Pamela (1974). 'Sex, race and class bias in census bureau reporting of occupations', *Public Data Use, 2,* 10-13.

Orwell, G. (1937). *The road to Wigan pier.* Harmondsworth: Penguin Books.

Osgood, C.E., G.J. Suci and P.H. Tannenbaum (1957). *The measurement of meaning.* Urbana: University of Illinois Press.

Osipow, S.H. (1962). 'Perceptions of occupations as a function of titles and descriptions', *Journ.Couns.Psychol., 9,* 106-9.

Ossowski, S. (1963). *Class structure in the social consciousness.* London: Routledge & Kegan Paul.

Ozanne, R. (1962). 'A century of occupational differentials in manufacturing', *Rev. of Econ. and Statistics, 44,* 292-9.

Packard, Vance (1959). *The status seekers.* New York: David McKay.

Parry, N., and J. Parry (1976). *The rise of the medical profession.* London: Croom Helm.

Parsons, T. (1971). *The system of modern societies.* Englewood Cliffs, N.J.: Prentice-Hall.

Parsons, T., and E.A. Shils (1962). *Toward a general theory of action: theoretical foundations for the social sciences.* New York: Harper.

Penn, R. (1975). 'Occupational prestige hierarchies: a great empirical invariant?', *Social Forces, 54,* 352-64.

Pineo, P.C., and J. Porter (1967). 'Occupational prestige in Canada', *Canadian Review of Sociology and Anthropology, 4,* 24-40.

Plata, M. (1975). 'Stability and change in the prestige rankings of occupations over 49 years', *J. Vocational Behvior, 6,* 95-9.

Prentice, M.J. (1973). 'On Roskam's nonmetric multidimensional scaling algorithm for triads', Edinburgh, Project on Occupational Cognition, mimeo.

Proshansky, H.M. (1966). 'The development of intergroup attitudes', in L.W. Hoffman and M.L. Hoffman (eds.), *Review of child development research,* vol. 2. New York: Russell Sage.

Quillian, M.R. (1968). 'Semantic memory', in M. Minsky (ed.), *Semantic Information Processing.* Cambridge, Mass.: MIT Press.

Rainwater, L. (1974). *What money buys: the social meanings of income.* New York: Basic Books.

Rapoport, Amnon, and S. Fillenbaum (1972). 'Experimental studies of semantic structures', in R.N. Shepard *et al.* (eds.), *Multidimensional scaling: theory and applications.* New York: Seminar Press.

Reeb, M. (1959). 'How people see jobs: a multidimensional analysis', *Occupational Psychology, 33,* 1-17.

Reiss, A.J., O.D. Duncan, P.K. Hatt and C.C. North (1961). *Occupations and social status.* New York: Free Press of Glencoe.

Roskam, E.E. (1968). *Metric analysis of ordinal data in psychology,* Ch. I. Nijmegen: Voorschoten.

——(1970). 'The method of triads for nonmetric multidimensional scaling', *Nederlands Tijdschrift voor de Psychologie, 25,* 404-17.

——(1972). 'Multidimensional scaling by metric transformation of data', *Nederlands Tijdschrift voor de Psychologie, 27,* 486-508.

——(1975a). 'Nonmetric data analysis: general methodology and technique, with brief description of MINI programs', Nijmegen: Department of Psychology Report 75-MA-13.

——(1975b). 'A documentation of MINISSA(N)', Nijmegen: Department of Psychology Report 75-MA-15.

Ross, J. (1970). 'Multidimensional scaling of attitudes', in G.F. Summers (ed.), *Attitude measurement.* Chicago: Rand McNally. 279-93.

Rossi, P.H., *et al.* (1974). 'Measuring household social standing', *Social Science Research, 3,* 169-90.

Runciman, W.G. (1968). 'Class status and power?' in J.A. Jackson (1968). Reprinted in W.G. Runciman (1970). *Sociology in its Place.* Cambridge: University Press.

Sarapata, A. (1966). Stratification and social mobility. In J. Szczepanski (ed.), *Empirical sociology in Poland.* Warsaw: Polish Sociological Publishers.

Sarapata, A., and W. Wesolowski (1960). The evaluations of occupations by Warsaw inhabitants. *Amer.J.Sociol., 66,* 581-91.

Schutz, A. (1972). *The phenomenology of the social world.* London: Heinemann.

Scott, W.A. (1969). 'The structure of natural cognitions', *J.personality and social psychol. 12*, 261-78.

Shanin, T. (ed.) (1972). *The rules of the game: cross-disciplinary essays on models in scholarly thought.* London: Tavistock.

Shepard, R.N. (1964). 'On subjectively optimum selections among multi-attribute alternatives', in M.W. Shelley and G.L. Bryan (eds.), *Human judgments and optimality.* New York: Wiley.

——(1969). 'Some principles and prospects for the spatial representation of behavioural science data', paper presented at Advanced Research Seminar on Scaling and Measurement, Newport Beach, California.

——(1972). 'A taxonomy of types of data and methods for analysis', in R.N. Shepard, A.K. Romney and S.B. Nerlove (eds.) (1972). *Multidimensional Scaling: theory and applications in the behavioural sciences.* New York: Seminar Press, 23-47.

Shepard, R.N., and J.D. Carroll (1966). 'Parametric representation of nonlinear data structure', in P.R. Krishnaiah (ed.), *Multivariate analysis.* New York: Academic Press.

Sherman, C.R. (1972). 'Nonmetric multidimensional scaling: A Monte Carlo study of the basic parameters', *Psychometrika, 37,* 323-55.

Shils, E. (1968). 'Deference', in J.A. Jackson 1968.

Siegel, P.M. (1971). 'Prestige in the American occupation structure', Ph.D. thesis, University of Chicago.

Simon, H.A. (1969). *Sciences of the artificial.* Cambridge, Mass.: MIT Press.

Siegel, P.M. (1970). 'Occupational prestige in the Negro subculture', in E.O. Laumann (ed.), *Social stratification: research and theory for the 1970's.* Bobbs-Merrill.

——(1971). 'Prestige in the American occupation structure', Ph.D. thesis, University of Chicago.

Sjöberg, L. (1972). 'A cognitive theory of similarity', Göteborg: Psychological Reports, *2,* 10.

Smith, M. (1943). 'An empirical scale of prestige status of occupations', *Amer.Sociol.Rev., 8,* 815-92.

Smyth, J.A. (1971). 'Utility and the social order: the axiological problem in sociology', *Brit.J.Sociol., 22,* 381-94.

Sommers, Dixie (1974). 'Occupational rankings for men and women by earnings', *Monthly Labor Review,* August, 34-51.

Sorokin, P.A. (1959). *Social and cultural mobility.* Glencoe: Free Press.

Sprague, J. (1976). 'Discrete linear systems as useful models for political analysis: three applications', paper presented at the Society for General Systems Research, Boston, Mass.

Spence, I., and J. Graef (1973). 'The determination of the underlying dimensionality of an empirically obtained matrix of proximities', *Mult.Beh.Res., 8.*

Stehr, N. (1974). 'Consensus and dissensus in occupational prestige', *Brit.Journ.Sociol., 25,* 410-27.

Stewart, A., K. Prandy and R.M. Blackburn (1973). 'Measuring the class structure', *Nature, 245*, No. 5426.

Super, D.E. *et al.* (1957). *Vocational development: A framework for research.* New York: Teachers College Press.

Sutton, A.J. (1971). 'The use of quadratic discriminant analysis for the measurement of profile distance in social perception', *Brit.J.Psychol. statistical section, 62*, 253-60.

Szczepanski, J. (1970). *Polish Society.* New York: Random House.

Tagiuri, R. (1969). 'Person perception', in Lindzey and Aronson (eds.), q.v., vol. 3.

Tajfel, H. (1969). 'Social and cultural factors in perception. In Lindzey and Aronson (eds.), q.v., vol. 3.

Tajfel, H., and A.L. Wilkes (1963). 'Classification and quantitative judgment', *Brit.J.Psychol., 54*, 101-14.

Transgaard, H. (1972). 'A cognitive system approach to methodology: an outline', *Quality and Quantity, 6*, 139-51.

Trabasso, T., *et al.* (1970). 'The representation of linear order and spatial strategies in reasoning', in Rachel J. Falmagne (eds.), *Reasoning: representation and process in children and adults.* New York: Wiley.

Treiman, D.J. (ed.) (1977). *Occupational prestige in comparative perspective.* New York: Academic Press (forthcoming).

Triandis, H.C. (1964). 'Cultural influences upon cognitive processes', in L. Berkowitz (ed.), *Advances in experimental social psychology*, vol. 1. New York: Academic Press.

Triandis, H.C., and L.M. Triandis (1960). 'Race, social class, religion and nationality as determinants of social distance', *J.abnorm.soc.psychol, 61*, 110-18.

Ulrich, G., J. Hechlik and E.C. Roeber (1966). 'Occupational stereotypes of high school students', *Voc.guid.quart., 14*, 169-74.

Vaughan, Michalina (1971). 'Poland', in M.S. Archer and S. Giner (eds.), *Contemporary Europe.* London: Weidenfeld & Nicolson.

Vodzinskaia, V.V. (1970). 'Orientation toward occupations', in M. Yanowitch and W.A. Fisher (eds.), *Social stratification and mobility in the USSR.* New York: International Arts and Sciences Press, Inc.

Waern, Y. (1971). 'A model for multidimensional similarity', *Percept. and Motor Skills*, 15-25.

Wagenaar, W.A., and P. Padmos (1971). 'Quantitative interpretation of stress in Kruskal's multidimensional scaling technique', *Br.Journ.Math.Statist. Psychol., 24*, 101-10.

Waites, B.A. (1976). 'Effect of the first world war on class and status in England: 1910-1920', *J.Contemp.Hist., 11*, 27-48.

Walker, C.J. (1976). 'The employment of vertical and horizontal social schemata in the learning of a social structure', *J.personality and social psychol., 33*, 132-41.

Walker, K.F. (1958). 'A study of occupational stereotypes', *J.applied psychol., 42,* 122-24.

Wallace, A.F.C. (1961a). *Culture and personality.* New York: Random House.

——(1961b). 'On being just complicated enough', *Proc.Nat.Acad.Sciences, 47,* 458-64.

Warner, W.L., Marcia Meeker and K. Eells (1949). *Social class in America.* New York: Science Research Association (republished 1960 by Harper).

Watnick, M. (1962). 'Relativism and class consciousness: George Lukács', in L. Labedz (ed.).

Wells, W.D. *et al.* (1957). 'An adjective check-list for the study of "Product Personality" ', *J.applied psychol., 41,* 317-19.

——(1958). 'A change in a product image', *J.applied psychol., 42,* 120-1.

Wesolowski, W. (1966). 'Changes in the class structure in Poland', in J. Szcepanski (ed.), *Empirical sociology in Poland.* Warsaw: Polish Sociological Publishers.

Wiggins, Nancy, and M. Fishbein (1969). 'Dimensions of semantic space: A problem of individual differences', in J.G. Snider and C.E. Osgood (eds.), *Semantic differential technique.* Chicago: Aldine.

Wilkinson, B.W. (1966). 'Present values of lifetime earnings for different occupations', *J.political economy, 74,* 556-72.

Willener, A. (1957). *Images de la société et classes sociales.* Berne: Imprimerie Staempfli.

Willings, D. (1971). 'What jobs are worth', *New Society 17,* (442), 435-7.

Wilson, D. (1969). 'Forms of hierarchy: a selected bibliography', *Gen. Systems, 14,* 3-15.

Wittgenstein L.(1958). *Philosophical investigations* (tr. G.E.M. Anscombe), 2nd edition. Oxford: Blackwell.

Wulf, F. (1938). 'Tendencies in figural variation' in W.D. Ellis (ed.), *A sourcebook of Gestalt psychology.* London: Routledge & Kegan Paul.

Yntema, D.B., and W.S. Torgerson (1961). 'Man-computer cooperation in decisions requiring common-sense', *IRE Transactions in electronics,* HFE-2, 20-6.

Young, M., and P. Willmott (1956). 'Social grading by manual workers', *Brit.J.Sociol., 7,* 337-45.

Zigler, E., and I.L. Child (1969). 'Socialization', in Lindzey and Aronson, q.v.

Zimbardo, P., and E.B. Ebbesen (1969). *Influencing attitudes and changing behaviour.* Reading, Mass.: Addison Wesley.

Name Index

Name Index

Subject Index